More Praise for *Contested Modernity*

'Written by one of the most astute scholars of the contemporary Gulf, this book presents an authoritative critique of the "ethnosectarian gaze" so often used in writing and thinking about Bahrain. Grounded in meticulous archival research and a fascinating retelling of Bahraini history, the book provides a wide range of fresh and compelling insights into debates around nationalism, identity, colonialism, and the production of knowledge. An indispensable work that breaks new ground in Middle East scholarship.'

Adam Hanieh, Reader in Development Studies, SOAS, and author of *Money, Markets, and Monarchies: The Gulf Cooperation Council and the Political Economy of the Contemporary Middle East*

'AlShehabi offers an insightful and a fresh perspective that challenges dominant narratives on contemporary sectarian politics in Bahrain and the other states of the Arabian Gulf. While situating the Arab Gulf countries within mainstream debates on Arab al-Nahda, the book provides well-argued analyses of the Gulf-specific colonial experiences and the colonial roots of "the modernized absolutist rule" in the region.'

Abdulhadi Khalaf, Professor of Sociology, Lund University

RADICAL HISTORIES OF THE MIDDLE EAST

SERIES EDITORS

Dr Mezna Qato, University of Cambridge

Dr Siavush Randjbar-Daemi, University of St Andrews

Dr Eskandar Sadeghi-Boroujerdi, University of Oxford

Dr Omar H. AlShehabi, Gulf University of Science and Technology

Dr Abdel Razzaq Takriti, University of Houston

OTHER TITLES IN THIS SERIES

Khalil Maleki by Homa Katouzian

For more information and details of forthcoming volumes, please
visit oneworld-publications.com/radical-histories

Contested Modernity

Sectarianism, Nationalism,
and Colonialism in Bahrain

Omar H. AlShehabi

ONEWORLD
ACADEMIC

Oneworld Academic

An imprint of Oneworld Publications

Published by Oneworld Academic, 2019

ISBN 978-1-78607-291-7
eISBN 978-1-78607-292-4

Typeset by Hewer Text UK Ltd, Edinburgh
Printed and bound in Great Britain by Clays Ltd, Elcograf S.p.A.

Oneworld Publications
10 Bloomsbury Street
London WC1B 3SR
England

Stay up to date with the latest books,
special offers, and exclusive content from
Oneworld with our newsletter

Sign up on our website
oneworld-publications.com

FSC
www.fsc.org
MIX
Paper from
responsible sources
FSC® C018072

To Esraa

CONTENTS

PREFACE

A shallow sectarian narrative continues to dominate discussions about Bahrain and the Gulf in academic circles and the media alike. This prompted me to embark on this project as a matter of immediate relevance and urgency. The first seeds were planted while excavating Bahrain-related documents in the British colonial archives. I realized how similar were the language and thoughts of early-twentieth-century British colonial officers to many writings in English on the Gulf today. Not only were the same ethnosectarian divisions and terminologies used, but the political coding and interpretations of society through such categories also remained remarkably constant. The difference was that the starring ensemble of ethnicities and sects kept switching in their roles of 'opposition' and 'loyalists' across time. Indeed, academic writings of our age often rely directly and uncritically on the British colonial archives for much of the resources and literature that form their views of Bahrain and the Gulf, so it is not surprising that they would adopt a similar outlook.

My initial focus was on tracing the roots of the ethnosectarian gaze that dominates narration on Bahrain and the Gulf, thoroughly critiquing it, and excavating the material and mental imprints the colonial experience had on the islands. This effort eventually materialized into a paper published in the *British Journal for Middle Eastern Studies*. My attention subsequently turned towards a goal that I came to view as much more important. I wanted to trace the rise of the first modern nationalist and trans-sectarian social and political movements in Bahrain, which emerged at a similar time as the first ethnosectarian mobilization on the islands. The roots of these movements have been completely neglected in the English literature. Just as the ethnosectarian gaze has dominated the discourse on Bahrain, it has also served to hide and obscure these other narratives. These first modernist movements, rich and varied in their thoughts and aims, were quickly and erroneously dismissed by British officers as 'Sunnis'. Nearly all of the English-language literature on Bahrain focusing on this period has followed in the same colonial footsteps, by similarly reducing these movements to broad ethnosectarian labels. In contrast, quite a substantial literary and political tradition flourishes in Arabic texts that continues to critique and draw inspiration from these first modernists.

Hence, in addition to analysing the roots of ethnosectarian mobilization in Bahrain, an equally important goal was to shed light on the thoughts and actions of these first individuals that brought and reshaped the al-Nahda renaissance in Bahrain and the Gulf. The primary aim of the book became narrating the complexities and currents of the first quarter of the twentieth century, when the first buds of nationalist, liberal, and Islamist thoughts and practices on the islands grew. Modernity did not take only one form in the Gulf, and it certainly was not only ethnosectarian.

*   *   *

This book's narration is aimed towards a general readership as well as an academic audience. Hence, for the sake of fluidity, I have minimized direct debates and engagements with the academic literature or placed them in the footnotes.[1] Wherever possible, I have placed hyperlinks to primary documents available online, particularly from the British colonial archives, in order to allow direct access and interaction with the original material.[2]

This work would not have been possible without the support of a great many individuals and institutions. Several friends and colleagues, as well as two anonymous reviewers and journal editors, gave their advice and comments on the article that was eventually published in BJMES. Whilst I had individually acknowledged their contributions in the article, I also feel that they need to be collectively acknowledged here.

The book is one of the first in the Oneworld series Radical Histories of the Middle East, and I am lucky enough to be on its editorial board. The great Abdel Razzaq Takriti proved a constant support as a dear friend, intellectual interlocutor, and commentator on this book. So has Mezna Qato, who continues to be a never-ending fountain and guide in my pursuit of knowledge. Eskandar Sadeghi-Boroujerdi provided great help both in his roles as editor in BJMES and as co-editor in this series, and so did Novin Doostdar, Siavush Randjbar-Daemi, Paul Nash,

1 Hence, explicit engagement with the debates in the scholarly literature on colonialism, sectarianism, Bahrain, and the wider Gulf has been minimized and approached indirectly throughout the arguments of the book. Citations and references are restricted to works that I directly used for information or arguments.
2 To keep the text simple, I have opted to employ simple transliteration without any diacritics throughout. In transliteration, the ' symbol is used to denote 'ain', while the ' symbol is used to denote 'hamza'.

and Jonathan Bentley-Smith. David Inglesfield's careful copy-editing of the manuscript deserves special praise. Talal al-Rash-oud, Hamad al-Rayes, Mahmood Almahmood, Nelida Fuccaro, Alex Boodrookas, Abdulhadi Khalaf, Ghasan Asbool, Bader al-Noaimi, Claire Beaugrand, and Toby Dodge have provided valuable commentary on different drafts of the book. I am particularly indebted to Ussama Makdisi for his thorough and insightful review of the text.

The arguments presented in this book were vastly enriched and nuanced by the constant discussions and debates I had with many brilliant individuals. I found myself constantly referring back to my brother, Saad, and his unrivalled grasp of the social history of Gulf notables. Ali al-Zumai deserves special mention for alerting me to the knowledge gap on al-Nahda in the region. Discussions with Omar Shweiki, Mazen al-Masri, Robert Carter, Ahmad al-Owfi, Sultan al-Amer, Wafa al-Sayed, Tareq al-Rubei, Raid al-Jamali, Rima Majed, Adam Hanieh, Sarah Kaiksow, Madawi al-Rasheed, Marc Valeri, Nader Kadhim, Rashid al-Jassim, and Nimr Sultani have also helped immensely in shaping my thoughts. Tanya Lawrence and Laleh Khalili have suggested helpful readings.

The initial ideas for the book materialized while spending time in UNC Chapel Hill as a Carnegie Corporation Visiting Fellow at the Carolina Center for the Study of the Middle East and Muslim Civilizations in summer 2015, a particularly fruit-ful time for which I am especially indebted to Charles Kurzman, Evelyne Huber, John Stephens, and John Pickles. Some work on the manuscript was done while completing a 2016 summer fellowship at the Middle East Institute at the National University of Singapore, for which I am grateful. The final touches on the book benefited from the 2017 conference 'Arab Traditions of Anti-Sectarianism' that was hosted by the University of Houston and Rice University, and masterfully organized by Abdel Razzaq Takriti and Ussama Makdisi.

The study was completed while I continued to work at the Gulf University for Science and Technology in Kuwait, my university base since September 2010. The largest institutional support continued to come from the Gulf Centre for Development Policies in Kuwait, particularly its board members Ali Khalifa al-Kuwwari, Ali al-Zumai, Jasem al-Saadoun, and Fahad al-Zumai. Special thanks are also due to Abdul-Wahab al-Enezi, my colleague at the centre, for his assistance in copy-editing the text. Many more have contributed directly or indirectly to this work, and I beg their forgiveness for not mentioning all here.

Above all, my greatest thanks goes to my mother, Aysha, my brother, Saad, my uncle Abdulaziz, and the rest of my family for their continued and unwavering support. The principles, traditions, and wide smile of my father, Hesham, continue to provide the energy and motive in all that I write and do. The period spent finishing this book was blessed through sharing its moments with my better half, Esraa al-Muftah, to whom it is dedicated.

INTRODUCTION: APPROACHING ABSOLUTISM, NATIONALISM, AND SECTARIANISM IN THE GULF

'*O*f *the whole population of about 100,000 souls, some 60,000, chiefly townsmen, are Sunnis and about 40,000, mostly villagers, are Shi'as.*'[1]

Thus did Lorimer, the legendary British colonial officer, begin his discussion of Bahrain in his famous *Gazetteer*, presenting his population census figures for the islands in the early twentieth century. Using 'Sunnis' and 'Shi'as' as the basic units of analysis when discussing Bahrain, the Gulf, and the Arab world more generally, remains the dominant mode of thought even in the twenty-first century.[2] It seems obligatory that any

---

1 Qatar Digital Library (henceforth QDL), 'Gazetteer of the Persian Gulf. Vol. II. Geographical and Statistical. J G Lorimer. 1908' [238] (265/2084), IOR/L/PS/20/C91/4, http://www.qdl.qa/en/archive/81055/vdc_100023515712.0x000042 (all links accessed on 11 November 2017).
2 'The Gulf' will be used to refer to the body of water between the Arabian Peninsula and Iran that is also referred to as the 'Arabian Gulf' or 'Persian Gulf' in the literature.

discussion of the region opens with a passage similar to the above. Such an ethnosectarian reading runs across the Western political spectrum, from the right to the left. The celebrated leftist intellectual Noam Chomsky, for example, would opine:

> Bahrain is about 70% Shiʿa, and it's right across the causeway from Eastern Saʿudi Arabia, which is also majority Shiʿa, and happens to be where most of the oil is . . . By a curious accident of history and geography, the world's major energy resources are located pretty much in Shiʿa regions. They are a minority in the Middle East, but they happen to be where the oil is.[3]

Disregarding the dubious evidence for these estimates,[4] the quote serves primarily to show how such sect-based readings of the region remain pervasive throughout the West, even within so-called progressive circles. Furthermore, these sectarian demarcations are usually intersliced with ethnic cleavages – Arab, Persian, Huwala, Baharna, Kurds – that are presented as

3 Noam Chomsky, speech at FAIR 25th anniversary meeting, https://www.youtube.com/watch?v=yY3yVQ0sxXo, minute 4:30.

4 Even if one were to adopt an ethno-sect statistical lens, there is little solid evidence to support, for example, that individuals who follow the Shiʿa faith are a majority in the Eastern Province of Saʿudi Arabia, particularly in the largest metropolitan area of Dammam, Khobar, and Dhahran. Similarly, all the largest cities located on the coasts of the other countries bordering the Gulf (the body of water around which the vast majority of the oil is concentrated), including those of Kuwait, Qatar, UAE, and Oman, would suggest an opposite conclusion to Chomsky's, with Bahrain, Bandar Abbas, and Basra being the three possible exceptions. Even the often quoted seventy percent figure in Bahrain lacks statistical evidence as a basis (the only official census of 1941 showed a fifty-two percent vs. forty-eight percent Shiʿa to Sunni split), and is mainly perpetuated by repeated recycling of the figure in Western academic and media circles.

primordial, clear-cut and unshifting identities that are products of age-old local rivalries – in the words of President Obama, 'rooted in conflicts that date back millennia.'[5]

This book seeks to destabilize such preconceptions and provide an alternative window of view. It takes as its case study a country that, as Chomsky's quote shows, has become a poster child for discussing ethnosectarian political practice and mobilization in the region. Specifically, it presents a new reading of events in Bahrain in the period of the first quarter of the twentieth century. This marked the first time in the island's modern history that overt mobilization based on ethnosectarian identities became a predominant feature of politics. Something changed during this period. Suddenly, the prescribed ethnicities and sects of the different groups became the paramount factor in politics, and political mobilization and practice became ethnosectarian.

Equally significant, and in many ways constituting a much more important goal of this book, is to reveal the other political thoughts, discourses, and movements that emerged during this period, and which such ethnosectarian readings have served to hide and obscure. This period also witnessed the rise of the al-Nahda renaissance in Bahrain, extending its currents from areas elsewhere in the Arab and Muslim world into the Gulf. The thoughts, writings, speeches, and actions of the individuals that formed this group laid the first seeds of Nationalism, Arabism, Liberalism, and Islamism in Bahrain and the wider Gulf. This first group of local modernist reformers, whose thoughts later came to dominate politics on the island throughout the twentieth century, have been completely

5 Barack Obama, 'State of the Union Address 2016', https://mic.com/articles/132466/state-of-the-union-transcript-2016-obama#.DDupWynlZ.

3

ignored in the English literature, being reduced by the British colonial officers and most writings since to labellings based on sects and ethnicities. To my knowledge, not a single study written in English has tackled this first group of al-Nahda reformers in Bahrain, whether within the literature on the Gulf or al-Nahda more widely in the Arab world. This is despite the extremely prominent and crucial role they continue to play in shaping the political and cultural scene of Bahrain and the wider Gulf, particularly the subsequent rise of Arab nationalist, Islamist, and leftist forces. Central to understanding these newly emerging thoughts and movements would be highlighting the actors, leaders, discourses, myths, spaces, and actions that led to their emergence and constituted their body of traditions that were produced, transmitted, modified, and carried across people, time, and space.[6]

The episodes covered in this book are important not only because they were the first modern case of sectarian and nationalist mobilization in the Gulf, but also because they occurred in a period that long preceded the advent of oil, the 'rentier state', or Islamism in the region, mantras that have become staple explanations in today's analysis of ethnosectarianism. Instead, this was a period that witnessed the fall of regional empires, both the Ottoman in Turkey and the Qajar in Iran, combined

6 Thus, although this book will draw on Hobsbawm's concept of invention of tradition by the state, it focuses more centrally on traditions as the produced and lived experiences and collective memories and discourses of political movements. For more on traditions in this sense see: Karma Nabulsi, *Traditions of War: Occupation, Resistance, and the Law* (Oxford: Oxford University Press, 2005). I have also benefited greatly from discussions on traditions of anti-sectarianism during the Conference on Arab Traditions of Anti-Sectarianism, convened by Abdel Razzaq Takriti and Ussama Makdisi in December 2017 at Rice University and the University of Houston.

with the planting of the first seeds of the emergent new states in the region. This was also a time that marked the height of colonial intervention in the Arab world, and Bahrain was ground zero for British presence in the Gulf. New modern discourses and modes of thoughts also began emerging, not least of which was al-Nahda, the literary and intellectual renaissance that swept across the Arab world in the nineteenth and early twentieth centuries.

Why did overt ethnosectarian mobilization emerge in Bahrain during this period? Why was it so marked in comparison to areas surrounding it, including those with a similar socioeconomic make-up such as Kuwait and eastern Saʿudi Arabia, which witnessed barely any similar bouts of ethnosectarianism during this time, and indeed up until the emergence of the Islamist wave in the 1970s? Were there other political discourses and visions that competed and interacted with ethnosectarianism? Equally importantly, how did observers that came from outside, particularly colonial officers from the West, come to read such societies mainly in ethnosectarian terms? Are there lessons and parallels that can be drawn out for other regions and time periods from what happened in Bahrain? These are the questions that will guide the book's narration.

First, though we must tackle a central question: what is meant by ethnosectarianism?[7] As some have noted, ethnosectarianism – which we will also refer to as sectarianism for short – can take on a multitude of meanings, and often the term serves more to obfuscate than illuminate. While the term

---

7 There is a burgeoning literature on sectarianism following the Iraq War of 2003 that is not possible to cover fully here. For a review of works related to the Middle East see: Fanar Haddad, ' "Sectarianism" and Its Discontents in the Study of the Middle East', *Middle East Journal* 71.3 (2017): 363–382.

'sectarianism' is usually associated with regions such as the so-called 'Middle East', Ussama Makdisi perceptively remarks that it is rarely used to describe the United States, where racial groupings and categorization also take on a central role in political practice.[8] For my purposes here, I take (ethno)sectarianism to mean political mobilization, practice, and discourse that is primarily defined in ethnosectarian terms and categories.[9] It is a process through which race, ethnicities, religions, sects,[10] and other such 'primordial' social categories take on the role of being the central factors in determining how political power dynamics are read and practised within a society, whether by the state or other social actors.

8 Ussama Makdisi, 'The Mythology of the Sectarian Middle East', Center for the Middle East at Rice University, 2017, http://www.bakerinstitute. org/media/files/files/5a20626a/CME-pub-Sectarianism-021317.pdf.

9 Hence, my main focus is not on tracing the history of the emergence and formation of particular sects or ethnicities as social identities, but rather on the mobilization of ethnicities and sects in the political arena. The two questions are obviously related, however, and the issue of social identity formation will be broached when relevant to the question of political mobilization based on ethnicities and sects. Furthermore, it should be clear that I am not focusing in this study on so-called 'casual' racism or sectarianism, as stereotypes and personal prejudices based on social markers certainly existed and continue to exist in Bahrain and many other areas of the world.

10 Many scholars prefer to use the term 'denomination' instead of sect, citing the fact that 'sect' historically referred to a specific type of phenomenon related to splits within the Christian Church in Europe following the Reformation. For our purposes, I use 'sect' in the wider meaning of religious denomination, given its current prevalent use in such a manner. For more see: Aziz al-Azmeh, 'Sectarianism and Antisectarianism', keynote address at the Rice University/University of Houston Conference on Arab Traditions of Anti-Sectarianism, 2017, https://www.strikingmargins.com/news-1/ 2017/12/20/prof-aziz-al-azmeh-sectarianism-and-antisectarianism? format=amp.

This book will argue that political practice that is primarily based on ethnosectarian readings in Bahrain is a product of the contestations and mobilizations that occurred in the period of increasing British colonial involvement in the early twentieth century. Two groups of factors will be put forward as playing a paramount role in shaping the conjuncture of the emergent sectarianism.[11] The first is by now a standard modernist reading of the rise of nationalism and sectarianism, but which has surprisingly been barely applied in the Gulf setting.[12] This reading emphasizes the overlaps, cleavages, and intersections between class, social background, geography, ways of life, and modes of thoughts across different individuals and groups, and the ways these have been transformed with the advent of new modes of production and economic activity in the 'age of capital'.[13] The new economies and technologies that emerged, particularly in transport and printing, had a profound impact on redrawing people's conceptions of space and time. The appearance of steamships and the printing press on the scene, coupled with new forms and organization of business and economic activities, led to increasing movement and geographical redrawing of the urban and rural social environment. These tectonic shifts had a marked impact on the ideas and discourses that defined how individuals came to articulate their

11 This work draws upon conjunctural analysis pioneered by Stuart Hall, where specific attention is paid to the 'condensation of forces during a period of crisis, and the new social configurations which result' and how they are articulated. For more see: Stuart Hall, 'The neoliberal revolution', *Cultural Studies* 25.6 (2011): 705–728.

12 Probably the most famous example is: Ernest Gellner, *Nations and Nationalism* (Ithaca: Cornell University Press, 2008).

13 Eric Hobsbawm, *The Age of Capital: 1848–1875* (London: Weidenfeld & Nicolson, 1975).

relationship with others around them, and these ideas in turn also impacted events on the ground in an inter-feeding dynamic. Particularly important in this respect will be the relationship between the ruling family and the residents of the agricultural villages and urban towns in Bahrain through the nineteenth and early twentieth centuries.

The other factor that this book will emphasize as playing a decisive role in the rise of ethnosectarianism is the colonial experience.[14] Especially crucial will be the role of the colonial experience in shaping the political system and the nature of the state in the islands. Two concepts will become paramount in understanding this colonial experience in Bahrain. The first is the colonial *ethnosectarian gaze*; a way of approaching and understanding local society that defined ethnosectarian cleavages as the main codes for evaluating the actions of local actors. Hence, the British employed a systematic approach to colonial rule that coded issues of local political power, practice, and discourse primarily through an ethnosectarian lens.

This gaze was complemented by a tendency towards marketing interference as 'benevolent imperialism', a hallmark of late British colonialism. As part of their 'civilizing' mission, British officials often displayed a noticeable concern about the treatment of certain societal segments that they identified using the ethnosectarian gaze, particularly minorities or groups they marked as being collectively oppressed or unfairly treated. In order to implement some form of perceived fairness in

14 In this manner, this book comes in a line of works that emphasize the importance of the colonial encounter in the production of modern sectarianism. For a book that makes a parallel argument regarding Ottoman Lebanon see: Ussama Makdisi, *The Culture of Sectarianism: Community, History, and Violence in Nineteenth-Century Ottoman Lebanon* (Berkeley and Los Angeles: University of California Press, 2000).

treatment between these different ethno-sect groups, ideas of consociations and proportionality were introduced in political practice.

The second central concept to understanding the colonial encounter is 'divided and contested rule',[15] which emphasizes the particular version of rule employed by the British at the height of their involvement in the island. With the advent of Lord Curzon's imperial 'forward policy' in the gulf, and increasingly to ward off other imperial interests, Britain actively divided sovereignty between itself and the local ruler, with actors on the island faced with at least two possible sources of jurisdiction. Britain took over jurisdiction of 'foreigners', while the ruler had sovereignty over 'locals'. The British defined these legal categories through an ethnosectarian lens, and increasingly so did other actors, creating a cross-pollinating dynamic between sectarianism and divided rule.

Thus, conceptions of ethnicities and sect overrode all other political identifiers and differences under the British colonial gaze in the early twentieth century. These ethnosectarian differences were framed as clear-cut primordial aspects of identity that then defined each person's political role and agency. In turn, they were sharpened and provided a legal formal footing by the institutions and classifications of the modern state, particularly under the dynamics of divided rule.

Of the many different forms of political mobilization that emerged at the social level, two different yet intermeshing forms are emphasized. One would be political mobilizations

15 As should be evident, this concept differs significantly in its nature and emphasis from the more common 'divide and rule', and is adapted from 'divided rule' developed in: Mary Dewhurst Lewis, *Divided Rule: Sovereignty and Empire in French Tunisia, 1881–1938* (Berkeley and Los Angeles: University of California Press, 2013).

based on ethnosectarian, identity-specific demands and grievances, with equivocal, sometimes even friendly views towards
British rule. The other, largely ignored or misrepresented in the
English literature, took a nationalist, trans-sectarian, anti-colonial tone, having its roots in an antithetical view of modernity
to that held by British colonialism. The discourse of this movement traced its root to the al-Nahda renaissance that arose
across the Arab world in the latter part of the nineteenth century.
These multiple visions of modernity would intermesh and clash
in 1920s Bahrain, with the contradictions and tensions
unleashed at the popular mobilization level continuing to
morph, collide, reshape, and cross-breed across Bahrain's twentieth century, their lingering effects and products felt until
today.

Finally, this book will also trace the roots and rise of modernized absolutism in Bahrain, through which domestic political
power was monopolized in a dynastic ruler, backed up by a
modern and rationalized system of governmental bureaucracy.[16] My main contention will be that Bahrain was the first
birthplace of modernized absolutism in the Gulf. As the system
of divided rule rapidly destabilized and fell apart during the first
two decades of the twentieth century, the British moved to
completely take over local rule, deposing the old ruler and
installing his more pliant son in his place. Concurrently, the old
order that relied on a balance of a localized and diffused constellation of power sources was wiped out, and a set of drastic
reforms aimed at rationalizing the state bureaucracy and
monopolizing power in its hands ensued. From the British

---

16 For a conceptual discusson of absolutism in Oman and the Gulf, see:
Abdel Razzaq Takriti, *Monsoon Revolution: Republicans, Sultans, and
Empires in Oman, 1965–1976* (Oxford: Oxford University Press, 2013).

point of view, Bahrain would rapidly become the role model of modernized absolutism for its neighbours in the Gulf.

Through its narration, the book aims to challenge the epistemic validity of the ethnosectarian assumptions that underline the majority of writings on Bahrain, the Gulf, and the wider Arab world, whether on the period in question or more generally. It provides a new reading of events in Bahrain at the dawn of the twentieth century, as well as of British rule during that period. It utilizes a wide range of Arabic sources, departing from the previous literature that has relied almost exclusively on British archives. Particularly, it becomes paramount to elucidate the role played by al-Nahda in Bahrain – something that has been completely ignored in English-language writings – through an extensive discussion of its central characters and the transnational flow of ideas between them.

Furthermore, the narration of events in Bahrain will be tied to the practices and writings on colonial rule elsewhere, showing the similarities, differences, and continuities displayed in relation to Bahrain. Finally, the book provides a novel interpretation of the rise of absolutist rule in Bahrain and the Gulf more generally by emphasizing its roots in the colonial experience and as a reaction to rising local movements of opposition. Thus, sectarianism, absolutism, and nationalism rose concurrently in a period of colonial divided rule that was defined by clashes of different forms and contestations of modernity. Ultimately, this radical interpretation of history aims to push and break through rigid and static conceptualizations of Bahrain and the Gulf. By doing this, I hope to contribute towards a historiography that is more deeply engaged and empathetic with the region and its people, freed from pigeonholing by their sect, ethnicity, or any other preconceptions.

1

THE ETHNOSECTARIAN GAZE AND DIVIDED RULE

L orimer's *Gazetteer* included Bahrain's first systematized attempt at a population census that his team conducted in the early 1900s. It is useful to begin by quoting the relevant passages in full:

The principality then contains . . . 4 towns with a population of 60,800 souls and 104 villages with a population of 38,275; in all 99,075. To these must be added about 200 non-Mohammadans at Manamah, making a grand total of 99,275 settled inhabitants. Of the whole population of about 100,000 souls some 60,000, chiefly townsmen, are Sunnis and about 40,000, mostly villagers, are Shi'ahs.

The largest community – for it cannot be called a tribe – in the principality is undoubtedly that of the . . . Baharinah, who compose nearly the whole of the Shi'ah community . . . The remainder of the people, except a few foreigners such as Persians and Basrah Arabs,

Hindus, Jews, etc., belong to various Sunni tribes or classes.[1]

Hence, in terms of 'primordial cleavages', Lorimer would apply the following divisions to the local population: at the 'community' level were the two great sects of Islam, Sunni (sixty percent) and Shi'a (forty percent). Sunnis were divided into Huwala and 'Tribes', while the local Shi'as were composed of Baharna. Added to those would be small groups of various 'foreigners' existing on the island.

Table 1: Sect-composition of the population of Bahrain in the early twentieth century according to Lorimer

Denomination	Towns	Villages	Total
Sunni	44,800	14,200	59,000
Shi'a	16,000	24,075	40,075
Non-Muslim	200	0	200
Total	61,000	38,275	99,275

Source: QDL, 'Gazetteer of the Persian Gulf. Vol. II. Geographical and Statistical. J G Lorimer. 1908' [238] (265/2084), IOR/L/PS/20/C91/4, http://www.qdl.qa/en/archive/81055/vdc_100023515712.0x000042.

Lorimer's categorizations were based on his readings of existing social identifiers at the local level. In Bahrain's setting, where the overwhelming majority of the population was Muslim and Arabic speaking, sect was the most obvious social cleavage, as even without the modern tools of censuses, one could immediately recognize that there was a sizable presence of both sects. Furthermore,

1 QDL, 'Gazetteer of the Persian Gulf. Vol. II. Geographical and Statistical. J G Lorimer. 1908' [238] (265/2084), IOR/L/PS/20/C91/4, http://www.qdl.qa/en/archive/81055/vdc_100023515712.0x000042.

at first sight, it seemed a relatively clear demarcation, with each individual being either Sunni or Shi'a (with a few cases of mixed marriages and conversions). As we will see, however, even this simple binary was in reality not so clear-cut, as there existed several *madhhabs*, or schools of jurisprudence, which complicated the rigid picture of only two distinct sect groupings.

Ethnic constructions are by nature more porous, vague, and less stable social categories.[2] To begin, it becomes necessary to give an overview of the different social group identifiers found within Bahrain's social landscape. Let us start with the Huwala.[3] Nowadays, the collective social consciousness uniting those who self-identify as Huwala could roughly be described as Sunnis with extensive historical, social, and familial ties across both sides of the Gulf, but who see their aspirations and identity anchored in Arab culture, thus considering themselves Arabs. This perception, of course, has been contested by different parties, as well as being porous and open to reshaping as a social construct. They would be termed at different times and by different actors as Arabs, Persians, Arabized Persians, or Persianized Arabs. Furthermore, as will emerge during this study, there would be contestation on the coverage and elasticity of Huwala as a social category, with the term sometimes used to exclude and at others to include individuals who would be classified as, for example, Khunjis or 'Awadhis.

2 As can be seen in various case studies, for example: Patricia M. E. Lorcin, *Imperial Identities: Stereotyping, Prejudice and Race in Colonial Algeria* (London: I.B.Tauris, 1995).

3 For more on the Huwala as a self-identified social group see: 'Abdulrazzaq Mohammad Seddiq, *Sahwat al-Fares fi Tarikh 'Arab Fares* (Beirut: Matba'at al-Ma'aref, 1993); Jalal Khaled Haroon Al-Ansari, *Tareekh 'Arab al-Huwala wal 'Utoob* (Beirut: Al-Dar al-'Arabiyya lel Mawsoo'at, 2011).

Similarly, the collective consciousness that unites those who today would self-identify as Baharna could roughly be summarized as Shiʿa Arabs whose roots lie in the agricultural and fishing villages of the islands of Bahrain.[4] Just like the case of 'Huwala', the term 'Baharna' would also be malleable and porous across time, facing contestation from different actors, albeit in different ways.[5] As will be shown, the term would sometimes be used to exclude and at others to include people identified as 'Hasawis', 'Qatifis', those with links to areas in Iraq (e.g. Helli or Basrawi), or those with links to parts of modern-day Iran (e.g. Muhammara).

Finally, 'tribal origins' is a social category whose members today would self-identify as individuals who belong to one of the tribes of the Arabian Peninsula. Tribes, of course, are a particular socio-economic formation in the Arab world that have been extensively written about, with the great Arab sociologist Ibn Khaldun describing them as the epitome of strong ʿAsabiyyah, or social solidarity based on shared kinship and group consciousness.[6] The most influential tribes in Bahrain are those of the ʿUtub, with the ruling family of al-Khalifa at the

---

4 For more on the Baharna as a self-identified social group see: Laurence Louër, *Transnational Shiʿa Politics: Religious and Political Networks in the Gulf* (New York: Columbia University Press, 2008).
5 One major difference that will appear in our text is that political mobilization based on 'Baharna' as a self-conscious socio-political group identity would frequently occur, while mobilization based on 'Huwala' as a self-conscious socio-political group identity would be extremely rare in Bahrain's modern history, with self-identified Huwala largely tending to politically mobilize based on more encompassing identities, whether nationalist, pan-Arabist, or Islamist.
6 Ibn Khaldun, *The Muqaddimah: An Introduction to History* (Princeton: Princeton University Press, 1969).

top of the pack.[7] However, in the context of Bahrain, being of 'tribal origin', regardless of the particular tribe, increasingly also takes on the form of a social marker that is used to identify a particular individual's background, similar to how 'Huwala' or 'Baharna' function.

While they shared a common religion and language, Lorimer treated each of the above social identifiers as different and clearly defined ethnic communities or 'classes' that made up the 'local' population. This was complemented by demarcating smaller groups of 'foreigners'. He identified the vast majority of foreigners as 'Persians', mainly Shi'a but also including some Sunnis, most of whom today self-identify as "Ajams', and who no longer would identify as 'foreigners' but as locals of Bahrain.[8] Being labelled as a 'foreigner', however, had strong legal, political, and social consequences in the times of Lorimer, as will become apparent in the following narration.[9]

THE ETHNOSECTARIAN GAZE

These ethnosectarian markers and identifiers, always malleable and shiftable as social constructs, obviously existed in Bahrain prior to the arrival of Lorimer, who used them as the basis for demarcation in his census. The demarcations as used by him, however, constituted a new form of knowledge and social

---

7 For more on al-Khalifa and the 'Utub see: Muhammad al-Nabhani, *al-Tuhfa al-Nabhaniyya* (Bahrain: unknown, 1923).

8 For more on the 'Ajams in Bahrain as a self-identified social group see: 'Tarikh al-'irq al-Farsi fil Bahrain', *Al-Waqt* newspaper, 28 October 2009.

9 Other social groupings that Lorimer mentioned under 'foreigners' have been skipped for brevity's sake due to their relatively smaller size of a few dozens. These included Indians, Jews, and Christians.

categorization. This was in line with colonial practice else-where.[10] In the words of one scholar, it was:

> [M]ade manifest in the activities of investigation, exami-nation, inspection, peeping, poring over, which were accompaniments to the colonial penetration of a coun-try. In ethnographic description and scientific study, in the curious scrutiny of the colonized by the colonizer, there was much of the attitude of the voyeur as well as of the map-maker. In writing, the gaze appears as bird's-eye description, and is embodied in the high vantage point or knowledgeable position taken up by a writer or traveller as he re-creates a scene.[11]

What most defined this colonial gaze in Bahrain was its ethno-sectarian lens, which was a systemic approach that saw ethno-sect cleavages as the underlying epistemic fault lines that shaped local society and its political power, practices, and discourse. Thus, the ethnosectarian gaze was a way of viewing and catego-rizing the social world, in which communities were primarily defined and composed of different sects and ethnicities. The local population, its actions, laws, and social make-up were to be analysed mainly based on ethno-sect divisions. The British focus on such demarcations emphasized differences in ethno-sects that they presented as contrasting and clear-cut (Sunni vs. Shi'a and Baharna vs Huwala vs. Tribes), rather than

10 There is a large literature on the use of colonialist knowledge for European imperial control, including in the Arab world, which it is not possible to cover here. What is usually considered the foundational text is: Edward Said, *Orientalism* (New York: Vintage, 1979).
11 Elleke Boehmer, *Colonial and Postcolonial Literature: Migrant Metaphors* (Oxford: Oxford University Press, 2005).

highlighting ethnic and religious commonalities (e.g. Muslim and Arab). Censuses, institutions, laws, forms of mobilization, and other apparatuses of power were to be organized mainly around these ethno-sect fault lines, which are elevated to become the most important markers on the political level.

Other socio-economic-political factors, such as kinship, class, geography, trade, and production relations take a back seat to these different 'primordial' elements. This does not mean that these other factors played no role. The British in fact displayed a knack for documenting different aspects of economy, society, and governance in excruciating detail. However, the basic building blocks that composed local society and its politics, from the British point of view, were to be distinct sects and ethnicities.

Just like other forms of orientalism, this ethnosectarian gaze, although originally based on the colonial reading of the local situation on the ground, would increasingly morph and take on a life of its own, similar to an artist's impression of real-life figures projected onto a painting, where the two increasingly resemble one another only tangentially. Unlike the painting, however, such ethnosectarian outlooks would interact and feed back into local events, generating real effects on the ground.

To illustrate this point further, let us return to Lorimer's section on Bahrain, in which he would continue:

> Although the Baharna are numerically the strongest class, they are far from being politically the most important; indeed, their position is little better than one of serfdom. Most of the date cultivation and agriculture of the islands is in their hands; but they also depend, though to a less extent than their Sunni brethren, upon pearl diving and other seafaring occupations.

The Huwala are the most numerous community of Sunnis; but they are all townsmen living by trade and without solidarity among themselves. Consequently, they are unimportant except commercially. The 'Utub, the Sadah and the Dawasir are the most influential tribes in Bahrain.[12]

These passages are revealing, for they not only show the primacy of the ethnosectarian as units of analysis in such a colonial gaze, where communities are primarily defined and constituted in such terms, but it also indirectly reveals the tensions within using such groupings as markers of political agency. For as Lorimer says, in contrast to tribes, the 'Huwala' are 'without solidarity among themselves' and the 'Baharna' are the weakest politically, implicitly pointing to the fact that organized political practice based on these social identifiers was not necessarily the norm between members of these groupings.

The resort of British colonial power, epitomized by Lorimer, to such ethnosectarian political classification was in no way surprising. It emerged out of the need to rule; and in order to rule, it needed to codify, order, and make legible those who were to be ruled.[13] Just like they did elsewhere, the British began mapping, classifying, and quantifying the minutiae of the geography of Bahrain and its history, culture, and society. A quick glance across the more than 4,700 pages of Lorimer's *Gazetteer* makes it clear that Bahrain was at the centre of British interests in the Gulf, as it received a particularly detailed and

12 QDL, 'Gazetteer of the Persian Gulf. Vol. II. Geographical and Statistical. J G Lorimer. 1908' [240] (267/2084), IOR/L/PS/20/C91/4 http://www.qdl.qa/en/archive/81055/vdc_100023515712.0x000044.
13 James C. Scott, *Seeing like a State: How Certain Schemes to Improve the Human Condition Have Failed* (New Haven: Yale University Press, 1998).

encompassing treatment compared to other areas. This was knowledge catered towards colonial rule par excellence. The population had to be governed, and this required identifying and codifying the population according to different stratifications and groupings that reflect both facts on the ground and provide manageable, clear-cut categories that are open to practices of government, and these were to be ethnosectarian.[14]

The British use of cadastral surveys and censuses heralded the entrance of modern techniques of government into Bahrain. Like those employed elsewhere in the empire, maps and censuses were systematically based on sharply defined categorizations, which were used to reductively simplify a complex social make-up into discrete, tangible categories, and to 'fix and officialise collective identities'. Thus, 'techniques of government' were tied to techniques of measurement.[15] The main underlying premise was that different categories of communities could be identified by governmental tools such as censuses and maps, enabling their quantification and comparison.

Furthermore, these social categories were treated as fixed, even racialized in accordance with the new ideas of racial theories in vogue in Europe in the nineteenth century,[16] as hinted by Lorimer's recurring remarks such as, 'the races inhabiting

14 Foucault's concept of governmentality is particularly relevant in this regard. For more see: Michel Foucault, *Security, Territory, Population: Lectures at the Collège de France 1977–1978* (Basingstoke: Macmillan, 2009). For an application of governmentality to census building in the US see: Matthew G. Hannah, *Governmentality and the Mastery of Territory in Nineteenth-Century America* (Cambridge: Cambridge University Press, 2000).

15 Dipesh Chakrabarty, *Habitations of Modernity: Essays in the Wake of Subaltern Studies* (Chicago: University of Chicago Press, 2002), 83.

16 Michael Banton, *Racial Theories* (Cambridge: Cambridge University Press, 1998).

Bahrain are generally insignificant in appearance and there is nothing remarkable in their character.'[17] Lorimer and other British officers routinely resorted to categorizing different groups of locals as 'races', 'breeds', and 'aboriginals'.[18] Hence, local social identifiers could only become intelligible once they had been filtered through a racialized lens that pigenholed them in Western-centric concepts and terminology, a practice that would dominate English-language discourse on Bahrain for generations and long outlast direct colonialism until this day.[19]

17 QDL, 'Gazetteer of the Persian Gulf. Vol. II. Geographical and Statistical. J G Lorimer. 1908' [241] (268/2084), IOR/L/PS/20/C91/4, https://www.qdl.qa/en/archive/81055/vdc_100023515712.0x000045.

18 QDL, 'Persian Gulf Gazetteer Part II, Geographical and Descriptive Materials, Section II Western Side of the Gulf' [67v] (137/286), IOR/R/15/1/727, https://www.qdl.qa/en/archive/81055/vdc_100023206838.0x00008a; QDL, 'Gazetteer of the Persian Gulf. Vol. II. Geographical and Statistical. J G Lorimer. 1908' [208] (231/2084), IOR/L/PS/20/C91/4, https://www.qdl.qa/en/archive/81055/vdc_100023515712.0x000020; Bill Ashcroft, Gareth Griffiths, and Helen Tiffin. *Post-Colonial Studies: The Key Concepts* (London: Routledge, 2013), 4–5.

19 There has been a tendency, for example, within some recent English-language scholarship to employ a modified version of this 'aboriginal' colonial discourse and paint the history of Bahrain and the Gulf in the following manner: the Gulf was a uniquely cosmopolitan contact zone, made up since time immemorial of heterogeneous ethnicities and sects. Bahrain was an exception, however, in that its population was solely composed of Baharna Shi'as, its indigenous inhabitants. The Sunnis, led by al-Khalifa, then invaded from thirty kilometres away and took over the islands in 1783, with some recent writings even depicting this as a case of 'settler colonialism', in a strange dislocation of the concept from its roots in European colonialism. Thus, the history of social agents that have interacted for centuries via a common religion, language, resources, and geographic space is racially recast into Western-intelligible categorizations, where 'Sunnis' role-play the white European settler-colonizers and 'Shi'as' the 'aboriginals'. (This echoes orientalist polemics that manipulate other episodes in the region's history in a similar manner, such as labelling the

Unlike such coding, however, social interactions on the ground are much more complex. To begin with, social identifiers such as ethnicities are porous categories open to interpretation and overlap, displaying what have been termed 'fuzzy boundaries'.[20] Given their nature as social constructs, there is inherent flexibility in such categories, in contrast to the rigid, discrete demarcations used in censuses.[21] Furthermore,

---

early expansion of the Arab Islamic empire as a form of settler colonialism that emerged from the Arabian Desert.).

A novel version of this discourse has also emerged since the late twentieth century as the subject of intense historical polemics in Bahrain and other parts of the Gulf, revolving around the recently adopted concept of 'the original population' (*al-sukkan al-asliyyoon*), particularly within circles that adopt ethno-sect-based political outlooks. Much energy has been expended by many sides on trying to 'prove' that their groups, tribes, and sects can claim to be the oldest and original 'natives' of Bahrain and the Gulf, with some even venturing into DNA-based scientific racism towards this goal. Lorimer's *Gazetteer* has become a cornerstone of many of the emergent narratives, taking on an almost sacred status as a reference. The logical and empirical fallacies of such an undertaking should be glaringly obvious, particularly in a region that featured the two sects of Islam (and many other denominations) ever since the religion's inception, as well as being home to interacting groups of people that relied on the region's sea, agriculture, and desert as a way of life for millennia. An empirical and analytic critique of such a sectarianized approach to history, and its supremacist undertones which are geared towards casting doubt on the legitimacy of 'the other' based on rigid conceptions of sects and ethnicities, can be found in: Nader Khadhim, *Taba'e' al-Istimlak* (Beirut: Al-Maktaba al-'arabiyya lel derasat wal nashr, 2007), 75–85; Sinan Antoon, 'Al-Sukkan al-asliyoon wal baqiyya: eshkaliyyat al-mustalah', *As-Safir*, 22 March 2016 http://assafir.com/article/482731.

20 Chakrabarty, *Habitations of Modernity*, 87.

21 The question of what defines an ethnicity has long vexed anthropologists and sociologists. Although British colonialists in Bahrain approached ethnic 'classes' in a rigid, racialized manner, many anthropologists today

ethnosectarian considerations were only one factor amongst many which influenced social interaction on the islands in the early twentieth century. Very often, they would not even be the most important factor in determining social and political interactions when compared to class, profession, geography, and kinship, in stark contrast to the primacy they were given in the colonial ethnosectarian gaze. As will be shown, British officials would often use problematic, contradictory, and confused definitions across time and agents. The inherent assumption that remained throughout, however, was that it was possible to objectively and discretely identify such ethno-sect groups, and that these groupings should serve as the main basis for political analysis and governance.

Categorizations of the type used in censuses are part and parcel of modern forms of government in any state. Most states classify populations under their control, for example, by such categories as 'citizen' vs. 'foreigner' and 'refugee' vs. 'migrant'. The important questions centre on what forms of modern rule practices become prevalent, and what kinds of categorizations, demarcations, and divisions are emphasized and elevated within particular states. In the case of British colonial rule in Bahrain, why were ethnosectarian differences the main codings and categorizations used to read, measure, and rule such communities? In other words, why were contrasting sects and ethnicities made the keys to understanding and drawing the political map in Bahrain from the British point of view? In order

---

tend to view ethnicity as a constructed and fluid social identity, whose members view themselves as a distinct social group based on a mixture of commonalities they believe they hold (in language, religion, ancestry, etc.), contrasted with perceived differences from other social groups they interact with. For more on ethnicity see: Thomas Hylland Eriksen, *Ethnicity and Nationalism: Anthropological Perspectives* (London: Pluto Press, 2002).

to excavate the emergence of such practices of rule based on ethnosectarian difference, it becomes necessary to periodize their appearance and their use. It becomes imperative to place in historical context British colonial rule that took shape in Bahrain during the first quarter of the twentieth century.

PERIODIZING LATE BRITISH COLONIALISM

That the British have used ethnosectarian cleavages as the basic units that defined practices of colonial rule will not come as a surprise to historians of other regions under the British Empire. The primacy of sectarian divisions has been well documented in British colonial rule in the Indian Princely States, the British Raj, Africa, and in South East Asia (e.g. Malaya and Burma). Divergent religions and ethnic identities were elevated and enshrined in censuses, laws, and institutions across a variety of settings and regions.[22] In India, British colonial rulers read and categorized the local population based on a multitude of religions and castes, each codified and enshrined by detailed and extensive laws and regulations.[23] In Myanmar (Burma), which was under the rule of the British Government of India, colonial officers governed society in the nineteenth century based on a classification of more than a hundred ethnicities and religions.[24]

22 Some examples include: Barbara N. Ramusack, *The Indian Princes and Their States* (Cambridge: Cambridge University Press, 2004), 212; Mahmood Mamdani, *Citizen and Subject: Contemporary Africa and the Legacy of Late* (Princeton: Princeton University Press, 1996).
23 Nicholas B. Dirks, *Castes of Mind: Colonialism and the Making of Modern India* (Princeton: Princeton University Press, 2011).
24 Adam Simpson, Nicholas Farrelly, and Ian Holliday (eds.), *Routledge Handbook of Contemporary Myanmar* (Abingdon: Routledge, 2017).

Indeed, systems of knowledge structured along racial and ethnic lines are a prevalent trait across colonialist power, stretching back to the Spanish colonization of Latin America.[25]

The last quarter of the nineteenth century represented the dominance of the 'age of empire', and by empire I am specifically referring to European powers.[26] What distinguished this period was the large expansion of European colonialism across the globe, particularly in Africa and the Arabic-speaking world. In contrast, this period also marked the decline of the traditional regional empires, as the Ottoman and Qajar dynasties were weakening and entering their last throes. The colonized world was yet to witness the advent of the League of Nations, and the ideals of equal and sovereign states were still distant but possible dreams. Thus, our story is set in that interregnum when Western colonialism was experiencing its height, while regional empires were decaying, and new ideas of liberation and freedom were emerging but yet to be put in widespread practice.

Direct British involvement in matters of local rule in Bahrain was a clear fact by the early 1900s, and the arm of the British Empire tasked with overseeing Bahrain was the Government of India. Lorimer himself was no stranger to British modes of colonial rule in India, as he came from a family with a long line of service in the British Raj. He himself was previously stationed in Punjab in the North-West Frontier Province.[27] He would

---

25 A foundational text in this regard is: Anibal Quijano, 'Coloniality of power and Eurocentrism in Latin America', *International Sociology* 15.2 (2000): 215–232.

26 Eric Hobsbawm, *The Age of Empire: 1875–1914* (London: Weidenfeld & Nicolson, 1987).

27 Fereydun Vahman and Garnik Asatrian, 'Lorimer, David i. In Persia', Encyclopedia Iranica, http://www.iranicaonline.org/articles/lorimer-david-i-in-persia.

collate his *Gazetteer* during the first decade of the twentieth century, when the 'forward policy' of active British expansion in the Gulf, penned by Lord Curzon, the Viceroy of India, was in full swing.

The political institutions the British would set up to rule the Gulf were formally under the Government of India, and nearly all of its staff would have previous experience of colonial rule in India similar to that of Lorimer. These 'Gulfites' as they were known, were mainly graduates from the India Political Service (IPS), a 'hierarchic group of Victorian gentlemen with numerous relatives serving here and there, particularly India, and very largely from the emerging Bourgeoisie, i.e. they went to public schools'.[28] These came to the fore after the closure of the East India Company in 1859, in the aftermath of the legendary 1857–1858 Indian Mutiny. Subsequently, control of India was transferred from the company to the British-run Government of India, leading to a restructuring of political rule.

The majority of these officers had family ties with the Indian subcontinent that stretched back for generations. Out of sixty-six Gulf Residents and Agents between 1858 and 1947, at least twenty-four had fathers who spent part of their careers in India.[29] At least twenty more had close relatives who served there, such as brothers or uncles.

Unlike scholarship on other regions under British colonialism, however, most of the existing Western literature on Bahrain has dealt with the British ethnosectarian gaze – epitomized by

---

28 Paul Rich, *Creating the Arabian Gulf: The British Raj and the Invasions of the Gulf* (Maryland: Lexington Books, 2009), 16. 'Public schools' is the term used in England for exclusive private schools, usually attended by members of the upper class.
29 Ibid., 54. These included: Knox, Meade, Prideaux, Prior, Shakespear, and Trevor, who will appear throughout this book's narration.

the colonial archives – largely uncritically, adopting nearly the same ethno-sect lens to read and interpret society. This has been a serious shortcoming, which this study aims to recognize and deconstruct. Approaching the colonial discourse through a critical lens suddenly turns the related British archives into an important treasure trove, not only as a record of historical events, but more importantly as a record of how the British saw and approached such events. Once this is done, the manic obsession of British officials with ethnosectarian analysis, common to different agents, decades, and institutions, becomes the glaring and systematic characteristic of the discourse found in the documents.

In addition to this ethnosectarian gaze, the other hallmark of British rule during this period was its marketing of its 'benevolent imperialism', through which it claimed that it was bettering the situation of subjects under its rule. As Dipesh Chakrabarty notes, it is one of the great ironies of the nineteenth century that just as the British became liberals at home, they also became imperialists abroad.[30] This juncture often manifested itself in a concern by British imperial officials about being fair to the different competing sections that – in their view – made up society in places under their rule. Social groups were often identified using ethno-sect categories, and in order to be fair while also recognizing each of their unique characteristics, ideas of proportionality and consociations were introduced in governmental practices.

Thus, as we will see, British officials often displayed a noticeable concern about the treatment of certain societal segments that they had identified using the ethnosectarian gaze, particularly minorities or groups they would perceive as being

30 Chakrabarty, *Habitations of Modernity*, 85.

collectively oppressed or unfairly treated. This does not mean that British officials did not partake in abuse and coercion themselves, as they frequently did. Furthermore, such concern was often born of a cynical instrumentalism to use the pretext of helping minorities in order to expand British influence. This does not preclude, however, that in some cases individual officials were moved by a genuine concern to alleviate the perceived plights of unfairly treated 'communities' under their rule.

The presence of a few dozen Indian subjects in Bahrain was the first opening that gave the British reason to intervene in local affairs in the Gulf, as they assumed the position of being their de facto protectors as a minority community.[31] As British involvement increased in Bahrain, this concern with the fate of 'minorities' would stretch to all 'foreigners' on the island, and to the 'Shi'as' within the local society, particularly the 'Baharna'.

This concern with comparative 'communal' welfare did not necessarily mean a move away from absolutist rule, which in many cases was actually strengthened and bureaucratized. British officials continued to view imperial subjects as primitive, backward individuals that were in need of guidance towards civilization, but who were nevertheless entitled to a modicum of relative fair treatment and the prevention of the worst excesses of 'despotic' rule, to be achieved by rationalizing and standardizing the latter. Each perceived 'community', identified and measured through censuses and other tools of quantification, had theoretically an equal right to be recognized and be

31 For example, Shaikh Jasim, the founder of the ruling dynasty in Qatar, tried to expel a group of Indians in 1882, but was forced by the British to apologize to them and to continue to host them. See: Rich, *Creating the Arabian Gulf*, 55.

treated fairly, with associated legal codes, institutions, and courts that represented them and their interests.

The implementation of this combination of the ethnosectarian gaze and benevolent authoritarianism has been traditionally ascribed to 'indirect rule', adopting a British-colonial term which refers to a situation in which 'native' rulers mediated British rule over locals, instead of direct rule by the metropole. This mode of rule was first practised in India and then extensively applied in the late nineteenth and early twentieth centuries across British colonial Africa, with the infamous apartheid system of South Africa being its most notable manifestation. As Jan Smuts, the South African prime minister, put it: 'the "native" would have to be ruled not just by his own leaders but through "native institutions".'[32]

'Ethnicity' was paramount in indirect rule, as the latter focused on ethnically defined 'customary' institutions and laws that supposedly built on native traditions. Key to 'ethnic' and 'customary' institutions was social difference and divisions. If each perceived ethnicity was to have its own customary institutions, then to begin with each ethnicity had to be recognized as different from the others. Consequently, social differences had to be emphasized in the local population and elevated to the status of distinct, even racialized, ethnicities. Rather than viewing the population as equal citizens, they were instead subjects, with each subject defined primarily through being a member by birth of a particular ethnicity or sect. Each of these ethnicities and sects should then have its own set of customary institutions of rule, which were formalized under the guidance of the

---

32 Quoted in: Mahmood Mamdani, 'Historicizing power and responses to power: indirect rule and its reform', *Social Research* (1999): 859–886, 870.

imperial power. In this manner, the apparatuses of the colonial state were organized based on ethnicity or sect, with the subject population fragmented into several ethnicized minorities, each with its own 'customary practices' that were enshrined into laws and institutions under supervision of the metropole.

This does not mean that indirect rule and the custom law it implied was a foreign conspiracy always defined from above, invented from thin air, and shaped by the colonialists; nor was it simply an acceptance and reflection of already existing practices in the 'native society'. Mahmood Mamdani has persuasively shown that the shift from direct to indirect rule entailed not only a recognition of the 'historicity of the colony and the agency of the colonized', but also an attempt at an analytical engagement with custom. This involved cultivating authoritarian elements of custom and distilling them into customary law:

> The point was to go beyond an understanding of custom in the singular to unravelling its many strands, thereby to identify the authoritarian strands so as to sculpt it and build on it, sanctioning the product officially as customary law. This sculpting and building, in turn, was done less by colonial administrators than by their 'native' allies (called 'chiefs') whose agency indirect rule did much to unleash . . . The authority of the chief has fused in a single person all moments of power: judicial, legislative, executive and administrative.[33]

Indirect rule was always a site of struggle between various forces. However, it should be recognized that the institutional context in which this contest took place was skewed towards

33 M. Mamdani, 'Historicizing Power', 874.

the interest of the colonialists first, and the native rulers they chose to deal with. 'Power, and hence, the encounter, was not equal.'[34] It is in this institutional setting of indirect rule that ethnosectarianism as discourse, knowledge, and practice was produced.

DIVIDED AND CONTESTED RULE

Indirect rule as a concept has been extensively applied and proved extremely useful in understanding the wider colonial landscape. However, it does posit some limitations, particularly in relation to what this book explores. Firstly, it implicitly assumes a somehow clear dichotomy between indirect versus direct rule. In practice, however, the line between the two can be blurry, with direct versus indirect rule becoming more of a spectrum, thus limiting its use as an analytic concept.[35] Furthermore, it can downplay the agency of local actors, including the local ruler, ignoring tensions between him and the colonial metropole, as well as tensions between the different imperial and international forces at play.

Instead, I find for our purposes that it is more useful to employ an adopted form of the concept of 'divided rule' from Mary Lewis, which approaches the analysis through the lens of sovereignty.[36] I will argue that the British colonial system in Bahrain institutionalized dual centres of authority and jurisdiction in the territory, where the British had 'co-sovereignty' with

34 Ibid., 873.
35 For a 'spectrum' of the types of indirect rule see: Michael H. Fisher, *Indirect Rule in India: Residents and the Residency System 1764–1857* (Oxford: Oxford University Press, 1998), 395.
36 Lewis, *Divided Rule*.

the local ruler. Co-sovereignty meant that the British allowed the local ruler to preserve his own system of customs, taxation, courts, coercive bodies, and religious institutions, while the British also introduced their own set of courts and structures of government that existed side by side with those of the ruler. British jurisdiction applied to those categorized as 'foreign' subjects, while the local ruler had jurisdiction over those deemed 'local' subjects.

I expand the term to 'divided and contested rule' (DCR), however, to emphasize that even the definitions of the jurisdictions of sovereignty were extremely contested in Bahrain. The local ruler and the British never agreed as to which subjects were to be considered 'local' vs. 'foreign', and thereby as to which would be under the ruler's vs. British control. These definitions would mainly be constructed and interpreted by the British along ethnosectarian lines, creating a legal and institutional basis for ethnosectarian political mobilization.

During the years 1900 to 1923, the British and local rulers struggled to reconcile the contradictions arising from this fragmentation and contestations of sovereign power in the new system. They, along with regional powers and local actors on the ground, would simultaneously manoeuvre through the ethnosectarian tensions created, reshaping and influencing the system from within. Over time, the cross-interaction between these different agents and the ensuing conflicts would destabilize the system of divided rule to the point where the British were no longer able to tolerate the situation. Political mobilization along ethnosectarian lines would reach a violent climax, leading the British to recalibrate the whole political system to one that more suited their needs.

2

POLITICS AND SOCIETY BEFORE DIVIDED RULE, 1783–1900

I n order to understand political practice in Bahrain during the period of divided rule, it becomes necessary to first recount the political history of the preceding period. As will be shown, politics on the islands was not always mainly defined and mobilized based on ethnosectarian considerations, and certainly not according to the ethnosectarian lines imagined by the British. Instead, political power was a product of the regional political practice of alliance and tribute payment under the ascending global British imperial might, while internally it was localized, highly personalized, and diffused. It was organized across urban-rural differences in economic organization and patronage, and was susceptible to a high degree of variance in its forms. 'Modern' bureaucratized governing practices were yet to take hold before the time of divided rule. However, it will be just as important to show that there existed local factors that, if placed in suitable circumstances, would provide fertile ground for political mobilization and practice that is primarily based on ethnosectarian lines. Repression and inequality were rife, and often would intersect with class, geography, social background, and sect.

During the narration, the reader will notice that when introducing new social actors, their ethnosectarian backgrounds are provided in parentheses. Rather than reinforcing the political primacy of these identifiers, they are mainly included to highlight that a purely ethnosectarian reading fails to provide an adequate explanation of political developments during this period.

REGIONAL SETTING: THE RISE OF TRIBAL ELITES AND *PAX BRITANNICA*

The story begins with the conquest of Bahrain by al-Khalifa in the late eighteenth century.[1] Regionally, this century marked the beginning of the decline of the Ottoman Empire, the most dominant force in the area. The Safavid Empire, the Ottoman Empire's main regional rival and the ruling authority in Iran, was not faring much better, and would be a spent force by 1736. As these regional powers waned, their grip on the frontiers of their empires correspondingly declined. In contrast, British imperial influence began steadily increasing in the region under the *Pax Britannica* that would span the globe for the next century. Taking advantage of these changing power structures, Arab tribes from the areas surrounding the Gulf began establishing their authority over ports and cities around its shores,

---

1 Hence, this study confines itself to the period from 1783 onwards, avoiding making any claims on the preceding epochs.

just outside the frontiers of these empires. Thus, tribal forces from the region emerged to replace previous rule by the imperial centre, heralding the beginning of what has been called the 'era of tribal elites'.[2]

Probably the most serious challenge to the Ottoman Empire to emerge out of this cycle of new forces was the al-Saʿud-ʿAbdulwahhab alliance that sprang from Nejd and crystallized itself in the first Saʿudi State of 1744.[3] The newly founded alliance would quickly establish its control over vast swathes of the Arabian Peninsula and the western shores of the Gulf. By the beginning of the nineteenth century, they had reached and sacked Karbalaʾ in Iraq, entered the Hejaz area, and were approaching the borders of Damascus.[4] Their ascending power was only checked by a major military campaign undertaken by Mohammad ʿAli, the ruler of Egypt, culminating in his sacking of the Saʿudi capital, Dirʿiyyah, and the destruction of the first Saʿudi state in 1818.

Other tribal political groupings and alliances emerged during this turbulent period. Notable within these were the ʿUtubs (Sunni), a coalition who established the port city of Kuwait at the beginning of the eighteenth century on the frontiers of Basra, then under Ottoman sovereignty. In a system that was to become a hallmark of their type of rule, they would

2 Khaldoun al-Naqeeb, *Society and State in the Gulf and Arab Peninsula: A Different Perspective* (Abingdon: Routledge, 2012), 76.
3 As many studies have noted it would be accurate to view the al-Saʿud and ʿAbdulwahhab alliance not as a tribe, but as a coalition originating from the urban areas of Najd. For more see: Rayed Krimly, *The Political Economy of Rentier States: A Case Study of Saʿudi Arabia in the Oil Era, 1950–1990* (Washington, D.C.: George Washington University, 1993).
4 Albert Hourani, *Arabic Thought in the Liberal Age 1798–1939* (Cambridge: Cambridge University Press, 1962), 38.

establish an urban centre characterized by a free port with low taxes in order to facilitate entrepôt trade, combined with a concentration on pearl diving as an industry. When a faction of the ʿUtub, including al-Khalifa, broke off in the mid-eighteenth century and moved to the Qatari peninsula a few hundred kilometres away, they followed a similar model there, focusing on developing the port and pearling city of al-Zubara from 1732, which would be replicated once again when al-Khalifa took over nearby Bahrain in 1783.

Table 2: List of prominent ruling families on the western coast of the Gulf

Region	Beginning of rule	Ruling family	First signed accord with British Empire
Abu Dhabi	1761	al-Nahyan	1820
Dubai	1833	al-Maktoum	1853
Sharjah and Ras al-Khaimah	1727	al-Qawasem	1820
Bahrain	1783	al-Khalifa	1820
Saʿudi Arabia	1744 (first Saʿudi state)	al-Saʿud	1915
Qatar	1847	al-Thani	1916
Oman	1744	al-Bu Saʿid	1798
Kuwait	1752	al-Sabah	1899

Bahrain was already convulsed by several successive changes and crises of power before the establishment of al-Khalifa rule in 1783. For most of the seventeenth century, the islands were ruled by the Safavid dynasty based in Iran, but the decline of that power at the beginning of the eighteenth century allowed for an invasion of Bahrain by the Yaʿariba from Oman (Ibadis) in 1717, which local lore recounts as a particularly destructive episode that laid waste to the islands.[5] Subsequently, Bahrain went through a period of unstable and frequently changing rule by different factions of Huwala forces (Sunni), who were able to expel the Ya'ariba from Bahrain. The last rulers before al-Khalifa were the al-Madhkurs, who also ruled Bushehr on the eastern side of the Gulf,[6] and who declared nominal allegiance to south Persian governors (Shi'as).[7]

It seems that al-Khalifa and their wider 'Utub coalition had already established connections with the islands of Bahrain before their conquest in 1783. Indeed, they were part of the forces that helped the al-Madhkurs take over Bahrain in 1753 from the previous rulers, and subsequently their ships were given permission to pearl dive free of taxes in seabeds considered part of Bahraini waters.[8] Furthermore, there are documents showing that the 'Utub owned palm groves in Bahrain at least dating back to the seventeenth century, where they would come and spend the hot summers under their shade.[9]

5 Yousuf al-Bahrani, *Lu'lu'at al-Bahrain fil Ijazat wa Tarajem Rijal al-Hadeeth* (Bahrain: Maktabat Fakhrawi, 2008), 425–428.
6 There is some dispute about the social grouping and sect of the al-Madhkurs, implicitly showing the malleability and the fuzziness of such classifications. They hailed from Oman before they took over rule and moved to Bushehr. For more on the al-Madhkurs see: Stephen Grummon, *The Rise and Fall of the Arab Shaikhdom of Bushire 1750–1850* (PhD thesis, John Hopkins University, 1986).
7 Mohammad al-Tajir, *'Iqd al-Li'al fi Tarikh Awal* (Bahrain: al-Ayyam, 1994), 100–102.
8 Ebrahim Khuri and Ahmad Jalal al-Tadmuri, *Saltanat Hurmuz al-'arabiyya al-mustakilla Vol. 2* (Ras al-Khaimah: Markaz al-Derasat wal Wath'eq, 1999), 222–223.
9 See for example a property document dated 1699 showing a member of al-'Utub buying a palm grove on the island of Sitra, found in: Rashid bin Fadhel al-bin, 'Ali, *Majmoo' al-fadha'el fi fan nasab wa tarikh al-qaba'el* (Qatar: Bader Publishing, 2007), 307.

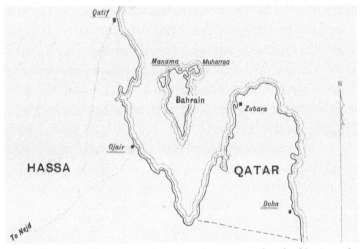

Figure 1: Map of Bahrain and surrounding ports, sketched by British officials in 1920
Source: QDL, 'Sketch map of Bahrain and surrounding ports' [113r] (1/2), IOR/R/15/1/319, f 113, https://www.qdl.qa/archive/81055/vdc_100023409102.0x000020, annotations by Omar AlShehabi.

The year 1783 has become part of the official lore of al-Khalifa in Bahrain. Accounts regarding the details of events differ. However, most recite that in retaliation against skirmishes that broke out between allies of al-Khalifa and residents on the island of Sitra (which lies on the easternmost frontiers of Bahrain's archipelago), al-Madhkur launched an all-out attack against al-Zubara in 1782. Back then, the latter was al-Khalifa's bastion on the Qatari Peninsula, approximately forty kilometres away from Bahrain's eastern coasts. The attack failed and the al-Madhkurs were roundly defeated. Their leader fled to Bushehr on the other side of the Gulf, and Bahrain was left in a state of political turmoil.

According to local historiography, the power feud on the islands was split mainly between two factions: the biggest one centred in the north around Jidhafs (Shiʿas), and their main rivals centred in the south around Bilad al-Qadeem (Shiʿas). The enmity reached a point where both factions were engulfed in bloody fights. After losing the feud, the faction in the south turned to al-Khalifa in al-Zubara, asking them to take over and rule the island and pledging them their support. Shaikh Ahmad ʿal-Fateh', the first of al-Khalifa's rulers, duly arrived, and it seems without much of a protracted fight, established himself as the political ruler of Bahrain.[10]

Sh. Ahmad did not base himself in Bahrain for the first twelve years of his rule, instead opting to move back and forth between the islands and his base in nearby al-Zubara.[11] He appointed members of the family of al-Bin-Rqayya (Shiʿa) as viziers and managers entrusted with his possessions and estates in Bahrain.[12] Upon his death, his sons and the allied tribes would relocate to the islands in 1794. The next two rulers of Bahrain, the two brothers Salman and ʿAbdulla, also continued their father's tradition by appointing Shiʿa ministers, as well as scribes, poets, and court writers.[13]

The regional politics of the first decades of al-Khalifa's rule were based upon the dictates of securing alliances through

10 N. al-Khairi, *Qalaʾid al-Nahrain fi Tarikh al-Bahrain* (Bahrain: al-Ayyam Publishing, 2003), 225–226; al-Tajir, *ʿIqd al-Liʾal*, 103–105.

11 Sh. will be used as an abbreviation to denote *Shaikh*, the honorific title by which members of the ruling family in Bahrain are usually called, in order to identify members of the al-Khalifa family in the narration.

12 Al-Khairi, *Qalaʾid al-Nahrain*, 228–237; al-Tajir, *ʿIqd al-Liʾal*, 107.

13 The main poet and scribe of al-Khalifa and their representative for the signing of the British imposed general treaty of peace and security in 1820 was Sayed ʿAbdulJalil Yasin al-Tabtabaei, a Shiʿa born in Basra. See: al-Khairi, *Qalaʾid al-Nahrain*, 228; Nader Kadhim, *Istiʿmalat al-Dhakira fi Mujtamaʿ Taʿaddudi Mubtala bi-l-Tarikh* (Bahrain: Maktabat Fakhrawi, 2008), 60–8.

tribute payment and pledges of allegiance.[14] Similar to the situation facing the previous rulers of Bahrain, their primary concern was to establish and sustain their authority over the scarce resources of the land and its people, in a regional political scene characterized by the intersecting presence of other tribal confederations and larger imperial powers. Alliances and rivalries could shift and alter quickly, with yesterday's friends being today's foes, including one's own kin. Towards this end, al-Khalifa were convulsed in many battles and tribute relations with different forces, particularly with the rulers of Oman, Najd, Iran, and most crucially the British Empire, which increasingly played the central role in shaping the regional political framework in which all the actors manoeuvred.

Shortly after al-Khalifa's takeover, forces from Iran tried to conquer the island in 1783 and 1785 but failed. In 1800, and after a previous failed attack in 1799, the Imam of Muscat (Ibadi) amassed a fleet with the intent of attacking Bahrain unless they paid him tribute, which forced the al-Khalifa rulers

---

14 This is a recurrent feature of political forces at the frontiers and intersections of empires. See the introduction of: Jane Burbank and Frederick Cooper, *Empires in World History: Power and the Politics of Difference* (Princeton: Princeton University Press, 2010). Onley calls this recourse to shifting alliances and allegiances in the Gulf 'the politics of protection'. This detaches such dynamics from the wider regional and global developments, decentring and sanitizing the crucial role of *Pax Britannica* in shaping the overall framework of the regional political system in which such alliances were formed. Such a reading makes it appear that the British imperial presence in the Gulf was mainly driven by invitations from the local forces to intervene in regional affairs and offer them protection, implicitly accepting the British colonial narrative of benevolent empire invited by willing protectorates, rather than emphasizing the centrality of expanding imperial ambitions under *Pax Britannica* in shaping the Gulf's dynamics. See: James Onley, 'The Politics of Protection in the Gulf: The Arab Rulers and the British Resident in the Nineteenth Century', *New Arabian Studies* 6 (2004): 30–92.

to flee back to al-Zubara.[15] The Omani forces were able to hold on to Bahrain for one year, after which the al-Khalifa allied with al-Saʿud and retook it in 1801, agreeing to pay a tribute to al-Saʿud in return. In 1805, they stopped paying them and allied themselves once again with the ruler of Muscat. In 1810, the Saʿudis attacked Bahrain and took the two ruling brothers of al-Khalifa, Salman and ʿAbdulla, as prisoners in Najd, and installed their own agent in Bahrain. (It is significant to mention that the three locals who accompanied the al-Khalifa brothers when they were taken to Najd were Shiʿa.[16]) Shortly afterwards, a cousin of the two brothers, ʿAbdulrahman, asked for help from the Sultan of Oman, and he retook Bahrain from al-Saʿud in 1811, paying tribute to the Omani ruler until 1815.[17]

At this point, al-Saʿud would start an alliance with the infamous Rhama bin Jaber al-Jalahma, who hailed from the same clan (ʿUtub) as al-Khalifa, and who for the next fifteen years would be the biggest external thorn in the side of al-Khalifa's rule until his death in 1826.[18] He would initiate several clashes, backed by al-Saʿud sometimes, and by the ruler of Muscat in others. From their side, the al-Khalifa rulers had by 1816 shifted alliances to al-Saʿud and al-Qawasem (Sunni, Huwala)[19] against the ruler of Muscat, who in turn allied himself with Rhama al-Jalahma.[20] By 1819, the Qawasem were crushed as a force by

15 Al-Tajir, 'Iqd al-Liʾal, 106.
16 The three were Salman bin Ruqayya, Altabatabaʾi, and Sayyed Yousif bin Sayyed Salman.
17 Onley, 'The Politics of Protection', 44–46.
18 Al-Tajir, 'Iqd al-Liʾal, 109–110.
19 Al-Qawasem were based in Ras al-Khaima and Sharjah in the modern -day UAE.
20 QDL, 'Gazetteer of the Persian Gulf. Vol I. Historical. Part IA & IB. J G Lorimer. 1915' [848] (1003/1782), IOR/L/PS/20/C91/1, http://www.qdl.qa/en/archive/81055/vdc_100023575946.0x000004.

the ever-encroaching British imperial might, which buttressed its pre-eminence by forcing the different powers in the Gulf to sign a peace treaty the following year. Intermittent threats of attacks by the ruler of Muscat against Bahrain would continue for the next few years, with the last big battle occurring in 1828, when al-Khalifa forces were able to repel the attacks. The British would then become the ultimate arbiter between al-Khalifa and the ruler of Oman, preventing the latter from making any further attacks.

The clashes between al-Khalifa and al-Saʿud took a back seat for a few years after the forces of Egypt's Mohammad ʿAli destroyed the first Saʿudi state in 1818, but al-Saʿud would soon return with the establishment of the second Saʿudi state in 1824. By 1833, their rising forces from Najd would reach the Qatif and Hasa oases in the eastern part of the Arabian Peninsula, perilously close to Bahrain. Encouraged by a request for aid by a group of notables from Qatif (Shiʿa), who preferred al-Khalifa rule over al-Saʿud, a faction of the al-Khalifa would block the port of Qatif and take over Tarut Island close by.[21]

By 1836, the Persian governor of Fars would also demand tribute from al-Khalifa, which made the ruler in Bahrain turn towards al-Saʿud once again for an alliance, thus ending the blockade on Qatif.[22] By 1839, the al-Saʿud presence had receded from the Gulf in the face of renewed attacks by the Egyptians, who in turn asked for tributes from Bahrain. Due to internal problems of their own, however, the Egyptians had to evacuate al-Hasa in 1840. This to and fro of political allegiance and

21 Kadhim, Istiʿmalat al-Dhakira, 64–65.
22 QDL, 'Gazetteer of the Persian Gulf. Vol I. Historical. Part IA & IB. J G Lorimer. 1915' [857-865] (1012-1020/1782), IOR/L/PS/20/C91/1, https://www.qdl.qa/en/archive/81055/vdc_100023575946.0x00000d.

tribute payment would continue for the next several decades in the shifting balance of power between the different tribal factions of al-ʿUtub, the Ottomans, al-Saʿud , Persians, and rulers of Oman, with the British Empire increasingly asserting itself as the strongest party that shaped the overall regional political framework. Al-Khalifa themselves would receive tribute from different areas and tribes, particularly on the Qatari peninsula, where they continued to hold sway over al-Zubara and its neighbouring areas, while more often they paid tributes themselves to larger regional powers.

It should be clear by now that an ethno-sect-based narrative on its own is unable to explain the political allegiances and movements that led to the establishment of al-Khalifa's rule in Bahrain, nor the regional intricacies that shaped their alliances during the first five decades of their rule. As Kadhim explains:

> [T]he conclusion we reach from all these historical examples is that there was no historical correspondence between sect and political positions ... Therefore, the proposition that there is an old correspondence between sect (Sunni/Shiʿa) and political position (loyalists/oppositions) is a historically incorrect proposition, because this history records that there were Shiʿa splits between opposition and loyalist, and Sunni splits between opposition (including military confrontation) and loyalists.[23]

More substantively, I also want to extend this conclusion to question the epistemological validity of giving primacy to sectarian cleavages as the most important units of political

23 Kadhim, Istiʿmalat al-Dhakira, 66–68 (my translation).

analysis. Not only is there little evidence that political stances directly correspond to sect, but there is little evidence that political practice and mobilization was formed mainly according to such sect considerations during this period.

INTERNAL WAR OF AL-KHALIFA

This conclusion is strengthened further by examining the internal socio-political dynamics within Bahrain. The history of Bahrain under al-Khalifa rule can be encapsulated, at least geographically, by the rise of the urban centres of Manama and Muharraq. In a system that was by now familiar from the 'Utub governance of al-Zubara and Kuwait, their rule in Bahrain would be based on the growth of port cities catered towards entrepôt trade and pearling.[24] Such cities were characterized by low taxes and an open outlook that encouraged the movement of people from the surrounding areas of both shores of the Gulf and Arabian Peninsula to the new urban centres.

Records of the early years of al-Khalifa rule in Bahrain are scant, but a 1790 report by Samuel Manesty and Harford Jones from the East India Company Residency in Basra is illuminating. After recounting the takeover of Bahrain by al-Khalifa seven years previously, they comment that there has been a considerable rise in trading and pearl diving in the islands, the latter being the primary source of employment, with the pearls then traded in India and Oman.[25] According to the report, the boom

24 I would like to thank Robert Carter for his thoughts on this matter.
25 QDL, 'Selections from State Papers, Bombay, regarding the East India Company's Connection with the Persian Gulf, with a Summary of Events,

in trade was driven by the relative stability of the internal rule, its openness and protection of traders coming to the islands, as well as levying no taxes whatsoever on mercantile trade. They were also able to profit from the declining trade in Basra, previously a regional hub, which had been hit recently by the plague and suffered from high taxes and instability due to European and Ottoman rivalries. In this respect, trade in Bahrain also benefited from the ʿUtub's use of their own ships that were able to sail all the way to India, allowing them to avoid stops in Muscat and other ports in the Gulf.

This internal relative economic prosperity under the rule of the first Shaikh of al-Khalifa began to wane after his death in 1796. By the turn of the century, al-Khalifa and their forces would be kept preoccupied for the next three decades by the previously enumerated skirmishes and clashes with al-Saʿud and the Omanis, beginning with the latter's takeover of the islands in 1800. Much more serious in terms of its impact on social conditions on the islands, however, was the internal war that engulfed the different factions of al-Khalifa by the beginning of the 1840s. Lasting for another three decades, its reverberations would reach far beyond the shores of Bahrain.

The roots of the internal rivalry can be traced to dual camps that grew out of the two sons of the first ruler, who split power after his death. Sh. Salman ruled over Manama and the neighbouring areas, while Sh. ʿAbdulla ruled over the Muharraq area. The first was the more dominant figure until his death in 1825, upon which the latter became the more influential Shaikh on the islands. Nevertheless, Sh. Khalifa, the son of Salman,

1600–1800' [241v] (482/540), IOR/L/PS/20/C227, http://www.qdl.qa /archive/81055/vdc_100023622976.0x000053.

continued to hold sway in the Manama area,[26] and after he died in 1834, his son Mohammad bin Khalifa (henceforth MbK) staked a claim over his estates. By this point, however, Sh. ʿAbdulla and his children had effectively become sole rulers. His reign seems to have been an unhappy period, characterized by misgovernment resulting from the vagaries of the personalized nature of rule, with many leaving the islands for elsewhere:

> The towns were in a state of rot and decay, and house rents had fallen to one-eighth of what they had been only a few years before. Six sons of the Shaikh pretended to exercise separate and independent power, and their attention was chiefly devoted to extracting money from merchants and other men of means . . . The result was a general exodus of the inhabitants to every quarter of the Gulf.[27]

The simmering internal rivalries between al-Khalifa members would soon violently explode. As the Egyptians withdrew from al-Hasa and al-Qatif in 1840, some notables in those areas renewed their calls of allegiance to al-Khalifa by sending for MbK to fill the power vacuum created by the Egyptian withdrawal. They preferred his rule to a potential return of al-Saʿud, and consequently he blockaded its ports.[28] This did not sit well

26 QDL, 'Gazetteer of the Persian Gulf. Vol I. Historical. Part IA & IB. J G Lorimer. 1915' [851] (1006/1782), IOR/L/PS/20/C91/1, https://www.qdl.qa/en/archive/81055/vdc_100023575946.0x000007.

27 QDL, 'Gazetteer of the Persian Gulf. Vol I. Historical. Part IA & IB. J G Lorimer. 1915' [858] (1013/1782), IOR/L/PS/20/C91/1, https://www.qdl.qa/en/archive/81055/vdc_100023575946.0x00000e.

28 Ibid., 865.

Al-Khalifa Rulers of Bahrain

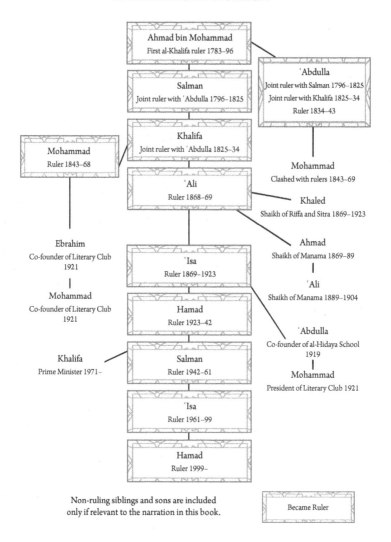

Figure 2: Family tree of al-Khalifa rulers and notable family members

with his great uncle 'Abdulla, starting a bloody rivalry between the two that would consume Bahrain, the surrounding areas, and eventually the region for the next quarter of a century.

War broke out between the two sides in 1842 and, after several battles, MbK had completely defeated his elder uncle by 1843 and assumed sole rule of the island.[29] 'Abdulla and his sons were scattered into the nearby areas in Sa'udi Arabia and Qatar, from which they would continue to scheme and launch attacks against MbK, often aligning with al-Sa'ud in their quest. A decisive battle was finally won by MbK in 1848, after which 'Abdulla lost hope and died shortly afterwards in 1849.[30]

The islands continued their economic decline during this period.[31] Many merchants left Manama, and the commercial fleets were reduced to a quarter of their size as they moved elsewhere.[32] The internal situation began to settle down after the defeat of the 'Abdulla faction in 1848, and it seems that the stability had allowed for some revival of economic and commercial affairs.[33] Conflicts were soon to erupt again, however, as the sons of 'Abdulla, particularly Mohammad bin 'Abdulla, began reaching out once again to the al-Sa'uds, in order to avenge and defeat MbK. During the 1850s, they would engage in several battles and raids on ships from Bahrain, all of which ended in failure.

29 Ibid., 867–872.
30 Al-Khairi, *Qala'id al-Nahrain*, 300–315.
31 Al-Tajir, '*Iqd al-Li'al*, 125–135.
32 Mahmood Almahmood, *The Rise and Fall of Bahrain's Merchants in the Pre-Oil Era* (Washington, D.C.: MA thesis, American University, 2013), 13–14.
33 This was evident, for example, to William Palgrave, who visited Bahrain in 1862: William Palgrave, *Personal Narrative of a Year's Journey Through Central and Eastern Arabia (1862–1863)* (London: Macmillan, 1871), 380–381.

However, the growing feud increasingly began sucking in several other regional players from Qatar and Sa'udi Arabia, and very soon it began involving even larger powers.[34] In his efforts to garner alliances against the Sa'udis, MbK reached out both to the Ottomans and the Qajar Empire in Iran at the same time, in order to pledge his allegiance. Local lore recounts the highly improbable tale that he raised both the Ottoman and Persian flags on top of the same fort, so that each was only visible to the respective party from their angle of vision. This immediately alarmed the British, who by now were pursuing a more vigorous trade and maritime policy in the Gulf. They finally decided to sign a treaty of 'protection' with MbK in 1861, a milestone in Bahrain's history. He agreed to abstain from aggression in the region, on promise of British support against any external attacks on the islands, including from the al-Sa'uds or the Ottomans. In essence, MbK signed over his ability to wage regional military campaigns to the British.

This treaty would prove to be his undoing, as matters turned sour in 1867 after a rebellion erupted in Qatar. Back then, al-Zubara and many of the tribes of the Qatari peninsula still pledged allegiance to al-Khalifa. In response to the unrest, MbK took as prisoner Jasem bin Mohammad al-Thani (Sunni), a notable of Qatar who eventually would become the founder of Qatar's modern ruling dynasty. Many tribes in Qatar took his arrest as a declaration of war.

The two sides met in the infamous battle of al-Damsa, which has become a landmark event in both Bahrain's and Qatar's historiography. Thousands amassed in both camps, and it became one of the bloodiest battles the Gulf witnessed in the nineteenth century. Local stories recount that the amount of

34 Al-Khairi, *Qala'id al-Nahrain*, 316–331.

dead bodies turned the sea red, with many refusing to eat fish for several months after the incident, in fear that they had fed on the human carcases.[35] The victorious army of MbK then marched on to and sacked Wakrah and Doha, the base of al-Thani. Even the rafters and doors of the houses were removed, with the overall damage estimated at 200 thousand Maria Theresa dollars.[36]

Although MbK never lost a regional battle, this victory in particular proved to be pyrrhic. The British saw the attack on Doha and Wakrah as a violation of the treaty they had signed with him, and a strong response was needed to maintain their authority over the gulf. They asked for a payment of 100 thousand dollars in compensation from MbK, and when he refused they sent their gunboats to the islands in September 1868, by which time MbK had absconded to the Qatari peninsula. The British duly deposed him, burned his fleet, and razed his main fort to the ground. They concluded a deal with his brother 'Ali, upon which he would become ruler of Bahrain.[37]

MbK was not to go down without a fight, however, even if it was against his brother. He amassed his forces and attacked his brother's troops in Riffa in southern Bahrain. Mohammad bin 'Abdulla, the exiled son of the previously deposed 'Abdulla, appeared for one final swansong, in which he played off the two brothers. MbK emerged victorious as his brother 'Ali was killed

35 May al-Khalifa, *Ma'a shaikh al-udaba' fil Bahrain Ebrahim bin Mohammad al-Khalifa* (London: Riad al-Rayes Books, 1993), 25.
36 QDL, 'Gazetteer of the Persian Gulf. Vol I. Historical. Part IA & IB. J G Lorimer. 1915' [892-894] (1047-1049/1782), IOR/L/PS/20/C91/1, https://www.qdl.qa/en/archive/81055/vdc_100023575946.0x000030.
37 QDL, 'Gazetteer of the Persian Gulf. Vol I. Historical. Part IA & IB. J G Lorimer. 1915' [895] (1050/1782), IOR/L/PS/20/C91/1, https://www.qdl.qa/en/archive/81055/vdc_100023575946.0x000033.

in battle, upon which the forces of Mohammad bin 'Abdulla, having finally been allowed back into Bahrain, sacked Bahrain's biggest cities of Manama and Muharraq.[38] Immediately, the British sent a gunboat to Bahrain, arrested both MbK and Mohammad bin 'Abdulla, and deported them to India. Upon consulting with local notables, Shaikh 'Isa, the son of the slain Sh. 'Ali, was chosen to be the new ruler in 1869, with the approval of the British.

THE REIGN OF SH. 'ISA BIN 'ALI: THE RISE OF PEARLING AND TRADE TOWNS

The reign of Sh. 'Isa bin 'Ali would span more than five decades, from 1869 until the climax of our story in 1923. Comparatively, the first twenty years of his rule was a period of internal stability and prosperity, enabled by the end of the civil war between the two al-Khalifa factions and the consolidation of rule under one person. This was in conjunction with the end of regional threats, backed by British imperial might after signing the 1861 treaty.

The islands would witness an unprecedented economic boom during the remainder of the nineteenth century. This was 'The Age of Capital',[39] with several technological breakthroughs making the world a truly global market for the first time. Particularly important was the invention of the steamship that led to 'spatio-temporal compression'.[40] The new technology would significantly alter people's conceptions of space and

38 Ibid., 898.
39 Hobsbawm, *The Age of Capital.*
40 David Harvey, 'Between Space and Time: Reflections on the Geographical Imagination', *Annals of the Association of American Geographers* 80.3 (1990): 418–434.

time, as different parts of the globe were connected together at increasing speeds. After the treaty of 1861 between Bahrain and Great Britain, the British India Steam Navigation Company included Bahrain in its stops, connecting the routes between Basra and India.[41] This made ports like Bahrain important intermediary links in British imperial trade. This was followed by the laying of a trans-oceanic telegraph structure, which created a market across the Indian Ocean.[42]

These game-changing technological breakthroughs were complemented by the huge increase in demand for pearls, with the rise of the nouveau riche in Europe and America concomitant with the age of capital. Although global demand for pearls existed previously, it was minuscule compared to the boom that would occur in the second half of the nineteenth century, creating an unprecedented rush for the white treasures, particularly for those from the Gulf. The total value of pearls exported from the Gulf tripled from almost half a million pounds in 1893 to 1.5 million in 1903–1904.[43] The centre of this trade in the Gulf became Bahrain, where the value of pearl exports quintupled from 180 thousand in 1875 to over a million pounds within fifteen years.[44] By the eve of the First World War in 1914, it would go up to nearly two million pounds.

This economic boom centred largely on the two urban centres of Manama and Muharraq. The two cities' growth

41 Sarah Kaiksow, *Threats to British 'Protectionism' in Colonial Bahrain: Beyond the Sunni/Shi'a Divide* (Washington, D.C.: MA thesis, Georgetown University, 2009), 17.
42 Fahad Ahmad Bishara, *A Sea of Debt: Histories of Commerce and Obligation in the Indian Ocean, c. 1850–1940* (Durham, North Carolina: PhD thesis, Duke University, 2012), 62–65.
43 Ibid.
44 Almahmood, *The Rise and Fall of Bahrain's Merchants*, 13–14.

reflected two distinct but intersecting economic ways of life. Muharraq would become the capital of pearl diving in the Gulf, and indeed the world, while Manama would become the main hub for commercial trade in Bahrain, driven particularly by the stopping of the British steamships in its port. Although built around two different technologies, production chains, and markets, these two economic spheres were intimately linked.

Pearl diving was the engine driving the economy. A hugely labour-intensive industry that also required large amounts of capital to finance its ships, it constituted the backbone of what Bahrain offered as exports to the rest of the world. This is where the second economic sphere would enter, as the resultant income from selling pearls abroad would fuel local consumption and demand. This would be met by rising import trade as well as services provided by local artisans. Thus, pearling was the main productive enterprise, while imports of merchandise created a wider link to goods and services from the rest of the world.

Since pearling was the main source of exports and hard currency for Bahrain, it was exempted by the ruler from taxes to encourage the activity. This was further aggravated by the fact that the industry by its nature was very susceptible to 'capital flight', given that ship owners could literally sail away to other port cities in the Gulf if taxation was too high or political conditions unappealing. This was not an uncommon phenomenon in the Gulf, as witnessed by the rise and fall of different port cities dotting its shores across the centuries.[45]

45 One of the most famous cases of this type of capital flight was '*Hijrat al-Tawaweesh*' (Migration of the Pearl Merchants) from Kuwait to Bahrain in 1910, due to the imposition of higher taxes by Sh. Mubarak (the ruler of Kuwait) on pearling enterprises. Three of the largest pearl merchants left for Bahrain with 250–300 of their ships that employed six thousand to

Hence, given the mobile nature of their industry and its status as the largest exporter, ship owners and pearl merchants were allowed to capture most of the surplus from pearl production, without much direct taxation from the ruler. In turn, the ruler would make the largest share of his income by extracting custom taxes on imports. In this manner, transnational merchants who wanted access to the local markets to sell their goods had to pay custom fees. These import taxes were kept relatively low by regional standards in order to encourage maritime trade.

Those engaged in trade and crafts services were concentrated in the urban areas of Manama, and to a lesser extent in Muharraq, often within their own districts and neighbourhoods.[46] As tradesmen, shopkeepers, and craftsmen, they were also expected to pay irregular forms of taxes and levies to the ruling family members in charge of the city in which they were active (*al-sukhrah*, see page 67). The rates varied not only across professions and traded goods but also across Shaikhs and time.

These economic taxes paled in comparison to the extremely repressive labour practices employed in pearl production, in which the majority of the population worked. Volumes have been written on the difficult conditions that faced the divers, both physically and socially. Diving was based on techniques that had remained relatively unchanged for centuries. This essentially relied on the ability of the diver to reach the

---

eight thousand men. This had such an effect on Kuwait's economy that the ruler himself had to go to Bahrain to ask that they return. For more on this episode and 'exit' strategies by capital more generally see: Saad Hesham Al -Shehabi, *The Evolution of the Role of Merchants in Kuwaiti Politics* (PhD thesis, King's College London, 2015), 66–75.

46 This, for example, applies to the shipbuilders of al-Naim district.

relatively shallow seabed and hold his breath while he collected pearls; then, after a few minutes, his assistant on the boat deck would pull him up by a rope. The physical pressures of the profession were particularly dangerous, harsh and damage inducing. As al-Rumaihi explains:

> The diver experienced great danger and discomfort not only from the attacks of sharks and sawfish but also from the masses of stinging jellyfish which swim at all levels and burned the body of the diver or in some cases even put out an eye. The 'bends' were a common affliction amongst the divers and produced severe pains in the joints, paralysis, or even death. Suppuration of the eardrums and rheumatism were also common amongst the divers. If the diver stayed down too long, he also often suffered from severe bleeding from the ears and nose.[47]

As if the physical strain of the profession was not enough, the socio-economic relations built around his labour were in many aspects even more taxing. A small minority were slaves. The vast majority, however, were deeply ingrained in a pervasive culture of debt running throughout all the echelons of the industry, from the divers to the ship captains (*nokhedhas*), and from the ship captains to financiers and pearl merchants. Infamously, most divers effectively mortgaged their life to the ship captains, to whom they usually would be tied for life. This was because divers did not live off monthly wages, but were instead paid a share of the profits at the end of the pearling

47 Mohammad Ghanim al-Rumaihi, *Bahrain: Social and Political Change Since the First World War* (London: Bowker, 1976), 71.

seasons. The pearling season, however, lasted only for a few months, and the harvest by its very nature was precarious and could fluctuate hugely based on weather conditions and the 'luck' of a particular ship. Divers could not depend solely on their uncertain returns at the end of the pearling season to sustain them with a constant income stream throughout the year. Therefore, divers were forced to take loans from the ship captains before the pearling season began, which then would have to be paid back at exorbitant interest rates. A diver was not allowed to work with another ship captain until his debt was paid off to the previous nokhedha, effectively tying him to the latter for life.

Rarely were divers able to pay off their debts, and in most cases they were illiterate and unable to read the accounts which were kept by the nokhedhas. If their debts were not paid off at their deaths, as was often the case, then their brothers and sons inherited the debt, with children entering the sea at single-digit years of age. In extreme cases, some captains would marry the diver's widow as payment towards the debt, and the diver's sons would become a servant in his household, to be then trained as divers when older.[48] In cases of dissent or rebellion, divers were often publicly flogged and crucified as a warning to others. In turn, the ship captain was also often in debt to financiers, who would have the right to take over his ship and even his house in case of non-payment, and in extreme cases he would be forced to become a diver himself.

This culture of peonage, which was managed across the port cities of the Gulf through an intricate system of debt documentation, served as an effective way for ship captains and

48 Ibid., 76–78.

financiers to control and discipline pearl workers and their labour.[49] This was particularly important since in theory pearl divers could abscond relatively easily, given the mobile nature of an industry based on ships. Furthermore, the organized and intensive labour involved in pearl diving made the industry highly susceptible to revolts and strikes, generating extremely repressive forms of labour control by the ship owners.

Still, the pearling industry formed the backbone of the economy, and provided the main form of sustenance for the majority of workers in the Gulf. This is evident from the large and growing stream of workers who would flow into Bahrain at the start of the pearling season from nearby areas in eastern Saʿudi Arabia, Qatar, or the Iranian side of the Gulf, seeking employment during this period. In the year 1926, for example, by which time the pearling industry was already in decline, there were more than twenty thousand workers employed in five hundred boats in Bahrain.[50]

The pearl-diving industry was mainly based in the city of Muharraq (and Hidd close by). Once al-Khalifa and the allied tribes moved permanently to Bahrain at the end of the eighteenth century, they established an urban centre at the southern tip of Muharraq Island, which would then become the centre for the pearl-fishing activities undertaken in Bahrain. The bastion of al-Khalifa rule until the climax of our story in 1923, Muharraq is probably the best indicator that political rule prior to the British arrival was not primarily guided by ethnosectarian considerations. Instead, its governance was based on the by

49 Pearl divers across the port cities of the Gulf needed to present written documents, called *Barwa*, showing that they were free of debt to ship captains, before they would be allowed to dive on the ships of other captains.
50 al-Rumaihi, *Bahrain: Social and Political Change*, 76.

now familiar 'Utub setup of administering port cities under the hegemony of tribal and urban solidarity.

If one looks at Muharraq from an ethno-sect standpoint, it is a largely Sunni city, with the island becoming the main place where both the tribes and Huwala concentrated. However, it would also have a smaller but notable Shi'a presence, both in terms of Shi'a Arabs and Persians. Just as was the case in the previous 'Utub cities of al-Zubara and Kuwait, rulers actively encouraged the movement of highly sought-after craftsmen, many of them Shi'a. Some of the latter moved with al-Khalifa from al-Zubara, while others migrated from the neighbouring eastern provinces of Hasa and Qatif. This phenomenon is best encapsulated by the al-Heyyach, al-Sagha and al-Bannayeen districts in Muharraq, which are named after the professions of the families that populated them: tailors, metalsmiths, and builders respectively. These districts became an integral part of the make-up of Muharraq, and they would arrange their living quarters and display a sense of solidarity in ways similar to other tribes present in Muharraq, even though by today's classification they would be considered 'Baharna'.[51] Under Lorimer's ethno-sect groupings, out of Muharraq's estimated population of 20,000 in 1904, half were classified as Huwala, 1,000 as of African descent, 1,500 as slaves, 900 as Shi'a Arabs, 100 as Shi'a Persians, and the rest of about 6,000 were from various Arab tribes.[52]

---

51 Al-Khater, *al-Qadhi*, 50. See also: Ahmad al-Baqshi, 'Al-Ehsa'yoon f Bahrain a w a set al-qarn al-'eshreen', https://malturath.word press.com/2013/04/12#/الع-القرن-أواسط-البحرين-في-الإحسائيون/-more-369.

52 QDL, 'Gazetteer of the Persian Gulf. Vol. II. Geographical and Statistical. J G Lorimer. 1908' [1270] (1381/2084), IOR/L/PS/20/C91/4, http://www.qdl.qa/archive/81055/vdc_100023515717.0x0000b7.

Al-'Utub and the allied families seemed to exercise an assimilative hegemony in Muharraq. Indeed, until today, and uniquely within Bahrain's historic regions, although a Muharraqi accent is instantly recognizable it is completely impossible to tell the sect or social background of the person from his accent. Furthermore, and uniquely amongst Bahrain, there is one cemetery where all different sects are buried, whereas other places have different cemeteries demarcated by sect.[53]

Muharraq was the capital of political power and pearl diving in Bahrain, while the other large city, Manama, lying only three kilometres away, was the trading capital. Manama would also develop at a tremendous pace during al-Khalifa's rule into the major urban centre of the islands by the beginning of the twentieth century. Largely a town that developed around trade and the servicing of trade, particularly after the arrival of British imperial steamships in the second half of the nineteenth century, the vast majority of the population that would move to the city came from Bahrain's villages and areas immediately surrounding the Gulf and the Arabian Peninsula. Although still a largely Arabic-speaking city built around the same concepts of tribal primacy seen in other cities established by the 'Utubs, it was also a hybrid frontier society that straddled both tribal ideals, the nearby agriculture villages, and far-flung trade routes across the Indian Ocean.[54] The latter were enabled

---

Once again, these numbers and classifications should be read with the required circumspection when dealing with such social categories.

53 Indeed, up until the 2011 protests, Muharraqis were famous for having a 'Muharraq first' identity that was elevated above other considerations, including sects and ethnicities.

54 Nelida Fuccaro, *Histories of City and State in the Persian Gulf: Manama Since 1800* (Cambridge: Cambridge University Press, 2009), 42.

by the new steam technologies that allowed steamships to dock at its port.

Within a few decades of al-Khalifa's rule, Manama had developed by 1836 into a sizeable town of four hundred shops surrounded by a wall with twenty-eight towers, rivalling the regional trade hub Bushehr.[55] However, the city would grow spectacularly during the last four decades of the nineteenth century, as Manama's population increased three times from about 8,000 in the early 1860s to approximately 25,000 in 1904. People poured in from the nearby agricultural villages of Bahrain, Hasa, and Qatif in the Eastern Province of Sa'udi Arabia, the eastern coasts of the Gulf, Najd in central Arabia, and Iraq, as well as from East Africa.

According to Lorimer's ethno-sect readings, out of a population of 25,000 in 1904, three fifths were Shi'a, of which the largest group were the Baharna (12,000 souls). There were also another 2,500 Shi'a Arabs, as well as 1,500 Shi'a Persians. In terms of Sunnis, the composition was made up of Huwala (5,000), 'Utub (500), Arabs from the Najd, Kuwait, and other nearby regions (1,900), individuals of African origin (1,500), slaves (800), and 50 Sunni Persians. There were also a very small but economically significant number of non-Muslims (200) composed of Jews (50), Christians (40), as well as dozens of Hindus, largely non-resident traders, whose numbers would fluctuate from 70 to 175 during the year according to the pearling season.[56]

---

55 Abdalla Yateem, *al-Manama al-madina al-'arabiyya* (Bahrain: University of Bahrain, 2015), 71–73.

56 The small numbers of non-Arabic speakers contrasted with an overwhelming majority of Arabic speakers, even within the inhabitants of that most 'cosmopolitan' city of Manama. Migrants from India to Bahrain and the rest of the Gulf were relatively few and limited to a few traders (e.g. Kuwait had only three Indian 'petty traders' in 1925 according to the British Political Agent), and their migrations were dwarfed by the opposite

Even though the population was overwhelmingly composed of Arabic speakers, an openness to trade with regions that lay far beyond the Gulf and Arabian Peninsula meant that many residents, particularly traders, could speak several languages.[57] Consequently, even though the residents of the city primarily hailed from areas surrounding the Gulf and the Arabian Peninsula, given their disproportionate involvement in trading activities across the British Empire's Indian Ocean trade routes, languages such as Farsi, Hindi, Swahili, and English would have a notable presence in written documents and the conduct of trade.[58]

---

movement of traders from the Gulf to India. While vibrant exchanges across the Indian Ocean demonstrate the openness in terms of trade and cultural outlook of the people inhabiting Bahrain, some of the recent literature exaggerates their impact to the extent of denying the centrality of Arabic language and culture in Bahrain and the rest of the western coast of the Gulf. In accordance with this discourse, Gulf society is painted as a largely cosmopolitan assemblage of migrating ethnicities, sects, and languages that was a cultural extension of the Indian Raj, but which was later Arabized by state-enforced nationalism. Such interpretations, however, run the risk of uncritically reproducing earlier colonial readings of the Gulf, which saw the region as a collection of different ethnicities and sects with few overarching commonalities. They could also potentially feed into a patronizing Western narrative that views people of the Gulf as not really capable of shaping their own identity, state, outlook, culture, and nation-building, requiring statal or outside forces to adopt any form of Arabism or nationalism. For more on the numbers presented here see: QDL, 'File 18/110 (B Series 18/12) Annual Report on the Working of the Kuwait Order in Council', IOR/R/15/1/308, http://www.qdl.qa/archive /81055/vdc_100022744559.0x000008.

57 For a description of Manama and its acquaintance with news from far-flung trade routes in the mid-nineteenth century, see: William Palgrave, *Personal Narrative of a Year's Journey Through Central and Eastern Arabia (1862–1863)* (London: Macmillan, 1871), 380–386.

58 For a study that analyses such documents extensively, see: F. Bishara. *A Sea of Debt.*

PERSONALIZED AND LOCALIZED POWER

Instead of overt ethnosectarian mobilization, urban political power and practice during this period seems to have been much more personalized, localized, and segmented across class, locality, professions, and kinship. Like the cities of Kuwait and Zubara under the rule of the 'Utubs, the urban space in the two main cities of Manama and Muharraq would have been governed by the ideals of tribal and urban solidarity rather than sectarian sentiment. The first was evident from the term used to denote urban quarters, *fereej*, which was originally used to denote tribal sections and Bedouin encampments.[59] In terms of the second, the success of the cities established by the 'Utubs depended primarily on two factors: the first was encouragement of pearling and commercial enterprise, particularly through low taxes and the provision of a functioning port, as well as maintaining a relatively open attitude towards people relocating into the new towns. The ability of a ruler to collect taxes and increase the number of subjects under his rule depended primarily on the commercial prosperity of the town, which in turn depended on its ability to attract people to trade and live in these towns. Thus, while residents in Bushehr in the early nineteenth century had to pay taxes to the local al-Madhkur rulers and the regional Fars governor, as well as to the central Qajar state in Iran,[60] residents in the urban towns of Bahrain had only one level of fiscal power to contend with. People poured in from the areas surrounding the Gulf and the Arabian

---

59 Fuccaro, *Histories of City and State in the Persian Gulf*, 29–30. The same reference provides an extensive study of the city of Manama.
60 Vanessa Martin, *The Qajar Pact: Bargaining, Protest and the State in Nineteenth-Century Persia* (London: I.B.Tauris, 2005), 39.

Peninsula, continuing an age-old phenomenon of movement across the shores and ports of the Gulf, but which accelerated at much more rapid rates in the nineteenth century.[61] Hence, access to the sea was essential for Manama and Muharraq, both for the movement of people and goods. Predictably, market-places developed as the main public space of the time. Individuals from the different skills, crafts, and professional and social backgrounds that spanned the commercial routes of the Gulf and the Indian Ocean would meet and trade in one concentrated area.

The second factor was the ability to establish supremacy in the functions of the coercive apparatuses. This entailed both having enough firepower to repel attacks by outside forces, as well as collecting taxes from subjects living within their areas of rule. Part of this setup was allowing for the growth of institutions that addressed internal conflicts and grievances. This was done through a bare-bones administrative structure character-ized by a dispersal of power through individuals, making the nature of rule in each area highly personalized and informal. Similar to other areas at the frontiers of the Ottoman and Qajar empires, central administration barely existed, and rule was not systematized and often dependent on the vagaries of particular individuals in charge.[62] Although this corresponded to a rela-tively thin layer of state apparatuses that residents had to navi-gate through, it could also often lead to instability and a

---

61 There is a large literature on the movements of people across the differ-ent ports and towns on both sides of the Gulf that date back millennia. See, for example: Khuri, Ebrahim and Ahmad Jalal al-Tadmuri, *Saltanat Hurmuz al-'arabiyya al-mustakilla* (Ras al-Khaimah: Markaz al-Derasat wal Wath'eq, 1999).

62 Ibid., chapter 2 for the case of Bushehr under al-Madhkur rule under the Qajar dynasty in the mid-nineteenth century.

precarious security situation, as well as the arbitrary use and abuse of power.

Each of the urban areas was assigned to a Shaikh from the ruling family who was in charge of its order and security, as well as collecting taxes for his personal use. Each Shaikh would have a group of armed men from non-tribal backgrounds under his command, called *fidawiyya*. Maintaining the coercive functions inside the urban quarters were the duties of the Amir al-Souk, the commander of the fidawiyyas, who generally was not from the ruling family, and whose tasks included prevention of unrest, collecting taxes, and solving petty disputes. The readiness to administer external protection and wage battles was assigned to the Amir Harb, or commander of war.[63]

The ruler himself was based in Muharraq, where he would meet in his Majlis with his consultants and visitors to reach decisions regarding administrative affairs.[64] His authority was that as *primus inter paris* between members of the ruling family, and was based on his ability to have other notable members of his family and the rest of society defer to his judgement, by their recognition of him as the ultimate arbitrator in political matters. Much of this authority was based on him having the largest revenues of all al-Khalifa members, which were sourced through his control of agricultural estates, customs taxes, and markets. This also meant that he should have the largest fidawi forces, which were financed by these revenues. There was no

63 Khalifa al-Ghatam, 'Amir al-souk', *Bahrain Historical and Archaeological Society*, 10 June 2016, https://www.youtube.com/watch?v=70t1Z8mXMqA. See also: Fuad I. Khuri, *Tribe and State in Bahrain: The Transformation of Social and Political Authority in an Arab State* (Chicago: University of Chicago Press, 1980), 51.
64 Ibid., 36–37.

centralized bureaucracy in the modern sense, with no distinction between a private and a public purse.

Although urban taxes were relatively low by Ottoman or
Qajar standards, they were not completely regularized, and
depended largely on the dispositions of the local Shaikh in
charge of the area. The first of these was customs taxes on goods,
which were introduced for the first time in a regularized manner
in 1860 through a customs house, directly under the ruler's
supervision.[65]

There was also an in-specie, in-kind tax called *al-sukhrah*,
levied on traders and craftsmen by the local Shaikh, with the
justification of providing protection (often from harassment by
his own forces). Beginning in the 1880s, the rulers resorted
increasingly to farming out the collection of such taxes, in
exchange for advances by the tax farmers (*dallalulun*), who
would keep the fees from sales themselves. In 1888, the ruler
outsourced the customs house to a Hindu family, while collection of taxes from the agricultural markets, meat markets, as
well as several of the real estates of Manama were farmed out to
merchants and notables from within the same social
communities.[66]

The administration of law came from many sources and
served several purposes.[67] It was also variable, shifting by
context, jurisdiction, and the personalities of the officials. There
was no monopoly of law that flowed down from the ruler, but it
instead flowed upwards with multiple sources of power and
legal authority. Apart from the ruler, this also included the

65 QDL, 'Gazetteer of the Persian Gulf. Vol I. Historical. Part IA & IB. J G
Lorimer. 1915' [928] (1083/1782), IOR/L/PS/20/C91/1, https://
www.qdl.qa/en/archive/81055/vdc_100023575946.0x000054.
66 Fuccaro, *Histories of City and State in the Persian Gulf*, 87.
67 See Khuri, *Tribe and State*, chapter 3, for an overview.

judges, the merchants, nokhedhas, mariners, village Wazirs, and British representatives. Each had their own source of legitimacy from which they derived their political and social power.[68]

The ruler's political legitimacy arose from the recognition from other members of his ruling family, notables, and surrounding regional powers. In contrast, another sphere of juridical power was that of Islamic law, encapsulated in the different Qadhis (judges) that would rule on matters of Islamic jurisprudence, including inheritance, divorce, and other civil and criminal cases. As there was no written civil code, each Qadhi had considerable authority in dealing with day-to-day cases according to his interpretation of Islamic law. Here sect considerations did play a considerable role, as different Qadhis and Mullahs would attend to the legal and social practices of each school of Islam, whether in terms of marriage, divorce, or burial.[69]

Importantly, it seems that *madhhab* played a more prominent role in terms of personal status issues than the sect categories of Sunni or Shiʻa per se. In Sunni Islam, there were four madhhabs, each referring to a different school of thought within Islamic jurisprudence.[70] The al-Khalifa followed the Maliki school of jurisprudence, while al-Shafiʻi had a strong presence among people of a Huwala background, and the stricter Hanbali school held sway with people with roots in

68 For more on diffuse power during this period, see: Bishara, *A Sea of Debt*, 350–355.
69 QDL, 'Gazetteer of the Persian Gulf. Vol. II. Geographical and Statistical. J G Lorimer. 1908' [248] (275/2084), IOR/L/PS/20/C91/4, http://www.qdl.qa/en/archive/81055/vdc_100023515712.0x00004c.
70 The four madhhabs in Sunni Islam are: Shafiʻi, Maliki, Hanbali, and Hanafi. Each school is named after the jurist who taught and practised them.

Najd.[71] Within Shiʿa Islam, the predominant madhhab was Jaʿafari. Thus, one usually finds individuals identifying themselves by reference to their madhhabs,[72] rather than the terms 'Sunni' or 'Shiʿa', which were less frequently used.[73] This was particularly the case with the former, as it seems that 'Sunni' as a clear-cut identity at the social and personal status level did not hold much sway. In this manner, it was the madhhab in the sense of a school of jurisprudence, rather than two strongly defined categories of Sunni vs. Shiʿa sects, which seems to have played a predominant role at the social level.

There were also different strands of traditions within each madhhab, which could sometimes manifest themselves in important social divisions and distinctions. Within the Jaʿafari madhhab, for example, there were significant doctrinal and practical differences between the dominant *Usuli* tradition of Shiʿa religious scholarship and practice, and the more conservative and literalist *Akhbari*. There was also a smaller group who followed the *Shaykhi* tradition, particularly within families that

71 Hanafi did not have a significant presence in Bahrain.
72 This practice seems to have held sway for hundreds of years. Thus, a religious scholar from Bahrain of the Maliki madhhab identified himself in a letter dated 1536 as ʿAbdulla bin Mahmood al-Maliki al-Ansari al-Bahrani. The name also shows how 'Bahrani' could also previously be used to identify individuals with connections to Bahrain regardless of sect, rather than being confined to a particular ethno-sect social group, as is currently the practice. See: Rashid al-Jassim, *al-Bahrain wa ʿumkuha al-ʿaraby wal Islami* (Bahrain: al-Dar al-ʿArabiyya lel Mawsooʿat, 2015). An image of the letter can be viewed at: Jalal Khaled al-Ansari, ʿAjdaduna al-Ansarʾ, *Shabakat al-Tawwash*, http://alharoon.blogspot.qa/2014/05/blog-post_27.html.
73 I am yet to come across local documents that predate the events of the early 1900s and the period of British divided rule that use the term 'Sunni'. Instead, the norm is to refer to the madhhab to which a person belongs. See, for example: Muhammad al-Nabhani, *al-Tuhfa al-Nabhaniyya* (Bahrain: unknown, 1923), 55.

had roots in the al-Hasa oasis in the Eastern Province. The debates between these different traditions could sometimes reach such a point of enmity that accusations of apostasy and heresy were levelled against each other.[74]

On the flip side, there were no rigid boundaries in terms of the Qadhis of each madhhab that people took recourse to in practice, with individuals often even referring to judges outside their sect to resolve their matters. Many members of al-Khalifa would prefer to turn to Shaikh Ahmed bin Harz, a Shiʿa cleric based in the village of Jidhafs, to resolve their personal and familial disputes. Shaikh ʿAbbas al-Sitri from the island of Sitra played a similar role, becoming a favoured adjudicator for some members of the ruling family. In return, many Shiʿa residents of Sitra would head to Shaikh Ibrahim Bukhammas in the fishing village of ʿAskar, a religious scholar of the Maliki school, to resolve their disputes.[75]

The case of Qasem bin Mehzaʿ deserves more attention, as he will become a primary character in the events to ensue. He was born around 1847 in the village of ʿAskar in the south of the island. He shared a milk kinship with the ruler Sh. ʿIsa bin ʿAli, with his mother breastfeeding both. Following in the footsteps of his father, who was the Imam of a mosque in Manama, he

74 The Akhbari tradition used to be more dominant in Bahrain prior to Safavid rule, which marked the ascendance of the Usuli tradition. For more on the different traditions see: Moojan Momen, *An Introduction to Shiʿi Islam: The History and Doctrines of Twelver Shiʿism* (New Haven: Yale University Press, 1985); Juan R. I. Cole, 'Rival Empires of Trade and Imami Shiʿism in Eastern Arabia, 1300–1800', *International Journal of Middle East Studies* 19.2 (1987): 177–204.

75 Interview with Hasan Radhi, a leading Bahraini legal expert and scholar who is from Sitra, 30 September 2017. For more on Shaikh Ahmed bin Harz see: al-Sayyed Hashem al-Sayyed Salman, *Ghayat al-Maram fi Tarikh al-Aʿlam* (Bahrain: Manshoorat Maktabat al-Madani, 2004).

travelled to pursue religious studies for a year in al-Hasa, back then a notable centre of religious learning in the Arabian Peninsula. He then spent another year in Mecca to perform the Haj pilgrimage and complete his studies. His close relation with the ruler would be cemented during the war of 1868, in which both he and Sh. 'Isa bin 'Ali participated in the battle that ended with the defeat and killing of Sh. 'Isa's father, Sh. 'Ali bin Khalifa.[76]

After the British deposed Sh. Mohammad bin Khalifa (MbK) and installed his nephew Sh. 'Isa bin 'Ali as ruler, bin Mehza' was eventually installed as the chief judge of Manama in 1875, a position he would hold for more than five decades until 1927. He would expand his jurisdiction to become the chief judge in Muharraq as well in 1911. Officially a follower of the Maliki school, the powers of bin Mehza' became legendary, with even the ruler having to think twice before encroaching on his spheres of jurisdiction. Bin Mehza' effectively monopolized the responsibility to adjudicate in many types of cases, including personal status, commercial, and criminal, for people who followed a diverse range of madhhabs.[77] These ranged from disputes over the usage of fishing traps (*hathras*), entitlement to common irrigation systems between farms, property, marriage, divorce, as well as cases of theft and murder.[78] He even adjudicated cases from outside Bahrain.

The pearling industry was a different arena of judicial references altogether, one not structured by Islamic legal precepts or

76 For more on his life see: al-Khater, *al-Qadhi*.
77 Ibid., 46–55.
78 QDL, 'Gazetteer of Arabia Vol. I' [360] (379/1050), IOR/L/MIL/17/16/2/1, http://www.qdl.qa/archive/81055/vdc_100023909212.0x0000b4.

al-Khalifa rule, but the logic of economic life, risk, and returns. Here, jurisdiction and matters fell to *ahl al-salifa* (people of the matter), established and headed by merchants and nokhedhas, where they governed according to ʿUrf, a 'malleable, unwritten body of customs and rules deeply embedded within the socio-economic hierarchies of what constituted mercantile custom'.[79] The difference in jurisdictions was also apparent geographically: the ruler was in Muharraq, while the mercantile tribunals were in Manama.

Inevitably, those who were dominant within mercantile activities, and had access both to the rulers through tax farming or extensive property activities, had a path towards becoming notables of the town.[80] Thus, trading notables within the city built their credentials through their connections with the local rulers, whether through tax farming or extensive trade contacts. This was increasingly done through connections to foreign governments as well, particularly the British, but also the Saʿudi Amir and the Qajar government, which had significant sway among the traders of Manama. Many Persian traders had long connections with the Qajari bureaucracy, a practice which continued in the Pahlavi era in the twentieth century, while some Najdi traders would establish connections as representatives of al-Saʿud.

The access to the corridors of power was complemented with solidifying social connections with the urban population, particularly those of a similar regional and familial background. This was done by providing social services, employment, or giving of charity. There was no formal planning or regulation of the built environment, with the cities growing in waves of

---

79 Bishara, *A Sea of Debt*, 353–355.
80 Fuccaro, *Histories of City and State in the Persian Gulf*, 89.

people moving into the different neighbourhoods, which were built with minimal central authority oversight. Given that there was no social welfare state to speak of, this allowed merchants to carry out these functions in neighbourhoods under their influence, where they would provide protection, representation, and welfare to people moving into the cities from the same areas as them.[81]

Another way that such notables had established themselves was through the sponsoring of religious institutions. Although both Shi'a and Sunni merchant notables of the cities sponsored and built mosques, there were some religious institutions that were particular to the Shi'a social scene. Prominent were the *Ma'tams* and *'Ashura'* processions, whose appearance in the public sphere as regularized institutions coincided with the economic boom of Manama in the last quarter of the nineteenth century.

Ma'tams were public houses dedicated to mourning the martyrdom of Hussein, the maternal grandson of the prophet who was killed in the Battle of Karbala', an event that is considered foundational to Shi'a thought and rituals. In practice, they also served as venues for social events such as marriages, funeral services, and religious commemorations. Although disputed, the first documented institutionalized Ma'tams in Bahrain are those of al-Mudaifa and Bin Rajab in Manama around the year 1875, followed in 1877 by Ma'tam bin Khamis in the nearby village of Sanabis.[82] As their names imply, they were established by notable merchant families, overtaking the Shi'a religious

---

81 Ibid., 99.
82 Mahmood al-Jazeeri, 'Al-Nashaba: Mudaifa' awwal Matam fil Bahrain', *Al-Wasat* newspaper, 14 October 2015, http://www.alwasatnews.com/news/1035536.html.

clergy as the main sponsors of religious institutions in the cities, with the latter playing a remarkably marginal role in the politics of the island in the period 1875–1923.

'Azas, on the other hand, were public processions of mourning during 'Ashura', the period in which the battle of Karbala' occurred. Each of the notable Ma'tams would sponsor a procession (*mawkeb*) that would begin from its doorsteps and then parade across the city, with the spectacle becoming one of the largest social events in the city. The first recorded public procession occurred in 1891 in Manama, with Ma'tam bin Rajab sponsoring the first mawkeb that led the processions.[83]

In this respect, ethno-sect affiliation did play a role within the urban milieu of the cities. In addition to religious services, the different urban quarters and settlement patterns were built on a variegated landscape of patronage, familial, geographic, professional, and sect social connections. These different social attributes intersected and articulated in various forms. Marriage was largely not only within sect, but also within groups of one regional origin, and often within the same families. Specialized skills and crafts often intermeshed with social and regional background, sect, and urban space. Baharna composed a majority of those trading in agricultural produce from the nearby villages, while Huwala disproportionally made up traders and the shopkeeping class, and Baluchis and individuals of African origin composed much of the fidawiyya armed forces. Migrants from Hasa and Qatif had a concentration in local crafts, while those from Najd gravitated more towards pearl trading.

---

83 Abdulla al-Madani, 'Kabeer al-'ajam fil Bahrain', *Al-Ayam* newspaper, 2 May 2014. http s: / / malturath.wor dp ress.com / 201 4 / 05 / 02 / كبـيـر العجــــم-في-البحــري /#more-1075; Mohammad al-Alawi, 'Bushehri: al-Manama 'asimat al-'aza'a al-Bahraini', *Al-Wasat* newspaper, 5 November 2014, http://www.alwasatnews.com/news/933706.html.

These identifiers were more marked in the case of Manama, due to its variegated social composition. However, such differences should not be overstated, as many professions involved a diverse group of social actors. Poor classes of all different sects and regional backgrounds were found working as pearl divers, builders, and construction workers, while petty shopkeepers and traders also encompassed the different social identifiers. Similarly, both Shiʻas and Sunnis of different social backgrounds engaged and interacted in pearl and import trading.

Thus, overall, one could say that the public space was characterized by a fragmentation of popular politics along a clientilist system made of intersecting lines of kinship, patronage, and locality.[84] Hence, up until the 1890s (more on which to come), there was a marked lack of overt political mobilization along ethnosectarian lines in either Muharraq or Manama.

LIFE IN THE AGRICULTURAL VILLAGES

There was a third prevalent economic mode of life in Bahrain. This was based on agricultural and fishing production in the villages scattered along the shorelines of the islands.[85] When the two sons of the original conqueror, Sh. Ahmad, took over at the helm, these various agricultural villages were distributed to high-ranking Shaikhs within the ruling family as benefices. This entitled them to treat them as fiefs during their life but without hereditary succession, as the ruler could redistribute such

---

84 Fuccaro, *Histories of City and State in the Persian Gulf*, 152–164.
85 For details on the types of lands under cultivation and their produce see: Khuri, *Tribe and State*, 36–41.

benefices once they died.[86] Each Shaikh had a high degree of autonomy and collected his own taxes and tributes in terms of bonded labour, backed up by his own armed forces, the fidawiyya.

Local social matters and disputes within each village were generally referred to local Qadhis and religious clerics, who would attend to the legal and social practices of marriage, divorce, or burial, with only more serious disputes and crimes referred to external adjudication.[87] Although social and familial connections did extend across villages, there is little evidence pointing towards forms of cross-village political mobilization or institutions, with each village largely treated by the rulers as politically autonomous. Political rivalries between villages were not uncommon, with the aforementioned enmity between the elites of Jidhafs and Bilad al-Qadeem that preceded the conquest of al-Khalifa being the most infamous.[88]

The relationship between the village and the al-Khalifa Shaikh entitled to the fiefdom was mainly one of tribute payment, as the Shaikh generally did not reside in the village, but remained closer to the corridors of power in Muharraq or Riffa, the town in the south of the island where many of the ruling family members resided. These tribute payments between the Shaikhs and the villages were largely mediated through *Wazirs*, village locals whose job was to be the representatives of the village to the Shaikh, providing a list of the

---

86 Khuri, *Tribe and State*, 43–46.

87 Some religious clerics amassed considerable influence within the villages in this respect, perhaps the most famous being Shaikh Khalaf al-'Asfoor. For more see: Khuri, *Tribe and State*, chapter 4.

88 The rivalry between Jidhafs and Daih is another example, as well as that between Diraz and the villages surrounding it, whose social imprints are felt until today.

numbers of individuals and palm trees in an area for taxing purposes. *Kikhdas*, on the other hand, were locals of the villages who were tasked with collecting these taxes.

Agricultural output revolved mainly around the cultivation of palm trees. There were two types of agricultural property titles: those directly administered by the ruling family Shaikhs, and those cultivated by private landholders and subject to tax, with the latter being the majority. Given that land was literally fixed in the ground, the threat of capital flight was minimal from the point of the fief-holding ruling family members. Furthermore, the harvest from palm trees was relatively stable and predictable. Finally, although labour absconding could happen, this possibility was mitigated by the immobile nature of agricultural work and the scarcity of other available options.[89] These factors combined to make the taxation of land, farmers, and agricultural produce much more feasible for the rulers compared to the pearling industry.

The two prevalent taxes were *regabiyya*, which was taken per male head of each household, and *al-sukhrah*, forced labour which required working for a certain period free for the Shaikh (corvée).[90] If a private landholder failed to pay his taxes, his holdings could sometimes be confiscated and become part of the Shaikh's private estates. These taxes not only created conflict between Shaikhs and those in villages under their fiefs, but also

89 As the upcoming quote from Lorimer shows, the possibility of agricultural labour migration was predominantly to al-Hasa and Qatif, and vice versa.

90 The practice of corvée has a long history of being enforced on workers in agriculture, with one of the most (in)famous examples in the Arab world being its extensive use by Mohammad 'Ali in Egypt. For more see: Roger Owen, *The Middle East in the World Economy, 1800–1914* (London: I.B.Tauris, 1993).

even between Shaikhs themselves, as some would complain that cultivators under their jurisdiction were forced into corvée on other estates.[91]

The relationship between the villages and the Shaikhs in charge seemed to vary across time and the Shaikhs in question, reflecting the personalized and extremely variable type of rule. While the reign of Sh. Mohammad bin Khalifa between 1842 and 1869 was marked by an unstable economic situation and constant warfare,[92] it seems that agricultural output experienced growth during the first two decades of Sh. 'Isa bin 'Ali's reign, with Bahrain becoming an exporter of palm products during this period.[93] Farmers were brought in from nearby al-Hasa to meet the work demand on agricultural estates under the jurisdiction of the ruling family and those owned by rich merchants of Manama.[94]

However, it seems that the situation had begun to break down by the last decade of the nineteenth century, once again in large part due to the precariously personalized and decentralized nature of rule. The death of the brother of Sh. Ahmad seems to have contributed significantly to this breakdown, as the ruler depended on him greatly for conducting matters of governance during a time remembered by contemporaries as relatively more benevolent and stable.[95] Areas under his jurisdiction were considerable, and upon his demise they returned to the ruler to redistribute, as was customary upon the death of

91 Khuri, *Tribe and State*, 41–49.

92 Al-Khairi, *Qala'id al-Nahrain*, 372–373.

93 Mubarak al-Khater, *al-adeeb al-Kateb Nasser al-Khairi* (Bahrain: Government Press, 1982), 6.

94 Mubarak al-Khater, *al-Qadhi al-ra'is al-Shaikh Qasem bin Mehza'*, (Bahrain: Government Press, 1975), 25.

95 Al-Khairi, *Qala'id al-Nahrain*, 393.

the fief holder. This distribution of real estate between members of al-Khalifa was a mechanism not only for exercising political power on the wider populace, but also to adjudicate and manage the balance of power and conflict between the different factions and brothers of the ruling family, who as we have witnessed frequently warred with each other. Indeed real estate continues to serve this function up until today (albeit in obviously modified forms).[96]

To address the new balance of power in the ruling family, Sh. 'Isa bin 'Ali gave primacy to himself, his children, and his brother Khaled in the new redistribution of land. The fiefs of the sons of the recently deceased Sh. Ahmad were reduced considerably,[97] and instead they were given salaries.[98] The decentralized nature of the rule seems to have led not only to a feud between the ruler and his nephews, but also to a considerable increase in abuse in many of the villages.[99] This was obvious to Lorimer at the beginning of the twentieth century:

96 Omar AlShehabi and Saleh Suroor, 'Unpacking "Accumulation by Dispossession", "Fictitious Commodification", and "Fictitious Capital Formation": Tracing the Dynamics of Bahrain's Land Reclamation', *Antipode* 48.4 (2016): 835–856.

97 Khuri, *Tribe and State*, 43.

98 QDL, 'Gazetteer of the Persian Gulf. Vol I. Historical. Part IA & IB. J G Lorimer. 1915' [912] (1067/1782), IOR/L/PS/20/C91/1, https://www.qdl.qa/en/archive/81055/vdc_100023575946.0x000044. The ruler had the agricultural estates of Muharraq, Sanabis, and Hidd under his control, while his brother Khalid controlled Sitra and Nabih Saleh. Each of the ruler's sons also had jurisdiction over particular areas, while Khalid's son Ebrahim controlled Jiblat Hebshi. The socio-political dynamics between the Shaikh in charge and the villages varied accordingly.

99 For an account of a contemporary see: al-Khairi, *Qala'id al-Nahrain*, 393.

They are subject to a constant Sukhrah or corvée which affects their persons, their boats and their animals; their position in regard to the land is that of serfs rather than of tenants at will ... Some of the Baharinah are in theory landowners, having been allowed in the past to purchase gardens and obtain Sanads for the same; but their estates are often resumed for no valid reason ... It does not appear that the Baharinah are ever put to death without a regular trial by a Qadhi ... If oppressed beyond endurance the Baharinah might emigrate to the Qatif Oasis, and a consciousness of this possibility is the principal check upon the inhumanity of their masters.[100]

Thus, by the 1890s repression seemed to have increased in many villages under the vagaries of personalized fiefdom rule and the whims of the individual Shaikhs. It is not surprising that the only documented instance of some form of organized opposition to this system of rule during the nineteenth century occurred during this period. Shubbar al-Setri tried to rally some fighters from al-Qatif and Bahrain. He also tried to obtain the support of Naser al-Din, the Qajar Shah, in his quest. However, he failed to gather the backing of religious clerics in Bahrain, and the Shah's support was not forthcoming, so this initiative quickly came to nothing.[101] With the exception of this event, there is a marked lack of documented organized revolts until the climax of our story in the twentieth century.

100 QDL, 'Gazetteer of the Persian Gulf. Vol. II. Geographical and Statistical. J G Lorimer. 1908' [249] (276/2084), IOR/L/PS/20/C91/4, http://www.qdl.qa/archive/81055/vdc_100023515712.0x00004d.
101 Hasan Abdalla, 'al-Wujood al-Britany wal Hukm al-ektaʻiy wal Islahat fil Bahrain', *Maraya Alturath*, 30 October 2015, https://goo.gl/UxztJu.

It is apt to say that life for the toiling classes in Bahrain, whether pearl divers or agriculturalists, was a harsh one. Both made for extremely repressive labour conditions, but the two economic activities would differ in significant ways. Although probably involving more extreme physical labour conditions, the divers' output relationship was mainly with the ship captains, with the Shaikhs of al-Khalifa generally staying out of pearl business. Since the industry was the main source of exports and hard currency, as well as being highly susceptible to capital flight, it did not make economic sense for the ruling family to impose high taxes and interfere in the industry. Indeed, pearl merchants and nokhedhas had developed their own methods and sources of legal custom to settle any disputes, and the al-Khalifa were seen as a last resort for pearl divers to complain to if the repression became too unbearable.

In the agricultural villages, in contrast, the beneficiaries of the extracted taxes were members of the ruling family, thereby creating a direct link of repression. The fixed nature of the land, the relatively stable harvest from palm trees, and the immobility of labour combined to make the taxation of agriculture much more feasible for the rulers compared to the pearling industry. Hence, while the songs of pearl divers frequently lament the harshness of their treatment by nokhedhas, the oral lore in the villages instead focuses on repression by the ruling family.[102]

102 An example of a song chanted by the divers' families as they waited on the shores for their return from the diving season went as follows:
'Don't you fear Allah, Nokhedha?
The rope tore their hands, Nokhedha
Don't you fear Allah, Nokhedha?
Sixty rupees, Nokhedha
Don't you fear Allah, Nokhedha?

Sect-wise, most of those involved in the pearling industry were Sunni, although there were also some who were Shiʻa. Many of the ship owners were from tribes and families with close social connections to the ruling family. The social background of the pearl divers was a variegated mix of tribal members, Huwala, Arabs from Najd, Baharna, as well as slaves and seasonal migrants from neighbouring areas who would come for work during the pearling season. On the other hand, farmers in the villages were almost exclusively composed of Shiʻa Arabs, the majority of which were Baharna but also including some from al-Hasa and al-Qatif.

Furthermore, pearl divers were primarily based in the urban centres.[103] Al-Khalifa's rule was in many ways symbiotically tied and concomitant to the rise of Muharraq and Manama, which grew into sizeable towns under their rule, and were where many al-Khalifa Shaikhs lived. In this manner, they were an integral part at the apex of the fabric of those cities. The situation differed in the agricultural villages. There is scant evidence available on what were the economic and class relations in the villages before the arrival of al-Khalifa.[104] One could make an educated guess, however, that it is unlikely that al-Khalifa brought in completely revolutionary and unprecedented class relations, or modes of production or extraction (although they

---

Meagre dates and rice, Nokhedha
Don't you fear Allah, Nokhedha?
May your eye be blinded, Nokhedha'
The song and many others can be found in: Waheed Ahmed bin Hasan al-Khan, *Aghani al-ghaws fil Bahrain* (Doha: Markaz al-turath al-shaʻbi, 2002), 79. Translation based on citation in: Almahmood, *The Rise and Fall of Bahrain's Merchants*, 22.
103 This also included the town of Hidd on the island of Muharraq.
104 See Khuri, *Tribe and State*, 27–28.

did probably modify the form of taxation). This could be surmised given the fact that the ʿUtub had properties and contacts with farms in Bahrain long before becoming rulers. They also had no previous experience of ruling over agricultural areas, instead relying extensively on scribes and viziers from the villages for administration during their first years of rule. Furthermore, comparable agricultural social relations of production existed in nearby areas of the Eastern Province, Iran, and Iraq.

However, this did not change the fact that the ruling family was seen as a ruling coercive force that was not from the villages. True, some farms in the villages were developed during the reign and through the sponsorship of the ʿUtubs, such as agricultural estates in the village of Malkiyya.[105] Furthermore, al-Khalifa members spent part of their summers on the farms, a common practice by many urban families who could afford it.[106] However, the al-Khalifas did not live in the agricultural villages, and nor did they engage in farming.[107] Instead, they were the ultimate coercive force over farmers, one that extracted production surplus from them via taxes. Thus, there were obvious cleavages between the rulers and those living in the villages in terms of profession, class, kinship, sect, and accent, combined

105 There is evidence to suggest that some estates in the village in their modern incarnation were developed under the patronage of Mubarak bin Khalifa al-Fadhel, a member of the ʿUtub, in the mid-nineteenth century (between 1834 and 1854, with the oldest documents dating to 1858). For more see: Bashshar al-Hadi, ʻAl-Shaikh Mubarak bin Khalifa al-Fadhel moʾasses qaryat al-Malkiyyaʾ, *Medwanat Bashshar al-Hadi*, 11 September 2010, http://bashaaralhadi.blogspot.com/2010/09/blog-post_11.html.
106 This practice of spending summer days on the farms is referred to locally as ʻ*yegayyeth*ʾ (summering).
107 They preferred to live in Muharraq, Manama, or their bastion of Riffa in the south of the island.

with a direct and unequal relationship of extraction between the two that often involved physical repression.

There were therefore significant differences in the experiences and socio-economic relations between those who lived in the towns and the villages. Perhaps the cleavages between the conditions of the urban vs. rural residents is brought into focus by the term '*Halayel*',[108] an extremely derogatory and offensive term still used by some urban Baharna of Manama to describe those from the villages. Indeed, marriages between Baharna of the city and those from villages remain contentious to this day. As a contrast, most Sunnis in Bahrain would not recognize what the above term means, let alone use it.

There were, however, also strong familial and trade links between many Baharna who lived in Manama and the villages, as many traced their ancestry before migrating to Manama to some of these villages. Many residing in the villages would also sell their produce in the markets of Manama and Muharraq.[109]

---

108 Although the origin of the term is unclear, its root seems to be in the world 'Halal', or permissible. There are at least two competing theories: 1. The term derives from the period of the Oman Ya'ariba rule, which was particularly devastating to the villages of Bahrain as many were destroyed, and thus the blood of villagers was 'Halal' to the Omani forces (Kadhim, *Isti'malat al-Dhakira*, 256); 2. The term derives from the fact that their labour is 'Halal' to the various al-Khalifa Shaikhs who controlled the villages as fiefdoms.

109 Consequently, just as when discussing other socio-economic categories, it is important not to essentialize and enshrine as absolute the distinctions between 'urban' and 'rural', thus replicating what British officials practised when discussing ethnicities and sects. As this narration has stressed, it becomes important to realize that within the broad trends highlighted, there were also complex linkages and overlaps between urban and rural areas, as well as differences within each. For example, villages and cities that were geographically close to each other had significant interactions, as was the case with Manama and Sanabis, with the latter known for its shipbuilding skills.

Hence, it is important to point out that there was strong overlap across class, social background, sect, and way of life (including experience of direct repression by members of the ruling family) across many of the agricultural villages of Bahrain. This was coupled with overlap in terms of sects and some familial relations between the Baharna of some villages and those of the urban centre Manama, even though there were also strong socio-economic distinctions between those living in villages and the urban quarters. These socio-economic links and differences, as we will see, would come to play an important role in the ensuing events.

CONCLUSION: LIFE AND POLITICS BEFORE THE ETHNOSECTARIAN GAZE

If one were to take a systematic bird's-eye view to measure and record the various ethnosectarian differences and cleavages in the social scene in Bahrain, then one could certainly find some to identify and codify. However, the first sentence of the previous paragraph becomes crucial: you would need to construct a bird's-eye view through modernist tools of measurement and demographic comparison – such as censuses and cadastral surveys – to systematically categorize such ethnosectarian differences. Most crucially, it would require constructing a particular reading of ethnosectarian categories, and subsequently elevating these categories as the most important politically, and imposing them on the social milieu. The earmarked ethnosectarian differences would need to be sculpted and generalized to become the primary variables in determining political processes and practices. There is little evidence to support that this existed in Bahrain in the period before 1900, nor that such an analysis alone would take us very far in under-standing the islands' social and political relations during the nineteenth century.

The ethnosectarian classifications as collated by Lorimer served to give political primacy to such groupings. Most of the complex social scene that we have outlined was reduced by the ethnosectarian gaze to two communities that the British imag-ined as forming the basic building blocks of the local popula-tion: there were the Sunnis, and there were the Shi'as. These two basic communities were intersliced by large blocks of different ethnic groupings, ruled overall by the al-Khalifa family. Thus was local society set up in the British understanding, and thus was it treated accordingly.

Equally crucially, while this gaze served to reveal and give primacy to these ethnosectarian divisions, it simultaneously also served to hide and relegate the rest of the social scene, both in terms of its complexities and commonalities. The vast major-ity of the population shared Islam as a religion and Arabic as a language. In turn, the social milieu was variegated by an intri-cate and intermeshing complex of class, profession, kinship, madhhab, geography, locality, as well as ties to the ruling elite and other foreign governments with influence in Bahrain.

As we outlined during this chapter, political power was char-acterized by a decentralized and personalized form of rule that was mainly built around administrating the port cities of Muharraq and Manama, and fiefdoms in the agricultural villages, while fending off any possible military threats from abroad. Regional politics were dominated by the exigencies of the shifting political alliances and tribute payment under the umbrella of *Pax Britannica*. Internally, political rule was not monopolized in a central bureaucracy, with power instead invested in different persons. This included the ruler, but also other members of his family with whom he would frequently conflict, as well as judges, pearl traders, ship captains, and religious clerics. Overall, it was a conjunctural balance of contested, localized, and geographically diffused forces. Principal in shaping the organization of these political forces were three economic modes of life: pearl production, trade, and agriculture. These three economic spheres were reflected geographically, with the first concentrated in Muharraq, the second in Manama, and the third scattered across the different villages dotting Bahrain's shoreline.

As long as the extended ruling family had supremacy in the coercive forces and taxation, then socio-economic relations – whether in the realms of madhhab, personal status, law, or work (trade, pearling, crafts, or agriculture) – were seen as different yet intermeshing domains that were allowed to regulate themselves according to their own logics of bargaining, consultation, and contestation, without much central oversight. There were no standardized and centralized laws and directives, and modes of regulation were highly contextual and could change based on the situation, the actors, and the time. Differences between these intersecting domains and actors were implicitly recognized and allowed to function according to their own dynamics, rather than applying any overt and systematized principle from the centre. Loyalty, not likeness, was the aim, whether through the use of carrots or sticks.[110]

Many aspects of this rule were personalized, cruel, unequal,

110 Thus, if one were to employ Burbank's and Cooper's scale of recognition of difference, exemplified by the Ottoman Empire, versus homogenization, exemplified by the Spanish Empire, this would fall closer to the first, with the obvious difference that there was no central imperial authority that issued formal edicts and laws. For more see: Jane Burbank and Frederick Cooper, *Empires in World History*, introduction and chapter 5.

and could appear arbitrary, but it was not primarily driven by any overtly religious or moralizing ideology with forced homogenization. There were no systematic campaigns within local society of forced conversions, mass killings, or expulsions of whole populations that were primarily driven by ethno-sect considerations.[111] However, raids, corvée, tax extractions, debt peonage, and physical force were common. Its particularities notwithstanding, many traits of this mode of rule were not novel compared to others that existed in the region.[112] Ultimately, it was based on maintaining rule pragmatically and opportunistically over small pearling/trading ports and agricultural lands with a diverse set of social agents using a minimal set of bureaucracy, in the midst of a regional setting filled with competing larger forces, in order to maximize the subjects and scarce resources that could be controlled and taxed.

This form of government shared with British colonial indirect rule its emphasis on differences in social subjects and the applicable modes of governance, rather than any systematic principle of equal citizenship. Unlike British indirect rule,

111 This is in contrast to other periods in the history of the Middle East, for example the forced conversions during certain periods of the Safavid Empire, or the mass killings and expulsions during the early Ottoman–Safavid wars, which were in large part framed by ethno-sect motives, albeit of a different form from those in the twentieth century that this book tackles. For more see: Rula Jurdi Abisaab, *Converting Persia: Religion and Power in the Safavid Empire* (London: I.B.Tauris, 2004); Stefan Winter, *The Shiites of Lebanon under Ottoman Rule, 1516–1788* (Cambridge: Cambridge University Press, 2010).

112 As a comparison one could look at the rule of the al-Madhkurs in Bushehr in the nineteenth century, the same family that al-Khalifa ousted and replaced as rulers in Bahrain: Vanessa Martin, *The Qajar Pact: Bargaining, Protest and the State in Nineteenth-Century Persia* (London: I.B.Tauris, 2005), chapter 2.

however, ethno-sects were not elevated above all other factors as the most important markers and divisions in the population and its mode of government, and these ethno-sect divisions were not engraved in formal laws and institutions issued by a centralized bureaucratic authority. However, the narration also emphasized that should a framework have appeared that elevated and enshrined such ethnosectarianism as the primary gaze of local politics, there were factors that would have provided strong impetus for political contestation to occur according to such readings of ethnicities and sect. Given the basic state administration setup and the localized and diffused mode of political power, such mobilization did not hold sway at the end of the nineteenth century. This is not surprising, given that many elements that facilitate the construction of modern political communities and the creation of their uniting mythologies and discourses – such as extensive road networks, censuses, the printed press, and schools – were still in their infancy in Bahrain during this era.[113] Instead, a different form of modernity was to produce its first buds on Bahrain's soil during this period: al-Nahda.

113 Benedict Anderson, *Imagined Communities: Reflections on the Origin and Spread of Nationalism* (London: Verso Books, 2006).

3

AL-NAHDA IN BAHRAIN,
1875–1920

THE RISE OF AL-NAHDA IN THE ARAB WORLD

The nineteenth and early twentieth centuries marked the rise of the al-Nahda renaissance across the Arab world, a movement of the intelligentsia that pushed for reform and modernization in Arabic thought and literature.[1] It was partly influenced by the increasing encounters between the 'West' and the Ottoman Empire, the latter stretching over vast swathes of Arabic-speaking land during this period. As Ottoman weakness and decline relative to Europe became very evident by the end of the eighteenth century, culminating with Napoleon's invasion of Egypt in 1798 and then the 1821 Greek War of Independence, a period of soul searching and change emerged throughout the

---

1 The foundational English text on al-Nahda, which this short introduction converses with, is: Albert Hourani, *Arabic Thought in the Liberal Age 1798–1939* (Cambridge: Cambridge University Press, 1962). For a seminal Arabic study see: Mohammad Jaber al-Ansari, *Al-Fikr al-'Arabi wa Sera' al-Addad* (Beirut: al-Mu'asasa al-'Arabiyya lel Derasat wal Nashr, 1999).

empire, epitomized by the Ottoman Tanzimat reforms of 1826 to 1875. These reforms aimed to reorganize the central government and overhaul military organization, tax collection systems, and private property law. Most importantly, moral and legal bases of reforms were introduced that began explicitly recognizing different ethnic and religious 'communities' throughout the empire, and granting them formal equality before the law as equal constitutive parts of the political community.

In Egypt, and in the aftermath of the chaos of France's withdrawal in 1801, Mehmet 'Ali rose to become the ruler, introducing a series of drastic reforms in the military, agriculture, transportation, and the wider economy. Railways were built, cotton production reorganized, and schools and training institutions multiplied, with political power hugely concentrating in his hands. He brought in Western experts to implement these reforms, as well as sending many from Egypt the other way to increase knowledge exchange. From this interaction emerged Egypt's first figures of al-Nahda, perhaps the most famous being Rifa'at al-Tahtawi, a prolific writer whose time in Paris influenced his writings deeply.[2]

In the Levant, and particularly in areas with a large Christian presence like Aleppo and the mountainous areas of Lebanon, missionaries from Europe and the United States had an increasing influence through their expanding monasteries and schools. A new educated intelligentsia emerged, who laid the foundations for an Arabic literary renaissance that formed the second mainstream within the early phases of al-Nahda.

The accelerator for the spread of the ideas was the growth of the printing press in the region during the nineteenth century, allowing for Arabic newspapers and periodicals to

2 For more on Tahtawi see: Hourani, *Arabic Thought*, 52–53.

be disseminated much more widely and in increasing volumes. Part of these new publications was pan-Islamic propaganda by Istanbul on the importance of the unity of the *Umma*. Other voices began to emerge, however, particularly in Egypt and Lebanon, and their writings over the last quarter of the nineteenth century would begin to reach the shores of the Gulf, particularly in Bahrain and Kuwait. This interaction was to have a profound effect on the development of literary and political thought and practice in both of these places.[3]

Through their readings and meetings with the figures of al-Nahda in the wider region, Bahrain's intelligentsia combined their ideas with local factors on the ground to produce their own own distinct trajectory. Just as with al-Nahda thought in other parts of the Arab world, these ideas and debates developed initially within a small group, part of a literate male elite who came from a class and background that allowed them to receive some form of education. Nevertheless, they somehow wanted to articulate the needs of their societies at that time, and their actions and ideas contributed to this impulse of change.[4]

As is the case with the earlier generations of al-Nahda in other parts of the Arab world, it is difficult to talk about distinct schools of thought in Bahrain during this time. The ideas put forward by this intelligentsia were still inchoate and evolving. More prominent were the thoughts and actions of individual personalities, and hence the focus of this discussion will

3 The spread of al-Nahda into Kuwait was as extensive and influential as that in Bahrain and is worthy of a wider study. For more on Kuwait see: Talal Al-Rashoud, *Modern Education and Arab Nationalism in Kuwait, 1911–1961* (London: PhD thesis, SOAS, 2017).
4 Hourani, *Arabic Thought*, preface.

necessarily be geared towards these individuals and their ideas rather than distinct schools of thought.[5]

AL-NAHDA RISES IN BAHRAIN

Probably the most apt period to initiate discussion of the emergence of al-Nahda thought in Bahrain would be the final quarter of the nineteenth century, and the place to begin this would be the Majlis of Sh. Ebrahim bin Mohammad. Born around 1850, he became famous as a collector of books and as a poet. His Majlis in Muharraq was to become a focal point for the emergent intelligentsia to meet and discuss literature, poetry, religion, and world events of the day.

Sh. Ebrahim was the son of the infamous Sh. Mohammad bin Khalifa (MbK), whom we encountered as the previous ruler of Bahrain in 1849–1869 and the main protagonist in the war with Qatar's al-Thani, leading to his deposition by the British. Nineteen years old at the time, Sh. Ebrahim remained in Bahrain as his father was exiled to Bombay. He was not to see his father again until 1883 in Mecca, where Sh. Ebrahim completed the Hajj pilgrimage and remained for three years to further his studies and spend time with his father. He then travelled to Basra and onwards to Bombay, which was then the centre of the Gulf's Indian Ocean trade, after which he returned to Bahrain. Sh. Mohammad died in 1890 in Mecca soon after his son had returned to Bahrain, still vainly hoping that he would be allowed to return from his exile to Bahrain.[6]

5 The list of individuals presented is in no way meant to be exhaustive, and given the dearth of current scholarship on the subject, it almost certainly has left out many individuals who deserve to be included.
6 May al-Khalifa, *Ma'a shaikh al-udaba' fil Bahrain Ebrahim bin Mohammad al-Khalifa* (London: Riad al-Rayes Books, 1993), 42.

The current ruler, Sh. ʿIsa bin ʿAli, was Sh. Ebrahim's first cousin, being the son of Sh. ʿAli bin Khalifa who was killed in the brotherly battle of 1869. The parents' feud did not prevent their two sons from being very close to each other, with Sh. ʿIsa marrying Sh. Ebrahim's sister ʿAisha, who herself would play a prominent role in ensuing events. In fact, and probably due in no small part to his father's past and his close relationship with the ruler, Sh. Ebrahim tended to generally steer away from overt political activity, concentrating instead on his literary endeavours and his Majlis.

This Majlis became an early focal point of the intelligentsia beginning in the late nineteenth century. It was open three times daily: in the morning, afternoon, and after the evening prayer. His considerable book collection served as an informal library to feed their emerging reading habits. Visitors would come to socialize or just to read his book and periodicals collection. The Majlis also had an extension for guests who wished to stay the night, particularly for visitors from Manama, who would cross the three kilometres of sea between the two islands in order to attend the Majlis's sessions.[7]

A frequent participant in Sh. Ebrahim's Majlis was ʿAbdulwahhab al-Zayyani, who, as our events will show, has a reasonable claim to being the father of modern Bahraini nationalism and demands for representative forms of government. He was born in 1863 to an elite family that arrived in Bahrain in the late eighteenth century with al-Khalifa. In 1879, he travelled to al-Hasa in modern-day eastern Saʿudi Arabia to further his education in what was considered back then a centre of religious learning in the Arabian Peninsula. He then continued his studies in Iraq, where he married. When he returned to Bahrain

7 Ibid., 63.

in 1883, his father, who was a famous pearl trader, opened a mosque with a religious private school, and entrusted his son as the Imam of the mosque and its main teacher. When his father died, he took over his pearl-trading business.[8] Thus, by the beginning of the twentieth century he had established himself as a notable teacher, religious scholar, and pearl trader from an elite family.

Al-Zayyani's private religious school was one of several that began sprouting throughout the nineteenth century in Bahrain's two main cities, Manama and Muharraq. These schools were distinct from the traditional *Kuttab*, which relied mainly on Quran recitation and memorization. They introduced a wider range of taught subjects, including *Fiqh* (Islamic jurisprudence), the principles of the Arabic language, and some basic mathematics, particularly for issues of wills and pearl trading, with some teachers even including some history or geography in their teachings. In essence, each of these schools was run by one individual, who chose the material that he would teach to his students. Many of these teachers were graduates of Ulaikura in India or al-Azhar University in Egypt.

One of the most famous of these schools was that of Ahmad bin Mehzaʿ, the brother of the previously encountered judge Qasem bin Mehzaʿ. He studied in al-Azhar from 1882 to 1887, and upon his return he asked the ruler to set up a school carrying the latter's name in 1891. He became the school's principal teacher, under whose tutelage many of the protagonists of our story would study.[9] One prominent student was Mohammad Saleh Ebrahim Khunji. Born in 1880 in Manama

8 Bashshar al-Hadi, 'Al-Madares al-Ahliyya fil Bahrain', *Sharʿia Teaching in the GCC Countries Conference*, http://www.rogulf.com/play.php?catsmktba=14.
9 Ibid.

to a family from a Huwala background, he enrolled in Ahmad bin Mehzaʿ's school and became a regular attendant of Sh. Ebrahim's Majlis beginning in 1898,[10] developing into an avid reader of its books and periodicals. He followed the example of his teacher by going to study in al-Azhar at the turn of the century, and upon his return in 1903 he started his own private school.

Khunji, Zayyani, and Sh. Ebrahim were all active founders of al-Hedaya, the first Arabic institutionalized modern school set up by locals in Bahrain, and a landmark of educational development in both Bahrain and the Gulf. Sh. Ebrahim was chosen to be the vice president of the Knowledge Council in charge of running and setting up the school. Zayyani was the second vice president, while Khunji was its secretary.

The president of the Knowledge Council was the ruler's son Sh. ʿAbdulla bin ʿIsa bin ʿAli. Sh. ʿAbdulla was born in 1883 to Shaikha Aisha, the sister of Sh. Ebrahim. His legacy seems to be one of a Jekyll and Hyde figure, as he became known as one of the most charismatic and politically inclined members of the ruling family, particularly through his involvement in education, in which he was actively involved throughout his life. He would also gain an unrivalled notoriety for committing several physical and sexual abuses throughout Bahrain, particularly during the period that constitutes the climax of our story in 1921–1923. His son Mohammad bin ʿAbdulla had an equal inclination towards politics, as well as being a regular attendant of the Majlis of Sh. Ebrahim. He was one of the most vocal opponents of the British presence in Bahrain, and the trio of Sh. ʿAbdulla, his mother, Sh. Aisha, and his son Sh. Mohammad, would become the bête noire of the British.

10 Ibid.

One of the closest confidants of Sh. 'Abdulla was Qasem al-Shirawi, described by the British Political Agency and its supporters as a 'dangerous political intriguer' and the 'cleverest rogue in Bahrain', an 'evil genius' who 'spares no pains to lessen the dignity and authority of the (British) Agency',[11] as he would actively promote such seditious concepts as the 'freedom of the nations'.[12] Born around 1880 in Muharraq to a family from a Huwala background, he gained fame as a notable poet. He worked in several jobs, entering the pearl trade business with al-Qusaibi, one of the famous trading families from Najd, before he became the manager of the port of Muharraq. By the second decade of the twentieth century, he seems to have had the ears of both the ruler and his son Sh. 'Abdulla, becoming the former's secretary. He joined Zayyani, Khunji, Sh. Ebrahim, and Sh. 'Abdulla as one of the members of the Knowledge Council running al-Hedaya school, holding the position of minute-taker.[13]

AL-HEDAYA SCHOOL

The project for modern Arabic education began gathering pace in 1918, when a principal was appointed to oversee the establishment of the school's first by-laws.[14] The project gained extra traction

11 QDL, 'File 5/10 Jasim Muhammad al-Chirawi and his uncle Ali bin Abdullah bin Muhammad on Black List' [26r] (53/98), IOR/R/15/2/104, http://www.qdl.qa/en/archive/81055/vdc_100023246775.0x000036.
12 Bashshar al-Hadi, A'yan al-Bahrain fil qarn al-rabi' 'ashar al-hijri, vol. 4 (Bahrain: Jam'iyyat al-Imam Maled bin Anas, 2008), 753-760.
13 Ibid.
14 The first principal was 'Abdulla Dahlan from Mecca, who left shortly after and was replaced by Hafedh Wahba. May al-Khalifa, Ma'at 'am min al -ta'leem al-nethami fil Bahrain (Beirut: Arabic Institute for Research and Publishing, 1999), 177.

after Sh. 'Abdulla bin 'Isa and Shirawi became the first people from Bahrain to visit the UK between July and October 1919. Their trip included a stopover in Egypt on the way back.[15] In both countries, they paid particular attention to visiting examples of modern schools to learn more about their education systems.

Upon their return, the Knowledge Council was established by fourteen members, all from notable families of Muharraq. The school began its teachings and activities in 1919 in the house of 'Ali bin Ebrahim al-Zayyani, a member of the same family as 'Abdulwahhab, who donated his house for the school's use. Al-Hedaya's first teachers hailed from Egypt, Syria, and Iraq, and its curriculum featured 'modern' subjects such as Arabic, history, maths, and geography. Although the curriculum also included religious studies, it seems these were ecumenical in form, with the school including some students of a Shiʿa background.[16]

Running the school mainly rested on contributions from locals, particularly wealthy merchants such as Zayyani, while the ruler donated land in 1919 on which to erect a permanent building. Often-recited lore recounts that during an event held to gather school contributions, a man came forward from the crowd, and after identifying himself as Mulla 'Abdulla ibn 'Ali, he exclaimed that he only had five rupees in his pocket, but that he wished for his name to be associated with this 'blessed venture'. The attendants were so delighted that they put his name as the first in the contributions book.[17]

---

15 May al-Khalifa, *Maʿa shaikh al-udabaʾ*, 107.

16 One of the most prominent was Ebrahim al-ʿUrayyedh, a famous poet, who enrolled at the school in 1922 at the age of fourteen, and then also became a teacher there in 1927. See: 'Portrait Ebrahim al-ʿUrayyedh', *Al-Wasat* newspaper, 20 October 2012, http://www.alwasatnews.com/news/166180.html.

17 Mubarak al-Khater, *al-ketabat al-uwla al-hadeetha li muthaqqafi al-Bahrain 1875–1925* (Bahrain: unknown, 1978), 75.

Al-Hedaya quickly attracted enmity. Ever since its original idea was floated, it had been heavily denounced by some Imams and religious clerics, who began circling petitions against it. From their viewpoint, such a school would bring in new, non-Muslim *beda'* thoughts and practices, garnering significant conservative opposition. However, Sh. 'Abdulla, Sh. Ebrahim, al-Zayyani, and the other main drivers of the project carried substantial weight in the community. They were also smart enough to obtain the green light from the one religious cleric whose opinion ultimately mattered. Judge Qasem bin Mehza' publicly defended it from his pulpit in the weekly Friday prayer sermons. They garnered his approval by convincing the judge that al-Hedaya was the seed of a religious school, which to his dismay he realized later on was not the case.[18]

The school had become the talk of the town given the controversy surrounding its affairs, and so the ceremony for laying the foundation stone of its new building became a notable event, with both the ruler and Judge Mehza' attending. After the ruler laid the foundation stone, Sh. 'Abdulla, Sh. Ebrahim, Zayyani, Shirawi, and Khunji each gave speeches in honour of the school's opening. The texts of these speeches are a great indicator of how the new thoughts of al-Nahda had a profound effect on the intelligentsia of Bahrain. Sh. Ebrahim's speech began:

> Eids and festivities are nothing except days of the year that carry reasons for happiness, joy and serenity for all nations (*al-Umam*). And is there an Eid more beautiful than the day when the whole people (*al-Sha'ab*) in all its classes, from its poorest to its ruler, partake in laying the

18 Al-Khater, *al-Qadhi*, 149–151.

first rock for knowledge in this blessed island? I feel as you feel that my heart is floating with joy and with great hopes, for we have planted the first seeds for the proper life, and our joy will be doubled when our seeds bloom, and our children are able to reap the blessings of knowledge and of living in a cultured society ... May God protect us all and guide us to what's good for the religion and the nation (al-Watan).[19]

Nations, classes, knowledge, and society, all presented within an ecumenical view of Islam that transcended any particular sect or madhhab. These were all concepts that marked a new discourse and mode of thought emerging in Bahrain, one that echoed those appearing elsewhere in the 'al-Nahda' age. Particularly impactful in this respect were the writings of Jamal al-Din al-Afghani and Mohammad 'Abduh, through their periodical al-'Urwa al-Wuthqa, (The Firmest Bond), published from Paris in 1884. Although it only lasted for a year, in which eighteen issues were published, it was nevertheless to have a wide-reaching impact throughout the Arabic-speaking world, including Bahrain.

One of the main issues to preoccupy 'Abduh, Afghani, and the emerging intelligentsia in Bahrain was the relation of Islam to modernity. Discussions abounded on how to reform and reinterpret the practices of Islam to make them a source of strength and accelerator of progress instead of weakness, in order to recapture the spirit of a long gone previous epoch of advancement and high civilization in Islam's early days. For Afghani, the essence of Islam was modern rationalism, as Islam fundamentally believed in the virtue of reason and encouraged

19 Al-Khater, al-Ketabat al-uwla, 69.

man to use his mind freely. Similarly for ʿAbduh, the tension between Islam and rational modernity was solved in that Islam was itself the embodiment of rational modernity, and what was needed was to revive and strengthen this inner essence.[20]

Thus, change was needed rather than continuity, with new ways of thought and action having to replace past conduct. Human welfare in the world centred mainly on the creation of civilization, and the Muslim world should be seen as one of these civilizations. There was no use denying that Europe was the current benchmark in this respect, and that it had reached its position through the application of education, science, and reason. The 'East' and the Muslim world once had a great civilization too, but which now was going through decline. In order to reclaim this lost glory, reform was essential.

Unity was paramount in this quest, where differences in sects could and should be overcome. Starting with al-Afghani, there was an emphasis on solidarity and ecumenical pan-Islamism, with reform of education and schools by introducing the new sciences to be the vehicle to achieve this renaissance. Equally important was a passion for the Arabic language and its literature, while it was also imperative to reform the language and make Arabic suitable to address and express the needs and ideas of the modern world.[21]

It is not surprising that al-Zayyani's speech at the opening ceremony of al-Hedaya school also focused on such themes, contrasting a bygone Islamic age of glory with the current phase of darkness, which had to be overcome by returning to the principles of knowledge and by forsaking disunity and ignorance:

20 Hourani, *Arabic Thought*, 123–126, 161.
21 Ibid., 150–158.

Do the seeds of ignorance, disunity, and discord bring joy and happiness? No, for history used to be the strongest witness to our past ancestors in the land and community of Muslims, for this was the cradle of civilization and learning, and a source of the lights of knowledge and eloquence. There emerged from us genius lawmakers, interpreters, doctors, engineers and skilled artisans in all arts and crafts ... Alas, our Arabic lands have now become infertile in knowledge and scholars, and we became foreigners to our noble language, until it nearly disowned us because we have not kept our word nor its true value. These sorrows have been with me for a large part of my life, but now I feel an unusual tremor of happiness and joy ... For we will make this happy day our biggest Eid to celebrate the founding of the world of new, glorious knowledge.[22]

Given his background as a religious cleric, perhaps no one exemplified the Islamic reformist strand of al-Nahda in Bahrain more than Zayyani. The other epitomizer of this Islamic reformist thought within Bahrain, Mohammad Saleh Khunji, wasted no time in corresponding with some of the Arabic periodicals of the day to inform them of the occasion, which evidently was one of tremendous pride for those involved. Khunji sent a letter to the periodical *al-Hilal* in 1919:

We would like to inform you that we have been successful in establishing an elementary school that we called 'al Hedaya al-Khalifiya', based on our desire to teach our children and educate them on patriotic principles ... We

22 Al-Khater, *al-Ketabat al-uwla*, 72–73.

have enclosed the texts of the speeches given at the ceremony, and we hope that you will be able to include what is possible from them in your esteemed newspaper.[23]

Khunji's decision to write to *al-Hilal* is revealing. Published in Cairo, *al-Hilal* was founded by Jurji Zaidan, a student at the Syrian Protestant College (later the American University of Beirut). It took the shape of a reader's digest that tackled a wide variety of topics of general interest, but with a focus on the arts, humanities, and social sciences.[24] Reflecting the ecumenical reformist streak within many of Bahrain's intelligentsia, the confessional background of Zaidan did not factor into Khunji's correspondence with *al-Hilal*, as he was eager instead to focus his attention on the common ground of 'patriotic principles'.

Indeed, *al-Hilal* became particularly popular in Bahrain in conjunction with *al-Muqtataf*, another reader's digest periodical founded in the late nineteenth century by alumni of the Syrian Protestant College, but with a particular focus on the natural sciences. Bahrain's intelligentsia began to correspond with both these periodicals as early as the 1890s, with the topics addressed varying considerably between religion, science, history, geography, current politics, and the interaction between East and West, reflecting the inchoate flow of ideas and the emerging thirst for any type of knowledge that was a hallmark of that period. Thus, Bahraini correspondences with *al-Muqtataf* sent in questions on the following: what is yawning and is it contagious (1903)? If a human being grew up with animals in

23 Ibid., 33–34.
24 All issues of both magazines can be browsed in: 'Arshif al-Majallat al-Adabiyya wal Thaqafiyya al-'Arabiyya', *Sakhr Software*, http://archive.sakhrit.co/AllMagazines.aspx.

the jungle, would they still be able to adapt to the manners of humans? There has been much talk about the Giaconda painting and its theft. So what is this picture and what is its history? (1914).[25]

Al-Hedaya school was the institutionalized form in which this al-Nahda quest for knowledge manifested itself in Bahrain. The first principal to oversee teaching at the school was the Egyptian Hafedh Wahba, who had a direct connection to the figures of al-Nahda in Egypt. Born in 1889, he enrolled at al-Azhar for higher learning under pressure from his parents. He disliked the place immensely due to its 'chaos' and 'dirtiness', remarking that superstitions and myths abounded in what was taught and read. However, he became exposed there to the teachings of Mohammad ʿAbduh, who had a profound effect on him, although he only spent a relatively short time under his tutelage before the latter's death.[26]

After becoming fed up with al-Azhar, he left and joined the recently established 'Sharia Judiciary' school, which was supposed to train and graduate a new set of judges that were more in tune with the requirements of modernity and the state. Once again, he found the place to be straitjacketing, and he left in 1910 for Istanbul to join the editorial team of *Al-Hilal al-Othmani* (*The Ottoman Crescent*), one of the newspapers funded by the Young Turks Party to spread Arabic propaganda throughout the Ottoman Empire. He eventually clashed with their goals and ideology, coming to the belief that the Arabs had the right to call for self-governance. Subsequently, he moved to India where he became acquainted with many of the trading families of the Gulf, including those from Kuwait. He moved to

25 Al-Khater, *al-ketabat al-uwla*, 20–40.
26 Wahba, *Khamsoona ʿaman*, 5–19.

the latter in 1914 to become an assistant principal and teacher in the first local institutionalized school in the Gulf region, the al-Mubarakiyya school, which had already opened back in 1912.

There was no love lost between Wahba and British colonial figures, as he had already been imprisoned by them once in Egypt and threatened with further imprisonment and expulsion in India for incitement against the colonial regime. It seemed this trend continued in Kuwait, where he managed to draw the ire of both the ruler, the infamous Sh. Mubarak, and the British Political Agent stationed there. The British occupation of Basra during the First World War led to a revolt in nearby Muhammara against its ruler Shaikh Khaz'al in November 1914, due to his perceived collaboration with the British. As the revolt threatened the rule of the Shaikh of Muhammara, the ruler of Kuwait ordered forces to be sent to support his beleaguered friend. A group of Kuwaiti notables objected vehemently, and it seems Wahba was encouraging them in their position. He was summoned to an angry audience with Sh. Mubarak in the presence of the British Political Agent, after which he swiftly left Kuwait. He was able to return, however, after the death of Sh. Mubarak in November 1915.[27] In October 1919, he moved from Kuwait to Bahrain to become the principal of al-Hedaya school, where as events in the next chapter will show, his habit of anti-British activity would continue.[28]

27 Al-Khater, *al-Qadhi*, 165–167.
28 Another notable anti-colonial figure who became one of the school's legends is the Syrian 'Uthman al-Hourani, the elder first cousin and mentor of the leading Syrian politician Akram al-Hourani. 'Uthman moved to Bahrain from Iraq after being kicked out of Syria after the French occupation of the country, the latter issuing an order for his execution. There is dispute, however, over the date that he arrived in Bahrain. While al-Bassam

THE COMMITTEE TO RESIST
BRITISH COLONIALISM

Indeed, 1919 could also be regarded as the year that marked the crystallization of resistance to British colonialism in institutional form within Bahrain's al-Nahda circles. The Committee to Resist British Colonialism (CRBC) was formed, reflecting the anti-colonial streak that had began emerging across the Arab world by the turn of the century. Europe, and Britain in particular, was no longer simply a role model as it was to the first generation of al-Nahda figures like Tahtawi, who compared it favourably as a source of inspiration to the Islamic world. Instead, and especially since the British occupation of Egypt in 1882 and the French takeover of Tunisia in 1881, it was now a threatening imperial power and a colonizer.[29] The preoccupation of the likes of Jamal al-Din al-Afghani with British colonialism in the late nineteenth century increasingly resonated with members of the intelligent-sia in Bahrain in the early twentieth century, as direct British meddling in local affairs increased dramatically.

Hence, if al-Hedaya and the associated Knowledge Council epitomized the 'education and knowledge' strand of the al-Nahda clique, then the CRBC epitomized the anti-colonialist strand running through them. There was some overlap between the two

---

(see below) contends that he arrived in Bahrain in 1921 and actively partic-ipated in the climactic events of 1923 through his position as a teacher at al-Hedaya, most sources hold that he only arrived in Bahrain in 1926. He became principal of the school and was eventually deported by British offi-cials in 1930. For more see: Khaled al-Bassam, *Rejal fi jaza'er al-lu'lu'* (Beirut: Arab Institute for Research and Publishing, 2007), 41–48. For the prevailing view see: Abdul Hamid al-Muhadeen, *al-Khurouj min al-'Utma* (Beirut: Arab Institute for Research and Publishing, 2003).

29 Hourani, *Arabic Thought*, preface, 81, 103.

groups. For example, both ʿAbdulwahhab al-Zayyani and Qasem al-Shirawi (and his brother Ahmad) were members of the CRBC, just as they were members of the Knowledge Council. The committee was not secret and its members were publicly known, but they had to keep their communications under wraps, as successive British officials kept a close eye on them. They accordingly resorted to the use of their children to relay messages to each other.

Officially as a group, it does not seem the committee achieved much beyond organizing meetings and discussions between its members. Each of its members, however, would eventually play an important role in the unfolding events in Bahrain. The eldest of the group was Ahmad bin Lahij. He was born in approximately 1860 to a family that belonged to the influential al-Nuʿaim tribe, allies and sometimes foes of the ruling al-Khalifa clan. Like many of the other intelligentsia, he was a pearl trader following in the footsteps of his father. He similarly spent significant time abroad, as he visited Iraq and Damascus for education during his youth and began frequenting India for selling pearls.[30]

Saʿad al-Shamlan shared a similar background to bin Lahij, and although he was younger than him by twenty years, he was to become the dynamo of the group. He was born in Muharraq around 1880 to a well-to-do family with strong connections to the ruling family. His father was a trader in pearls and woods, but primarily a religious scholar who was very close to the ruler; so close that he would conduct the royal family's marriage ceremonies and act as an adjudicator in their familial and marital affairs, issues that he had extensive experience with through his seven marriages.[31]

30 Al-Hadi, *Aʿyan al-Bahrain*, 81.
31 Fouziyya Matar, *Ahmad al-Shamlan seerat munadel wa tareekh watan* (Beirut: Arab Institute for Research and Publishing, 2009), 36-44. Also: al -Hadi, *Aʿyan al-Bahrain*, 337.

Like many we encountered previously, his son Sa'ad entered the private religious school of Shaikh Ahmad bin Mehza'. He then travelled to al-Hasa to further his education, just like Zayyani before him. Upon his return to Bahrain in 1898, he took up pearl trading with his father, and moved from Muharraq to Juffair, an area on the mainland not too far from the capital, Manama. Like his father, he had a good relationship with the ruler and his family, particularly his two sons, Hamad and Mohammad, the first of which would become ruler by the end of our story. This, as we will see, would not stop Sa'ad from becoming one of the most vocal critics of both his and British rule.

The youngest member of the committee was 'Abdulla al-Zayed, who would be labelled by his compatriots as the 'genius of Bahrain'. In a recurring pattern, he was born in 1894 to a notable family that was involved in pearl trading. He was a student at Khunji's school that opened after the latter's return from al-Azhar, after which al-Zayed joined his father in his pearl trades in Bombay starting in 1918. There he struck up friendships with several other youths from across the Gulf, including Kuwait, Jubail, and Oman, and his interest in developments and thoughts across the Arab world correspondingly intensified. Due to its status as the main commercial hub in Asia, Bombay would become a focal point for meetings of al-Nahda figures from the different cities of the Gulf, as well as from India and other parts of the Arab world. Ideas, periodicals, and gossip regarding the latest events of the times would be exchanged and spread far across the Indian ocean and the Arab world.[32]

32 Mubarak al-Khater, *Nabeghat al-Bahrain 'Abdulla al-Zayed* (Bahrain: Government Press, 1988), 48–57.

Starting at a young age, al-Zayed became infatuated with the Majlis of Sh. Ebrahim. As one of the youngest attendees, he grew up under the wings and tutelage of the older crowd of the Majlis. He quickly stood out as excelling in literature and poetry, and he was one of the first of the group to learn English, accomplishments that he would put to great effect when he established the first periodic newspaper in Bahrain in the early 1930s.[33] He particularly epitomized that strand within al-Nahda reformist thought that focused on literary reform in Bahrain. Before this renaissance, poetry and prose in Bahrain, like elsewhere in the Gulf, was characterized by a verbose descriptive genre that was heavy on style and light on substance.[34] Al-Nahda established a new approach that emphasized simplicity, clarity, and directness in style. This literary renaissance in Bahrain was to be crystallized in another institution that was founded around 1919, the Literary Club, and al-Zayed was to be its first secretary.

THE RISE OF SOCIAL CLUBS

In essence, it seems the Literary Club in Muharraq was a formalized extension of the Majlis of Sh. Ebrahim, as all of its members were visitors of the latter. The first president of the club was chosen to be Sh. Mohammad bin ʿAbdulla, the nineteen-year-old son of Sh. ʿAbdulla bin ʿIsa, no doubt due to his social standing as the grandson of the ruler.[35] The club began hosting icons of the al-Nahda literary renaissance during their

33 Ibid., 87–8.
34 A great example of this would be: Othman al-Basri, *Sabaʾek al-ʿasjad* (Doha: Hasan al-Thani Centre for Historical Studies, 2007).
35 Al-Khalifa, *Maʿa shaikh al-udabaʾ*, 103–106.

visits to Bahrain, most notable of which were Amin al-Raihani from Lebanon, Mohammad al-Shanqiti from Mauritania, 'Abdulaziz al-Tha'alebi from Tunisia, and Khaled al-Faraj from Kuwait.[36]

Al-Raihani's visit to Bahrain in 1922 is illuminating in this respect. Born in the village of Freika in Lebanon, he was one of the al-Nahda third-generation figures associated with *al-Mahjar*, or migrants to the West. He moved to the United States, where he studied law and dabbled in acting. While there, he seems to have experienced a negative mental reaction and decided to return to the region. He began travelling through the Arabian Peninsula on an invitation from the King of Hejaz, and based on these travels he would write his famous *Arab Kings* travelling memoirs.[37] One of his visits was to Bahrain, which according to him positively proved wrong his previous misconceptions of backwardness and underdevelopment. He first attended the ruler's Majlis, where he opined that the goal of his travels and writings was to galvanize and unite the Arabs. He then visited the Majlis of Sh. Ebrahim, and was subsequently hosted by the Literary Club. A large celebration was held there in his honour, as he was feted with poems and speeches recited by several members. Al-Zayed's speech was the finale:[38]

36 'Abdulaziz al-Tha'alebi (1876–1944) was a notable Tunisian political and religious writer who became one of the leaders of the fight against French colonialism. Mohammad al-Shanqiti gained fame as a reformist religious scholar, while Khaled al-Faraj made his name as a poet who spent a considerable part of his life in Bahrain. For more see: al-Khater, *al-Ketabat al-uwla*.

37 Amin al-Raihani, *Muluk al-'arab*, 1925.

38 Al-Khater, *Nabeghat al-Bahrain*, 143–147.

Hello to the son of Lebanon, to the clearest example of Independent Arab Life. Your visit here is a true honour... a ray of light that we have arisen from our slumber to explore. It is the breeze that we had almost lost hope of it blowing: the breeze of the city, the breeze of freedom, and the breeze of living Arabism that was re-sent to rejuvenate the world, cleansed from the baggage of tradition.

Even though al-Raihani was Christian, his sect-affiliation was of secondary concern to the al-Nahda group, who were much more interested in emphasizing national belonging and intellectual accomplishement. After his slightly inflated salutation that was filled by the now established al-Nahda themes of Arabism, rejuvenation, freedom, and revolt against tradition, al-Zayed continued:

Sir, you carry in your conscience an Obligation that you must carry out for the east in general and the Arab world in particular. You must enlighten the west to the souls of easterners... Tell them, that I have visited Egypt, Hejaz, Yemen, Iraq, Nejd and Bahrain, and I saw there people who have shrugged off the dusts of laziness and prepared themselves to labour. People that long to shake your hands as friends... but who will not accept under any circumstances that you become their masters and them your slaves. The eastern world has been awoken by events and alerted by catastrophes, and so it has risen again to reclaim its lost glory.

In this early phase of his life, al-Zayed was one of Bahrain's intelligentsia who most embodied that strand in al-Afghani's and

'Abdu's thought of confrontation between East and West, where the Arab and Muslim world was experiencing a sense of rejuvenation in which it aimed to establish itself as on par with the West, instead of being under its colonial domination.

By the time of Raihani's visit in 1922, Arabic periodicals of al-Nahda had been present in Bahrain for nearly five decades, with their first arrival coinciding with the movement of merchants throughout the trade routes of the Indian Ocean in the last quarter of the nineteenth century. Thus, Sh. Ebrahim's library at his Majlis had several periodicals dating back to the 1870s. Those who studied in al-Azhar, such as Ahmad bin Mehza' and Khunji, further brought with them periodicals upon their return. Bin Mehza', for example, brought back a full set of al-'Urwa al-Wuthqa upon his return from al-Azhar in 1887, three years after the periodical first came out.[39]

The importation of these periodicals became much more regularized by 1890 due largely to the efforts of Muqbil al-Thukair. Originally from 'Unaiza in Najd in modern-day Sa'udi Arabia, he left his home town around 1870 and travelled to Bahrain in search of a livelihood. Despite his modest beginnings, he entered the world of pearl trading, and by 1890 he had established himself as one of Bahrain's most successful pearl merchants. During this time, he became a regular visitor to Sh. Ebrahim's Majlis. Upon the insistence of the Majlis's attendees, he became the first to regularly import and sell these periodicals, beginning in 1895, and he very quickly also became a frequent correspondent with them.[40]

Al-Thukair seems to have had a particular inclination towards pan-Islamist and anti-colonial causes. This led him to

39 Al-Khater, al-ketabat, 11–16.
40 Al-Hadi, A'yan al-Bahrain, 960–963; and al-Bassam, Rejal fi, 11–18.

set up, with Khunji,[41] the Islamic Literary Club in mid-1913, as a way of countering what they saw as the rising threat of American evangelicals in Bahrain. The club was made up of two classes, to which they brought in a disciple of Mohammad 'Abduh from Basra to run, teaching religion and some modern sciences.[42] Al-Thukair also became an active campaigner for different pan-Islamic and anti-colonial causes in the wider Muslim world. During the First World War, he led a campaign to gather donations for the Ottomans, followed by another campaign for the Libyan Mujahedeen in their fight against Italian colonialism. His fortunes quickly declined in 1917, however, as several bad deals forced him into bankruptcy. He left Bahrain a poor man in 1917 and headed back to his home town of Najd without witnessing the climax of our story, but this was not before leaving a lasting imprint on the flow of al-Nahda ideals into the islands. (He also laid a claim to being the first person to bring a car to Bahrain in 1910, and the famous French jeweller Jacques Cartier rode in it with him during his trip to Bahrain.)[43]

This growing circulation of periodicals began to stimulate a transnational exchange of ideas across the Arab world and the Indian Ocean. There were differences in the preferences of the readers, depending on their particular inclinations. The more nationalist and anti-colonialist oriented Qasem al-Shirawi, for example, preferred the Egyptian *al-Liwaa'* (*the Standard*) because of its anti-colonial and nationalist sentiment. When the periodical's founder, Mustafa Kamil Pasha, died in 1908,

---

41 Yousuf Kanoo was also a co-founder.

42 Al-Bassam, *Rijal fi*, 14–18.

43 Abdul Rahman al-Shubaili, 'Muqbelan min al-Thukair', *Asharq al-Awsat* newspaper, 20 November 2011, http://archive.aawsat.com/details. asp?section=19&article=650680&issueno=12045#.WNEX3PmGM2w.

Shirawi ran crying to the Majlis of Sh. Muhammad, knowing that its attendees would be the only ones who would understand his grief.[44]

The periodical that was by far the most influential on the early group of al-Nahda figures in Bahrain was *al-Manar*, published by Rashid Rida, who would have a particularly strong connection with the rising intelligentsia in the islands. Born in a village near Tripoli, Lebanon, in 1865, he benefited from a modern education at the recently established Ottoman schools, which began to teach curricula involving French, as well as Arabic and Islamic sciences. Reading *al-'Urwa al-Wuthqa* had a profound effect on him, inducing him to become 'Abduh's disciple and biographer. He left the Levant in 1897 and headed to Cairo, where he began publishing *al-Manar*, which was to become his life for the next four decades until his death in 1935. He used *al-Manar* to disseminate his polemics and musings on Islamic doctrine, as well as ongoing events in the world. For the latter, he relied extensively on relayed news sent to him by his readers from across the Islamic world, creating a transnational network of followers and participants. Most popularly, he devoted a section to *fatwas*, where readers could send in their questions on any moral or practical questions to which he would provide answers, and this latter was to become a particular favourite of its readers in Bahrain.

In terms of thought, he would continue to espouse views similar to those of his mentor, where he would contend that Islam has at its core the principles of reason, civilization, and prosperity, but if these were deviated from, it would result in weakness, barbarity, and decay, which is why the Muslim Umma had fallen behind. Increasingly over time, however, Rida

44 Al-Khalifa, *Ma'a shaikh al-udaba'*, 71.

became suspicious of Sufism and similar strands within Islam, and his thoughts and outlook were drawn closer to teachings of Ibn Taymiyya and to Wahhabi doctrine.[45]

Bahrain's intelligentsia enthusiastically took to Rida's periodical and thoughts, with correspondence dating back to *al-Manar*'s inception year. The letters continued to reflect the general eagerness for all kinds of knowledge, and the fact that al-Nahda figures in the Gulf looked westward in the Arab world for inspiration and guidance during this period. Al-Thukair sent a question in 1903 asking: in areas on the periphery of the Islamic world such as the Gulf, what are Muslims to do if Ramadhan was adjudged to have started on a particular date, and this date was discovered later on to be different from that in more central locations such as Egypt and the Levant? Should the fasting dates be immediately switched to coincide with the central locations, or should they be kept as originally judged? Alternatively, Khunji sent a question in 1911 asking: what are comets, and where do they come from?[46]

Nasser al-Khairi was one of the most prolific correspondents with these periodicals. More importantly, he has a strong claim to being the first modern historian from Bahrain, on whose writings this study relies significantly. He was born and raised in Manama, but he had extensive interaction with the intelligentsia of Muharraq. Indeed, Khairi was one of the closest friends of Sh. Mohammad, the son of Sh. Ebrahim, whose Majlis he would frequently attend. He was one of the founders of the Literary Club, a venture dear to his heart, where he would leave his work in the evening and travel by boat to Muharraq to

---

45 Hourani, *Arabic Thought*, 224–228.
46 Al-Khalifa, *Ma'a shaikh al-udaba'*, 41–43.

attend its sessions, frequently sleeping over in Sh. Ebrahim's guesthouse.[47]

A black man, his background differed uniquely from the rest of the intelligentsia. His family was classified as 'al-Mawali', which were families of freed ex-slaves. Born in 1876, his father died while he was still young, upon which his grandfather brought him up with limited means. This background makes it even more remarkable that he was able to pursue scholarship and schooling from a young age. He began studying at one of the local Kuttab, and when his abilities shone through, he then entered the school of Ahmad bin Mehza', where he studied for three years.

During this time, he also began attending the American missionary school in Manama, the first modern institutionalized school in Bahrain that opened in 1896 (of which more will be said later). His tutor Shaikh Ahmad gave his blessing to his attending, as 'whoever learns a people's language, has insured himself against their machinations.'[48] During his three years of study at the missionary school, he learned English, which at a time of booming trade and when the vast majority of the population was illiterate would come in handy for him professionally. He began his first job working as a clerk for a trader in Manama in 1903, after which he became a clerk with Sh. Mohammad bin Ebrahim in 1914, during which time their strong friendship began. He then became an employee in the newly founded Manama municipality in 1919 that will figure prominently in the events of the next chapter. During this period and up until his death in 1925, he would work on his uncompleted magnum opus on the history of Bahrain, *Qala'id al-Nahrain fi Tarikh al-Bahrain* (*The Pearls of Bahrain's History*).

47 Al-Khater, *al-adeeb al-kateb*, 6–20.
48 Al-Khater, *al-Qadhi*, 125.

His time at the American missionary school was to have a strong impact upon him. He developed a continuing fascination with the periodicals that the missionaries provided in their library. Top of his list of favourites was *al-Muqtataf*, which was available in the missionary school given that it was written by Lebanese Christians who were graduates of missionary schools themselves. In 1910, he began corresponding with the periodical. Given his social background, it is telling that his first question centred on Islam's view on slavery, and whether it was favoured or looked down upon. This also probably shows the influence of attending the missionary schools, which frequently used the issue of slavery as a focal point in its evangelizing. His subsequent letter in 1911 shifted focus to his interest in history, asking about who discovered the pearl banks in the Gulf. This was followed in the same year by another letter inquiring on who had conquered the islands of Bahrain in ancient history, a topic which was to become part of the focus of his own historical writings.[49]

In 1913, Khairi joined with nine other individuals[50] from Manama, including Sa'ad al-Shamlan and Mohammad Saleh Khunji, to form a public library under the name *Maktabat Iqbal Awal* (Awal Rising Library).[51] This was to function as a counterpoint to the missionary library, as its attendance began arousing local suspicion. They rented a shop and converted it into a library to house their books and gatherings, and after a few months, this library was rebranded into a literary club under the

49 Al-Khater, *al-adeeb*, 33–36.
50 This group included Mohammad Saleh Yousuf, Nasser al-Khairi, Mohammad al-Urayyed, Khalil al-Moayyad, Mohammad al-Tajir, 'Ali al-Fadhel, Mohammad Ebrahim al-Baker, 'Ali Kanoo, Sa'ad al-Shamlan, and Salman al-Tajir.
51 Awal is an historic name for the islands of Bahrain.

name *Nadi Iqbal Awal* (Awal Rising Club). This proved to be a landmark in several aspects. They were in effect the first non-missionary public library in Bahrain, and (along with the Islamic Literary Club) the first formalized literary club on the islands. Its composition was mixed in terms of sects, with three Shi'a and seven Sunni members. Khunji was elected as the president, and Nasser al-Khairi as its secretary.[52]

Mohammad 'Ali al-Tajir was another founding member of the club and, like Khairi, he was one of the first modern historians from Bahrain. Like many others of the intelligentsia enumerated here, he came from a pearl merchants' background, where he used to travel with his father to India to sell pearls. Unlike the others we have described so far, he was Shi'a. He began his studies between the local Kuttab and religious schools, as well as spending time in the Persian school in Bombay. After returning to Bahrain, he specialized in property dealings, and he became one of the financial contributors to al-Hedaya school. He eventually opened a private library around 1920–1921, which became a stopover point for pearl traders and scholars to gather and discuss issues of the day.[53] His magnum opus, *'Iqd al-Li'al fi Tarikh Awal* (*The Pearl Necklaces of Awal's History*), still stands as one of the major treatises on Bahrain's history during this period, a testament to the number of notable historians and writers to have emerged from the small group that was involved in setting up the club.

The first lecture at the club was delivered by its president Mohammad Khunji, and the speech's text sheds light on the

---

52 Al-Khater, *al-ketabat al-uwla*, 136.
53 Wesam al-Sebe, 'Mohammad 'Ali al-Tajer, hekaya min al-madhi', *Al-Wasat* newspaper, 17 December 2013, http://www.alwasatnews.com/news/838698.html.

nature of thoughts circulating within the club's intelligentsia during that period. It begins by stating that Islam is the one true religion, whose oneness and truth was carried by all prophets, and its central tenet is the belief in the oneness and uniqueness of God alone without any other equivalents. This part of Islam, which deals with all manners of the soul and its morality, can be defined as 'religion', which does not change across time, place, or prophets. On the other hand, there are various ways for prophets to communicate these central tenets of religion, depending on their circumstances in different places and times. This second part that has to do with the politics of humans and their civil aspects is called 'Shari'a' and does change from time to time:

> As for that part (Shari'a) that has to do with reforming the social circumstances that are pursuant to civilization (*Hadara*) and advancement ('Umran), which we said could change across circumstances, it is very possible that the laws and principles that were set in earlier times might need to be added to, subtracted from, or reformed.

Hence, the 'religion' aspect is the same across time and space, while the Shari'a principles can vary spatio-temporally, to which he now turns his attention on how to decipher these changes:

> The sources of these principles are the holy book, the *Sunna*, and *ijtihad* arising from consultation (*musha-wara*) over the matter, which should be between people who have knowledge and experience of what is good for the *Umma*, which are referred to in the holy book as *Ulul Amr*. Sh. Mohammad Rashid Rida said, 'What is meant

by Ulul Amr are the people that the Umma trusts to provide solutions, including its scholars and leaders in the military, and public occupations such as trade and industry and agriculture, as well as the leaders of workers and parties and the editors of respectable newspapers. Obedience to them in this case is obedience to Ulul Amr.[54]

Several themes come up in this speech, which apparently had many of those attending staring in bewilderment and incomprehension. The first is exalting Islam as the one true religion, which seems to be an acknowledgement of the type of debates members of the club were having with missionaries during that period. Secondly, it is pertinent to our discussion that an ecumenical view of Islam dominates the text, one that transcends different sects. The focus of the speech instead is on highlighting that principles and conduct of earthly matters are distinct from the core of religion, and the former can and should change over time, in order to ensure that civilization and advancement ensue in the Umma. Finally, Ulul Amr is interpreted broadly and in a distinctly modern manner as essentially the rule of experts, and these experts were not only the traditional religious scholars and the ruler, but also included political party leaders, union heads, newspaper editors, and experts in industry, agriculture, and commerce. Shura was needed based on modernist conceptions, according to the directions of Shaikh Rida, who is brought in to support such a viewpoint. Since Bahrain at this point had neither political parties, nor unions, nor local newspapers, it is not surprising that some members of the audience found the speech a bit confusing.

54 Al-Khater, *al-ketabat al-uwla*, 63–66.

The club was obviously bringing in radical ideas by the standards of the time. Members of the club were derogatorily referred to by their detractors as '*asriyyoon* (those of the times' zeitgeist). This 'being of the times' was to bring an abrupt and unhappy ending to the club after only a few months of its existence. At the end of 1913, the members of the club decided to perform the Hajj pilgrimage in Mecca. They asked Nasser al-Khairi to send a set of questions regarding Hajj to Rida's *al-Manar* periodical, to which he had written previously. Once again, it is noteworthy that differences in sects and madhhabs between the members did not factor as a prominent issue regarding these correspondences or performing the pilgrimage together, with the letters focusing instead on a more encompassing view of Islam. He sent seven questions in total, and they centred mainly on the validity and reasons for certain rituals in Hajj and Islam, including kissing the black stone at the *Ka'ba*, offering sacrificial lambs, and whether these are considered a form of idolatry.[55]

Rida duly replied in an extensive answer, which he began by commenting that he senses the influence of Christian missionaries in these questions. The questions continued to occupy Rida and *al-Manar*'s readers for several subsequent issues, with many criticizing him for engaging with such questions whose goal was to defame Islam.[56] When the periodical in question was published and reached the hands of the stern judge Qasem bin Mehza', who does not seem to have shared the openness and reformist appeal of his brother Shaikh Ahmad, he 'lost it'.

---

55 Question sent on 4 Sha'ban 1331 by Nasser Mubarak al-Khairi, *al-Manar*, Volume 16, Issue of Ramadhan 1331. Found in *al-Maktaba al-Shamila*, version 3.64, http://www.shamela.ws.
56 See *al-Manar* Volume 16, thul Hujja 1331, 960; and Volume 17, Muharram 1332, 80.

Given that the members had set up the club without asking for his permission in the first place, he ordered its closure.[57] The members were branded by some in the community as the 'nine heads who were spreading corruption in the land'.[58] This was in reference to a Quranic verse telling the story of the nine heads of the town of Thamud who tried to assassinate the prophet Saleh, but who were punished by God and his angels by being killed instead.[59]

For his particular intransigence, Judge Mehza' wanted to have Nasser's nose cut to make an example of him, which fortunately he was dissuaded from at the last moment. The fortunes of the president of the club, Shaikh Mohammad Saleh Khunji, worsened in the aftermath of the incident, as students stayed away from his school. The school was disbanded and he was unable to get any other jobs, so he had to leave for Bombay in search of opportunities there.[60]

THE AMERICAN MISSIONARIES
AND THE PERSIAN SCHOOL

Discussion of al-Nahda would not be complete without addressing the significant role that the American missionaries played in the intellectual developments in Bahrain. Indeed, they were to arrive in Bahrain even before there was a direct British white presence on the ground. The mission was founded in 1890 at the New Brunswick theological seminary in New

---

57 'Al-Khater, *al-Adeed al-Kateb*, 85–90.
58 'التسعة الرهط المفسدون في الأرض', al-Khater, *al-Qadhi*, 138.
59 وَكَانَ فِي الْمَدِينَةِ تِسْعَةُ رَهْطٍ يُفْسِدُونَ فِي الْأَرْضِ وَلَا يُصْلِحُونَ, *Surat al-Naml, The Noble Quran*, 27:48.
60 Al-Khalifa, *Ma'a shaikh al-udaba'*, 72.

Jersey under the name of the 'The Arabian Mission', with the stated aim of Christianizing the Arabian Peninsula. The first mission in the Gulf region was established in Bahrain by Samuel Zwemer (1867–1952), who first arrived in 1893 as a young missionary in his twenties. He would stay for twenty years, coming back to visit frequently even after leaving. He was a driven man and a prolific writer, completing more than fifty books about his experiences in the Arabian Peninsula. He married Amy Elizabeth Wilkes, whom he met in Basra in 1899, and moved with her to Bahrain.

Bahrain was chosen to launch the mission due to the protection that Britain could afford to Western subjects, as well as its cities' relatively cosmopolitan atmosphere. In addition, it was judged to be a disease danger zone due to the high heat and humidity, which they perceived to be ideal for evangelizing purposes. 'It was the most unhealthy place in all the areas,' with cholera, malaria, dysentery, and smallpox widespread. In their dedication to their cause, two of the Zwemers' daughters died from cholera in one week in Bahrain.[61]

Initially, the missionaries focused on evangelizing to recently freed slaves and their families, as well as taking care of a handful of recent converts fleeing persecution from other areas in the Gulf, particularly from Basra. They hoped to reach a wider audience using three chief means: providing institutionalized education, disseminating literature, and providing medical services.[62] Zwemer began in 1894 by opening a small bookshop that also acted as a public library, the first in the region, which became known as the library of the missionaries. This became

61 Lewis R. Scudder, *The Arabian Mission's Story: In Search of Abraham's Other Son* (Grand Rapids: Wm. B. Eerdmans Publishing, 1998), 153.
62 al-Khalifa, *Ma'at 'am*, 23–24.

the library that Khairi frequented with other members of Nadi Iqbal Awal before opening their own club.

Judge Qasem bin Mehzaʿ, who held a lot of sway in Manama, was furious at first at the presence of the missionaries and vehemently objected, but the British Gulf Political Resident and the ruler allowed them to remain. The reaction of the city dwellers seems to have been mixed. Zwemer was able to mingle freely without any threat of violence, roaming through the town on his bike, even though many looked at him with suspicion. He used to debate youths on the street regarding Islam, telling them that he came to their land as their guest, and if they did not accept him then he was the guest of God. They would retort that he was neither their nor God's guest, but the guest of the Devil. 'The Devil's guest' stuck as his moniker, and his bike, which was the first to enter Bahrain, was called *Khail Eblees* (the Devil's horse).[63]

His wife, Amy, opened the first institutionalized school in Bahrain and the Gulf in 1899 under the name The Acorn, also becoming its first teacher. It was an all-girls school to begin with, with a boys' school following suit in 1902. Thus, institutionalized female education began in Bahrain before male education. It first concentrated on teaching freed slaves from Muscat and recently converted Christians who had escaped from Iraq, as well as accepting some local students. Enrolments were very small: until the early 1900s they barely exceeded more than two dozen and were frequently in the single digits.[64] Next, Zwemer set his sights on opening a hospital. After several unsuccessful attempts at obtaining permission to buy a plot of land from the ruler, he was finally granted the right in 1901 with

---

63 Al-Khater, *al-Qadhi*, 110–115.
64 Al-Khalifa, *Maʾat ʿam*, 28–60.

the aid of heavy British pressure, and the hospital was duly built in 1902, the first of its kind in the Gulf.[65]

In its primary aim of converting the people of Bahrain to Christianity, the missionary school was an unmitigated failure, with less than a dozen converts over its existence. However, its impact through education and medical practices was profound. Foremost was its effect on Bahrain's intelligentsia of the time, many of whom would study and read there, as well as duel with the new ideas, practices, and even objects brought in by the missionaries. As we saw, discussions regarding Islam versus the evangelizing missions came to occupy a central role within al-Nahda circles, in marked contrast to their avoidance of intra-sectarian polemics within Islam.

The second school to open after the Acorn in Bahrain was set up by and catered for the 'Persian' community. Although small as a percentage of Bahrain's overall population, they had a significant influence on trade, particularly in the cities (Lorimer's count shows a total of 1,650 out of Bahrain's population of approximately one hundred thousand, overwhelmingly concentrated in Manama and Muharraq). In 1913, as news spread that the 'Bahrain Order in Council' was to be implemented by the British to formalize their rule in the islands (the next chapter), a group of Persian traders based in Bahrain decided to open a private school for boys. This was a time of rising anti-British sentiment in Persia, particularly in the aftermath of the encroaching British control over economic matters under the rule of the Qajar Shah.

Mohammad Ardakani was a trader deported that same year

---

65 QDL, 'Gazetteer of the Persian Gulf. Vol I. Historical. Part IA & IB. J G Lorimer. 1915' [936] (1091/1782), IOR/L/PS/20/C91/1, https://www.qdl.qa/en/archive/81055/vdc_100023575946.0x00005c.

by the British from Bahrain to India due to his anti-British writings in Persian newspapers. While in India, he somehow managed to obtain a copy of the draft of the Bahrain Order in Council (BOIC) even before it was published. He opened a printing press there, and duly sent the copy of the BOIC to Persian notables in Bahrain to alert them that under the BOIC's edicts they would be placed under British jurisdiction. He recommended that a school be set up with the utmost urgency in order to strengthen Persian nationalist sentiment and culture within the Persian community in Bahrain.[66]

Following on the advice of Ardakani, a group of Persian traders set up a committee to establish and supervise the school, which was mainly run on donations and contributions from Persian merchants, as well as payments from Iran's government. Its first name was *Ittihad Melli* (National Unity School), and it was located next to Ma'tam al-'Ajam, the main Ma'tam for Persians.[67] Its curriculum focused on teaching Persian language, poetry, and history, as well as science, maths, geography, Arabic, and English. Most of the pupils were children of Persian traders, with a few admitted from the poorer Persian classes, as well as a handful of Arabs, the latter being required to pay for tuition. The total enrolment was small, although not insignificant, standing at forty-seven in 1915.

As was common with the emergent modern nationalist schools at the time, many of its principles and practices were geared towards instilling forms of order, discipline, and punishment, with a strong focus on an ethos of Persian patriotism.

---

66 Al-Khalifa, *Ma'at 'am*, 105–106.
67 The founders were 'Abdulnabi Kazerooni, 'Abdulnabi Bushehri, Mirza Hussain Dasthi, 'Abdul Qasem Shirazi, 'Abbas Bushehri, and Mirza 'Ali Dasthi. The last was the principal of the school. See: ibid.

Uniforms were introduced in 1919 based on the 'Qajar' dress code, and later on scout groups were formed that conducted public parades throughout Manama in official dress while carrying Persian state flags and banners, much to the chagrin of the local rulers and the British officials.[68] In this manner, the school could be seen as the first institutionalized embodiment of nationalism in Bahrain, even if it was concentrated within a tiny portion of the population. In contrast to the inchoate Arab nationalism and Islamism which was still in the process of formation at the end of the 1910s, Persian nationalism had by then taken a much more concrete form in Iran. This began in the early 1890s with the Tobacco Protests against the award of a monopoly in tobacco provision to a British firm.[69] In tandem, the emergent Persian nationalism within a small but influential part of the population would play a crucial role in the explosive events that would ensue in Bahrain.

CONCLUSION: BAHRAIN IN THE AGE OF AL-NAHDA

The period 1890–1920 was particularly consequential in terms of the germination and cross-fertilization of new 'modernized' modes of thought and discourse in Bahrain. Institutionalized schools with modern curricula, libraries, and literary clubs began to emerge for the first time, and periodicals from the wider region reached Bahrain more regularly. The ideas and writings of al-Nahda started to be increasingly debated in

68 Ibid., 107–129.
69 For more on the tobacco protests and the 'constitutional revolution': Vanessa Martin, *The Qajar Pact: Bargaining, Protest and the State in Nineteenth-Century Persia* (London: I.B.Tauris, 2005).

Bahrain, combined with the rise of Persian nationalism and American missionaries.

The discussion in this chapter focused primarily on articulating the thoughts and lives of the individuals who embodied the rise of al-Nahda in Bahrain. The interactions between these individuals formed overlapping circles that spread across literary, educational, anti-colonial, as well as Islamic reformist spheres of thought. Most of these individuals were part of the male elites of society, frequently being pearl traders themselves. They were also very close to the ruling family (and some were members of the ruling family). The extent and spread of these ideas remained within a limited circle, given that neither a regular printing press nor modern schools had been established widely in Bahrain. Thus, written documents by non-elites are almost non-existent from this period, so the ideas and events enumerated here almost exclusively revolve around the perspectives and actions of the literate notables of society.[70] Given the class background of most of these individuals and the events of their age, their debates and thoughts focused mostly on issues of education, freedom, administrative reform, and independence, while issues of social justice, inequality, and class, although present, were not as

---

70 It is thus important to emphasize that the descriptions of the 'non-elites' presented in this book, whether female or male, urban or rural, farmers or pearl divers, are mostly based on accounts by other actors. This is a near universal feature within the literature due to the lack of literacy and directly written documents by non-elite groups (although oral traditions such as songs and poetry do provide an excellent window). Consequently, most 'speaking' is done on behalf of the subaltern, an issue that this book has to grapple with just like the rest of the literature on this period. This remains a crucial area in need of further work. For more see: Gayatri Spivak, 'Can the subaltern speak?', in Rosalind Morris (ed.), *Can the Subaltern Speak? Reflections on the History of an Idea* (New York: Columbia University Press, 1988), 21–78.

prominent. If one were to focus on ethno-sect identities, most of those listed above were Sunni, although there were some Shiʿas too (e.g. al-Tajir). However, the writings of this group provided a non-sectarian discourse, influenced by the al-Nahda movement, and this discourse was that of anti-colonialism and ecumenical Islamic reform.

During this period, the Ottoman and Qajar empires, for so long the established powers in the region, were undergoing radical restructuring and entering their last throes. The eruption of the First World War in turn cast doubt on the supposed civilizational supremacy of Europe, and then raised the question of who was to lead the Muslim and Arab world given that the Ottoman *Khilafa* was no longer around. This was coupled with an explosive growth in the cities of Manama and Muharraq in the period before the war, with the rise in demand for pearls resulting in unprecedented income flowing into Bahrain. A harsh recession and famine checked this growth during the years of the war, after which the economic situation would rebound strongly. All these intermeshing factors would combine to set the background to the convulsive events of the early 1920s. Before narrating these events, however, we need to turn towards the most important variable in shaping the field in which they unfolded: the imposition of direct British rule in Bahrain.

4

CONTESTING DIVIDED RULE, 1900–1920

PAX BRITANNICA BEFORE DIVIDED RULE, 1800–1900

B ritish presence in the Gulf dates back to at least 1763, when the East India Company opened branches in Basra and Bushehr, installing a Resident in the latter on the eastern side of the Gulf. As British and French imperial rivalry intensified with Napoleon's invasion of Egypt in 1798, threatening French inroads into the Arabian Sea and the Gulf, the British quickly moved to cement their hegemony over these maritime routes to India. The East India Company's Resident signed a treaty with the Sultan of Muscat in that same year, in which he promised not to permit French presence on his lands. This was followed by the 1800 treaty, which allowed the British to post an Agent in Muscat. British officials then moved to sign treaties with the Qajar ruler of Persia that also excluded the presence of French troops. Thus, imperial and military intrigues with other European powers over the maritime routes to India, rather than any direct trade interests in the Gulf, formed the background for the expansion of the British presence in the region at the turn of the nineteenth century.[1]

In order to cement their influence in the region, however, the British had to contend with the rising force of al-Qawasem from Ras al-Khaimah (in modern-day United Arab Emirates), back then the strongest local force in the Gulf. Their repeated clashes with British ships constituted a real threat to the latter's hegemony over the region's maritime routes.[2] Under the pretext of fighting piracy, a large naval expedition was sent to lay siege and attack the fleet of al-Qawasem at their base in 1809, causing significant damage but failing to wipe them out completely. As skirmishes continued to simmer over the next few years, the British sent another expedition in 1819 which this time destroyed al-Qawasem's fleet and base in Ras al-Khaimah.[3]

This was quickly followed by imposing the signing of the General Maritime Treaty of 1820 on local powers. The treaty specified the cessation of hostilities between the British and the subjects of the different signatory rulers, with ships of the respective parties able to use each other's ports. The vessels under the jurisdiction of the local rulers were required to carry flags recognizable by the British government. The ruler of Bahrain was a signatory to the treaty, constituting the first official legal manifestation of British relations with the al-Khalifa.[4] Hence, using the banner of eradicating piracy, British imperial

1 Mubarak al-Otabi, *The Qawasim and British Control of the Arabian Gulf* (PhD thesis, University of Salford, 1989), chapter 4.
2 Ibid., chapter 6.
3 Sultan al-Qasimi, *The Myth of Arab Piracy in the Gulf* (Abingdon: Routledge, 1988).
4 An informal agreement to remain neutral in the battles between al-Khalifa and the Omani Sultan was signed previously in 1816.

forces domesticated the local powers and cemented their ultimate control over the waters of the Gulf and the Arabian Sea,
mainly as a means of monopolizing the Western maritime
routes to India. *Pax Britannica* was to rule supreme for the next
hundred years. In return, the rulers on the western shores of the
Gulf received official recognition from the British Empire, helping them to avoid the fate of the rulers of other small Arab emirates in the Gulf, who would eventually be gobbled up by larger
powers in the region.[5]

Next came the first maritime truce of 1835, backed up and
administered by the British, which was an experimental ban on
warfare between the different rulers of the Gulf for six months
during the pearling season. The truce proved so successful for
pearling affairs that it kept being renewed by the parties. Given
that the British were the mightiest imperial power in not only
the region but also the globe, they kept receiving formal protection requests by the different local rulers, including al-Khalifa.
Initially, the British tended to see no overall benefit to providing explicit commitments to any local power, but the war
between the rival factions of al-Khalifa in the mid-1800s would
change that.

As the war reached a crescendo in the 1840s, Britain became
worried that the situation was threatening *Pax Britannica*'s
stability in the Gulf and drawing in a large number of regional
actors, including al-Sa'ud of Najd, al-Sabah of Kuwait, al-Thani
of Qatar, the Ottomans, as well as Iran. They signed a treaty of
suppression of the slave trade with Bahrain in 1847, and British
'protection' was finally awarded in 1861. This was to counter

5 This would be the fate of the al-Madhkurs in Bushehr, who would be
swallowed up by the Qajari Empire in the mid-nineteenth century, and the
al-Ka'abis in Muhammarah, taken over by the Shah in 1921.

Shaikh Mohammad bin Khalifa's (MbK) pledge of allegiance to both the Persians and the Ottomans against the resurgent Sa'udis. Worried that this meant other imperial powers were encroaching on its turf, Britain offered MbK protection from external hostilities, requiring in return that he himself cease from maritime aggression in the region.[6]

The treaty stipulated that British subjects be able to reside and trade in Bahrain. Furthermore, British extraterritorial jurisdiction was established within the islands, stipulating that Britain's representative would adjudicate all legal cases involving British subjects and dependants.[7] Consequently, the 1861 agreement was significant in that it gave Britain sovereignty over British subjects in Bahrain, which as we will see would play a primary role in creating a system of divided rule and dual jurisdiction. Theoretically, there were now two legally recognized sources of sovereignty within the same land, with each covering different subjects. British jurisdiction at this point only covered British subjects, who numbered a few dozen souls, mainly traders, from India.

The encroaching imperial influence was buttressed when British naval forces bombarded Bahrain in 1869 and forcibly replaced MbK after his deadly feud with his brother. Based on the requests of local notables, they agreed to Sh. 'Isa bin 'Ali taking over the helm as the new ruler: his reign would span the next half-century until the climax of our story in 1923.[8] As the

6 QDL, 'Gazetteer of the Persian Gulf. Vol I. Historical. Part IA & IB. J G Lorimer. 1915' [881-902] (1036-1057/1782), IOR/L/PS/20/C91/1, https://www.qdl.qa/en/archive/81055/vdc_100023575946.0x000025.
7 James Onley, *The Arabian Frontier of the British Raj: Merchants, Rulers, and the British in the Nineteenth-Century Gulf* (Oxford: Oxford University Press, 2007), 119–121.
8 Kadhim, *Isti'malat al-Dhakira*, 65.

British became increasingly worried about encroaching imperial rivalry in the Gulf from the Ottomans, the French, and even
the Americans, they forced Sh. 'Isa in 1880 and 1892 to sign
treaties of exclusivity with the British, which bound rulers of
Bahrain not to enter into treaties or negotiations or establish
diplomatic ties with any other international power.[9]

At a similar time, the Foreign Jurisdiction Act was passed in
London in 1890, which stipulated the conditions for exercising
jurisdiction over territories subject to British control.[10] The act
made it lawful to exercise jurisdiction in a foreign country in the
same manner as if that jurisdiction was acquired by 'cessation or
conquest of territory'. Furthermore, the act conferred on the
Crown the ability to obtain jurisdiction over British subjects
residing in any country that was seen as lacking a regular government. Thus, the latter part of the nineteenth century would
gradually see rising encroachment by Britain on the ruler's turf
and increasing involvement in Bahrain's internal affairs.

In terms of actual British physical presence in Bahrain, this
can be dated back at least to 1816, when a system of 'Native
Agents' was set up to administer Britain's mainly commercial
interests in the islands. Native Agents were established and
influential merchants with financial and political connections
to the local rulers of the Gulf. Given that Britain had no white
'British' officers present, this system allowed the British to tap
into local politics and business 'on the cheap' as a means of
increasing the influence of the empire locally.[11]

---

9 QDL, 'Gazetteer of the Persian Gulf. Vol I. Historical. Part IA & IB. J G
Lorimer. 1915' [922] (1077/1782), IOR/L/PS/20/C91/1, https://
www.qdl.qa/en/archive/81055/vdc_100023575946.0x000025.
10 Hassan Ali Radhi, *The Bahrain Judiciary* (London: Kluwer Law
International, 2003), 58.
11 Onley, *The Arabian Frontier*, 130–140.

This system of Native Agency under British jurisdiction would see the first seeds of divided rule and the colonial ethnosectarian gaze being implanted in the political system of Bahrain. Ethno-sect considerations played a fundamental role in the choice of Native Agents. Although heavily immersed in the local setting, they were nearly always chosen from ethno-sect groups that the British considered 'foreign' subjects in Bahrain. Initially, the Native Agents were Indian, but based on 'covertly racial views' due to their perceived unsuitability and lower status, the British in the 1820s switched to Native Agents from the surrounding regions, all of them Shi'a, with particularly strong connections to Iraq and Iran. In Bahrain, they were drawn nearly all from one family: al-Safar. Of the thirteen Native Agents, only two were born in Bahrain. Once again based on covertly racial views, the British would switch in 1900 from Native Agents to the employment of white English officers as Political Agents, confirming the primary role that racial and ethnic perceptions played in the Agency system.[12]

Before the treaty of 1861, the Native Agent did not have any legal powers except being protected as a British subject, and he had to refer any legal cases to the Gulf Political Resident in Bushehr. Given the rising trade in the region, most cases were of a commercial nature. 'Mixed cases' involving both locals and British subjects would be adjudicated by the ruler or the previously mentioned Majlis al-'Urf that specialized in trade disputes. There were very few cases involving British subjects before the arrival of steamships, however. With the treaty of 1861, there was a legal basis to establish a British Agency court on the island, and the ruler was legally not supposed to have jurisdiction over

12 Ibid.

mixed cases. In practice, Majlis al-'Urf continued to adjudicate such cases, with the British opting to rely on the extensive, localized knowledge within this institution. In time, case proceedings on mixed cases by the Majlis would end up being held in the Native Agency. In this manner, trade relations and Majlis al-'Urf formed the main vehicle for contact between British imperial concerns and locals.[13]

Tensions arising from the dual jurisdiction implied by the treaty began to surface almost immediately, although these cases were few until the 1890s. In 1873, the representative for the British India Steam Navigation Company in Bahrain, 'Abdulla bin Rajab, who was entitled to British protection because of his position, was arrested on the ruler's order for assaulting local subjects. The Resident at Bushehr ordered his release, which the Shaikh did after protests, even though he admitted that the charges seemed to be valid.[14]

By the mid-1890s, and as trade increased considerably in Bahrain to the point where it became the main hub in the Gulf, these tensions arising from encroaching British sovereignty became much more frequent. As Lorimer put it:

Trade increased and flourished in a remarkable degree. The attention of the British government, whose influence in Bahrain was now more powerful than before, was turned chiefly to schemes of *internal* improvement and reform, and precautions against political competitions on the part of European powers. *Any distinction between*

---

13 Ibid.
14 QDL, 'Gazetteer of the Persian Gulf. Vol I. Historical. Part IA & IB. J G Lorimer. 1915' [921] (1076/1782), IOR/L/PS/20/C91/1, https://www.qdl.qa/en/archive/81055/vdc_100023575946.0x00004d.

British policy and the general course of events in Bahrain is
henceforward impracticable.[15]

In August 1897, a wealthy local merchant named Sayyed Khalaf, whose social background would be classified as Shi'a Baharna, went bankrupt and was placed in the custody of the ruler's chief clerk, Sharida. Sayyed Khalaf escaped and sought refuge with the British Native Agent. Sharida entered the Agency and forcibly removed him. The acting British Native Agent, Khan Mohammad Sharif 'Awadhi, protested and reported it to the British Resident at Bushehr.[16] Although the Resident saw that Khalaf had no right to British protection given that he was considered a 'local' subject, the Resident viewed entering the Agency as a serious offence, and he imposed a fine on Sharida and got him to apologize.[17]

Another example, probably more serious from the British point of view, was a developing crisis in 1896–1897 concerning Bahrain becoming a regional clearing house for arms. What complicated the situation was the personal profiting of the British Native Agent and the ruler, as well as a British-Persian firm, Messrs. Fracis and Times. The Shaikh had granted a concession to the Native Agent and the aforementioned company to import arms for his own use.[18] However,

15 QDL, 'Gazetteer of the Persian Gulf. Vol I. Historical. Part IA & IB. J G Lorimer. 1915' [926] (1081/1782), IOR/L/PS/20/C91/1, https://www. qdl.qa/en/archive/81055/vdc_100023575946.0x000052. The emphases are my own.

16 He was deputizing for the Native Agent at the time, Mohammad Rahim al-Safar.

17 Radhi, *The Bahrain Judiciary*, 59.

18 QDL, 'Persian Gulf gazetteer. Part 1. Historical and political materials. Précis on arms trade in the Persian Gulf.' [16v] (32/70), IOR/L/PS/20/C237, http://www.qdl.qa/en/archive/81055/vdc_100023515244.0x000022.

the Native Agent and the company took the opportunity to start selling thousands of rifles to other parties and neighbouring areas, making Bahrain a hub for the regional arms trade. This alarmed the Shaikh, who wanted to withdraw the concession and confiscate the arms from the firms, but he was afraid of British repercussions given that British protected subjects were involved. Furthermore, it seems the Native Agent and the company had a falling-out regarding payment, upon which they raised civil suits against each other in Basra. This was also compounded by complaints made by the Indian family in charge of customs against the Native Agent, in which he was accused of bringing in imports without paying them the due rates.

From its side, Britain was facing problems with arms and rebellious tribes on the North-West Frontier in India, and had convinced the Shah of Persia and Sultan of Muscat to impose an arms prohibition. It would have smacked of contradictions and hypocrisy if its Native Agent in Bahrain had then become a primary seller in the region.[19] The issue ended with the British returning the arms to the company and withdrawing its concession, although it did not allow the ruler to confiscate the arms, since there might have been legal reservations regarding the ruler confiscating from a 'British' firm.[20]

This same company was also shortly afterwards the subject of a violent attempted robbery, in which its local security guard was hurt.[21] The British Resident perceived that the ruler was reluctant to act against the attackers, and they intervened

---

19 Onley, *The Arabian Frontier*, chapter 6.
20 QDL, 'Gazetteer of the Persian Gulf. Vol I. Historical. Part IA & IB. J G Lorimer. 1915' [932] (1087/1782), IOR/L/PS/20/C91/1, https://www.qdl.qa/en/archive/81055/vdc_100023575946.0x000058.
21 Radhi, *The Bahrain Judiciary*, 59.

directly and applied fines that were paid to the company and the local security guard attacked. Accusations that the Native Agent was unable to perform his duties steadily increased during this period, including by British subjects themselves, reaching the point where the Gulf Political Resident personally requested that the Native Agent be replaced.[22]

These events serve to illustrate that not only were British Agents and authorities exercising jurisdiction over British subjects, but their encroachment also began to extend to 'local' subjects in a sporadic manner. An even earlier significant case involving British 'protection', particularly from a sect-relations perspective, occurred in 1891. Following its rapid spread throughout Iraq, Iran, and parts of India during the nineteenth century,[23] the Shi'a public procession of Muharram took place for the first time in Bahrain's modern history. It was held in Manama under the patronage of the 'Persian' Mirza Mohammad Isma'il, the local agent for the British India Steam Navigation Company, a position that placed him under official British protection.[24] The event marked the establishment of an

---

22 The Government of India, however, would be unconvinced.

23 Yitzhak Nakash, *The Shi'is of Iraq* (Princeton: Princeton University Press, 2003), 142–143. Charles Rathbone Low, a British lieutenant in the Indian Navy, provides descriptions of the processions in Lingah in Iran and Lucknow in India during the mid-nineteenth century. His writings are also notable for his brief and rather bigoted accounts of Bahrain sometime in the 1860s. He did not provide descriptions of Muharram processions on the islands, however, as it seems they were yet to be established in Bahrain: Charles Rathbone Low, *The Land of the Sun* (London: Hodder and Stoughton, 1870), 231–258.

24 Fuccaro, *Histories of City and State in the Persian Gulf*, 169. Unfortunately, records are scant. From their perspective, British officials did not deem the event or any of its surrounding circumstances noteworthy for mention in either the Political Residency annual administrative reports or Lorimer's *Gazetteer* entries for the period: QDL, 'Persian Gulf Administration Reports

open-air tradition that has since then become an important marker in the annual public calendar of many cities and villages of Bahrain.

The period of the 1890s also witnessed increased British interest and encroachment on another area of the ruler's jurisdiction, that of customs. In 1899, the Political Resident visited Bahrain to try to impose a customs official from the Indian civil service on the Shaikh. The ruler instead extended the contract with the Indian family already in charge until 1904, causing the Residency to withdraw its support for the latter, as their operation was 'not to the advance of British interests in Bahrain'.[25]

Mixed into this cocktail were the increasing calls by other regional powers to exercise jurisdiction over those whom they considered their own subjects, emulating the British model of granting protection, which the latter had by now introduced across several of the major trading ports of the Gulf. The Qajar government in Iran renewed calls for the sovereignty of Bahrain as a Persian protectorate in 1886, and began demanding compensation and the ability to exercise protection for those they deemed 'Persians' across the Gulf. The Ottoman government also put forward similar demands.

The switch from a Native Agency system to a Political Agency headed by white British officers finally occurred in 1900. As part of the reorganization, the new Political Agent in Bahrain would now report to the Gulf Residency in Bushehr,

---

1883/84 – 1904/05' [120r] (244/602), IOR/R/15/1/709, https://www. qdl.qa/archive/81055/vdc_100023373226.0x00002d. For a list of agents of British India Steam Navigation, a company which later came to be known as Gray McKenzie, see: Onley, *The Arabian Frontier*, 276.

25 QDL, 'Gazetteer of the Persian Gulf. Vol I. Historical. Part IA & IB. J G Lorimer. 1915' [943] (1098/1782), IOR/L/PS/20/C91/1, https:// www.qdl.qa/en/archive/81055/vdc_100023575946.0x000063.

who in turn answered to the Government of India. This was based on Lord Curzon's Forward Policy formulated at the close of the century, in which the Viceroy of India advocated for increasing ground presence in the Gulf to counter heightened imperial rivalry in the region. As trade boomed in Bahrain and it became the stop of many traders, the British wanted to ensure their supremacy on the islands by fending off any perceived Ottoman, French, Persian, and American encroachments. British moves were further hastened by rising tensions opened up by the system of divided rule of the 1861 treaty, including increasing accusations of favouritism by the Native Agent and his inability to protect British interests. This shift to the Political Agency system, however, would only serve to deepen the tensions and contradictions of divided rule.

IMPOSING DIVIDED AND CONTESTED RULE

Britain sent an officer with the rank of Assistant Political Agent to Bahrain in 1900, the first permanent white British officer on the Arabian side of the Gulf.[26] A new power was in town, and unlike before, where it limited itself to maintaining hegemony over the region's waters and facilitating its trade; this time it was focused on increasing its powers and jurisdiction domestically. This new source of sovereignty would be reflected geographically, between 'Bait al-Dawla' (the House of the State), the name of the Residency of the British Political Agent in Manama, vs. 'Dar al-Hukooma' (the House of the

---

26 Gaskin was acting Assistant Political Agent in 1900, and was followed by Predaux (1904–1909), who would also later serve as Political Agent and Political Resident.

Government), the residence of the ruler Sh. 'Isa in Muharraq. Very soon, it was to become very clear which of these two had the upper hand.

In 1904, Lord Curzon toured the Gulf Arab areas, with Bahrain being a primary stop in his trip, underlying the increasing importance of the islands in British imperial policy. In the same year, the Assistant Political Agent in Bahrain was upgraded to the rank of Political Agent, and the situation did not take long to become contentious. By all accounts, this was a watershed year in the history of Bahrain, and the sparks of the convulsive events were, on the surface, two unremarkable incidents, but upon closer inspection they pushed all the buttons for the British, particularly regarding the issues of divided rule and the ethnosectarian gaze. Both happened in Manama, which as we saw in the previous chapters, had a socio-demographic make-up that could make it more susceptible to such issues.

The two skirmishes involved followers of Sh. 'Ali bin Ahmad, the ruler's nephew who effectively ran the affairs of Manama, on whose jurisdiction 'Bait al-Dawla' was encroaching. In the first incident, some of his followers tried to enforce *al-sukhrah* tax on local employees of a German merchant named Wonkhaus, then the only European merchant in town, who was under British protection.[27] He complained to the British Agent and the German council for reparations. In the second, a fight broke out between 'Persians' working for one of the leading merchants in Bahrain, and the fidawiyya strongmen of Shaikh 'Ali. The Qajar Shah's government in Persia sent protestations

---

27 QDL, 'Gazetteer of the Persian Gulf. Vol I. Historical. Part IA & IB. J G Lorimer. 1915' [937] (1092/1782), IOR/L/PS/20/C91/1, https://www.qdl.qa/en/archive/81055/vdc_100023575946.0x00005d.

to the British, claiming 'Persians' as its own subjects.[28]

Lord Curzon, who now took a keen interest in Bahrain, advocated 'vigorous measures' against the local ruler.[29] The British Political Resident in Bushehr arrived on a battleship in February 1905. The ruler's son Hamad was taken on board as hostage, along with Sh. Qasem bin Mehzaʿ, the judge of Manama, and his brother Ahmad, the notable religious scholar whose school graduated many of the al-Nahda figures. They burned Shaikh ʿAli's ship and flogged his fidawiyya publicly, while his house was ransacked and its contents set ablaze in front of the watching crowd. Shaikh ʿAli himself was arrested and banished to Bombay for five years.[30]

This was a calculated move. Most importantly, it publicly undermined all the political sources of power in the local regime: the ruler, the Shaikh in charge of Manama, the fidawiyya, the religious clerics, and the judges. This was a public show of force and humiliation, and a declaration that there was a new power in town, and this power was above any other.

This event would prove significant in many other respects. Besides publicly declaring a new, supreme sovereign, the British also claimed jurisdiction over the protection, affairs, and judicial matters of all 'foreigners', expanding the domain of their sovereignty beyond the previous realm of 'British subjects' only. In this manner, they argued that adjudicating the case of

28 QDL, File 791/1904 Pt 3 'Orders-in-Council: Bahrain' [86r] (176/199), IOR/L/PS/10/28/3, http://www.qdl.qa/en/archive/81055/vdc_100026682266.0x0000b1. See also: QDL, 'Gazetteer of the Persian Gulf. Vol I. Historical. Part IA & IB. J G Lorimer. 1915' [939] (1094/1782), IOR/L/PS/20/C91/1, https://www.qdl.qa/en/archive/81055/vdc_100023575946.0x00005f.

29 QDL, 'File 9/1 Institution of Reforms & Sunni opposition intrigues' [166r] (348/504), IOR/R/15/2/127, https://www.qdl.qa/archive/81055/vdc_100023321443.0x000095.

30 Al-Tajir, 'Iqd al-Liʾal, 150. See also: al-Khater, al-Qadhi, 65.

the 'Persians' in the fight incident fell under their jurisdiction, to which the ruler protested in vain that they were local Muslim subjects under his jurisdiction.

Thus, there was a new sovereign power in town, and this power saw itself as having jurisdiction over a significant proportion of Bahrain's population. Individuals were either to be classified as 'foreigners' or 'local' subjects, with 'foreigners' falling under the jurisdiction of British rule, while 'locals' would be under the jurisdiction of the ruler. The crux, however, was that 'foreigner' was not a predefined category, and hence would become a site of contestation, with massive consequences in terms of sovereignty and how individuals were treated. The term would become an 'apparatus', upon which contestation would occur and institutions, discourses, mobilizations, and practices would strategically form.[31]

The British held that any 'subject' of a government other than that of the local ruler would count as a 'foreigner'.[32] By this definition, anyone who was to be considered a subject of the governments administering 'Iraq' (then under Ottoman rule), 'Hasa' (Ottoman), 'Qatif' (Ottoman), Persia (Qajar), Najd (Al-Sa'ud), would be considered a 'foreigner' and under British jurisdiction. Given the cultural, geographic, and familial links of the people who resided or worked in Bahrain, the vast majority of the population had some familial connection with at least one, and frequently more, of these regions. To compound the issue, in many of these regions there were yet to emerge modern state bureaucracies, let alone state borders, emigration offices, nationally recognized

---

31 Apparatus is used in the Foucauldian sense of *dispositif*.
32 It is important to note that there was no talk of 'citizens' among British officials during this epoch of colonial rule in Bahrain, with the discussion largely revolving around 'subjects'. For more on citizens and subjects under British colonial rule see: Mamdani, *Citizen and Subject*.

naturalization policies, or passports.[33] The population of the islands would also fluctuate throughout the year, with many pearl divers flowing into the island from these areas during the pearling season. Furthermore, as previously elucidated, nationalism and the factors leading to national identity formation were still in their infancy and yet to be crystallized concretely.

In this context, the British turned to employing ethnosectarian analysis to identify the different subjects. 'Huwala', 'Baharna', and individuals from tribes associated with al-Khalifa were considered by British officials to be subjects of the local ruler, while 'Hasawi', 'Qatifi', 'Persian', 'Najdi', 'Baluchi', and 'Indian' were considered 'foreign' subjects under British jurisdictions. These social categorizations became markers that defined the groups in which each individual would fall, and these groups would then shape who was 'foreign' or 'local' and thus subject to British jurisdiction. The interplay between divided rule and ethnosectarianism was firmly set in motion, with each feeding into the other.

A close textual reading of the British documents becomes useful in this respect, and the extensive archives from this period fortunately provide a wealth of material to deconstruct the British colonial gaze. Such an endeavour should constitute how the archives are primarily to be read: as a well-documented testimony to the colonial ethnosectarian gaze of British officials and not as the authoritative reading and interpretation of events in the islands, as previous studies have tended to do. Once such a critique is employed, the manic obsession with ethnosectarian analysis becomes glaringly evident, as it is revealed as the defining framework for the different institutions and individuals of the British Empire that dealt with Bahrain, regardless of differences in policies and opinions between them.

33 Khuri, *Tribe and State*, 87.

The other recurring feature that stands out is the practice of 'benevolent imperialism', which usually was read and interpreted through an ethnosectarian lens. British officials in Bahrain showed a consistent concern towards alleviating any perceived undue cruelty between the different competing ethno-sect categories that – in their view – made up society under their rule. In this vein, Assistant Political Agent Prideaux wrote to Major Cox, the Political Resident, regarding the 1904–1905 events:

> Shaikh 'Isa, I think, should be told emphatically that no disputes between Shi'as and Sunnis are henceforth to be referred to the Sharia Court, any more than disputes between Hindus and Mahommedans are. The Shi'as, who are mostly Persians, in the absence of the Shah's Consular representatives naturally look to us for protection, and as the British Government are interested in the welfare of all classes in Bahrein, they cannot view with equanimity the injustice even of making Bahrein Shi'as (who are all Persian by origin) submit to the jurisdiction of a religious court other than their own.[34]

The above quote illustrates several important points. Firstly, and most obviously, it highlights the ethnosectarian gaze that the British employed, reading events primarily in terms of Sunnis, Shi'as, Persians, etc. The person's identity is primarily reduced to their sect and ethnicity, which in turn would define their standing as 'foreigner' or 'local', and which subsequently

---

34 QDL, File 1508/1905 Pt 1 'Bahrain: situation; disturbances (1904-1905); Sheikh Ali's surrender; Question of Administration Reforms (Customs etc)' [238r] (481/531), IOR/L/PS/10/81, http://www.qdl.qa /en/archive/81055/vdc_100027013014.0x000052.

would have repercussions on their legal, social, and political standing. The plight of these different ethnosectarian groups is then used to justify benevolent imperialism. The quote also serves to highlight the confusion, vagueness, and porousness between the different ethno-sect categories the British employed, sharply illustrated by the statement, utterly farcical from today's viewpoint, that all Shi'as are Persian. Since the British considered 'Persians' to be 'foreigners', and foreigners fell under the jurisdiction of the British, it served their purpose to define as large a group as possible as Persians and thereby as foreigners. Finally, the quote serves to show how 'nationality' fed into ethnosectarianism, which in turn fed into divided rule and vice versa, creating an interconnected dynamic.

Such statements were frequently made, and the implied views on sectarianism were pervasive within the different institutions and officials of the British Empire concerned with Bahrain. Although these officials would often put forward conflicting viewpoints and policy recommendations for the different sections of the India Government, Whitehall, and Political Agents and Residents on the ground, the ethnosectarian gaze was a uniting feature between them all. Thus, Trevor, then the Political Agent, and who would also serve later as the Political Resident, would comment on the same incident that '[s]ome Persians were attacked by Shaikh Ahmad's men and the affair developed into a Sunni-Shi'a fight. Several Persians were severely wounded, and Persian shops and houses were closed. Persians have complained to Persian authorities.'[35]

35 QDL, File 1508/1905 Pt 1 'Bahrain: situation; disurbances (1904–1905); Sheikh Ali's surrender; Question of Administration Reforms (Customs etc)' [257r] (519/531), IOR/L/PS/10/81, http://www.qdl.qa /en/archive/81055/vdc_100027013014.0x000078.

To sharpen the point, it is worth contrasting the British documents with the writings of local historians from that period. One of the most perceptive was Nasser al-Khairi, the al-Nahda figure who wrote Bahrain's first modern history monograph. The word he used to describe the 1904 events was '*fitnah*': strife. In Islamic tradition, 'fitnah' is a state of significant tumult and deviation from the righteous path, reserved for situations of heightened turmoil, encapsulated by the Quranic verse: 'and fitnah is greater than killing'.[36] Using such terminology to refer to the events of this period reflects their gravity and extreme character in the lives of people experiencing them. With remarkable vision, Khairi writes:

> This ominous crisis . . ., which due to its grave events and enormous lessons, it is apt to say was the beginning of a new political era in Bahrain, and the start of an important overthrow in the shape of the government, its system, and the principle of dividing the people of the land (al-Ahali) into nationals versus foreigners, and external versus internal.[37]

This division between 'foreign' and 'local' was put in practice right after the events of 1904. By 1909, British officials had decided that they needed stronger legal grounds for this practice of divided rule, and consequently wanted to codify this jurisdiction in writing somehow. The solution they concocted was to force the ruler to send a formal letter stating that foreigners were worrying him, and that he would be grateful to the British Government if they would 'relieve him from the

---

36 والفتنة أشدّ من القتل, Surat al-Bakara 1:191.
37 Al-Khairi, Qala'id al-Nahrain, 416.

responsibility of exercising jurisdiction over foreigners in his island'. The Shaikh had no choice but to sign this letter.[38]

The ruler, however, was not about to lie down and accept the erosion of his jurisdiction without a fight. His manoeuvre would be to contest what was meant by the word 'foreigner'. He insisted that his interpretation of the word 'subjects' covered not only 'locals', but also subjects of other Arab governments.[39] The British did not see matters with the same eye, and a contestation developed regarding the word 'foreign' and who counted as local subjects, with each side trying to include as many individuals under their jurisdiction. This was a fight over sovereignty, and rule was not only divided, it was contested.

Thus, by 1923, the British Political Agent would claim that although there were only 550 British subjects (mainly Indian) in Bahrain out of roughly 100,000 residents, the number to whom British jurisdiction applied, including 'foreigners' under British protection, amounted to 40,000, increasing in the diving season to 60,000–70,000 as workers poured in from areas across the Gulf.[40] British jurisdictional claims had now extended to approximately half of the islands' population.

This dispute between the ruler and the British opened up the avenue for other regional forces to enter the fray. Three would come to play a primary role: the Ottomans, the Qajar Dynasty in

---

38 QDL, 'File 18/56 I (B 70) The Trucial Coast Order in Council; File 18 /51 I (B 70) The Ottoman Order in Council, 1910; File 18/131 I (B 70) The Foreign Jurisdiction (Military Forces) Order in Council, 1927' [22r] (54/250), IOR/R/15/1/295, http://www.qdl.qa/en/archive/81055/vdc_100023842168.0x000037.

39 Radhi, *The Bahrain Judiciary*, 72.

40 QDL, File 951/1912 Pt 2 'Bahrein Order in Council' [18r] (40/534), IOR/L/PS/10/249, http://www.qdl.qa/archive/81055/ · vdc_100035092757.0x000029.

Iran, and the rising force of al-Sa'ud. King 'Abdulaziz ibn Sa'ud had become the ruler of Najd by 1906, heralding the beginning of the third Sa'udi state. He would take over the Eastern Provinces of Qatif and Hasa from the Ottomans without a fight in 1913. This was followed by signing the Treaty of Darin with the British in 1915 that recognized him as the ruler of Najd.

He would come to use the contradictions exploded by divided rule in Bahrain to his own end. The ruler of Najd would first side with the British, giving them jurisdiction over 'Najdis'. He would then switch in 1913 and formally in writing hand over jurisdiction to his subjects from Najd and Hasa to the ruler of Bahrain.[41] He would then go back and hand jurisdiction over his subjects to the British in 1920.[42]

Ibn Sa'ud even reached the point of directly contesting the British monopoly on extraterritorial sovereignty in Bahrain, appointing an agent, al-Qusaibi, who would try to issue passports and act as a consul, causing the British great ire and anxiety.[43] The ruler, in his turn, also tried to play off regional and imperial rivalries, opening negotiations with the Ottomans to be under their protection during the First World War.[44]

Given their superior coercive force, the British were generally able to push forward their claims, although not without resistance. The administration report of the Political Agency for the year 1918 shows that there were some matters of concern

---

41 Radhi, *The Bahrain Judiciary*, 73.
42 QDL, 'Historical Summary of Events in the Persian Gulf Shaikhdoms and the Sultanate of Muscat and Oman, 1928–1953' [25r] (54/222), IOR/R/15/1/731(1), http://www.qdl.qa/archive/81055/vdc_100023415995.0x000037.
43 QDL, 'File 61/9 (D 109) Nejd passports' [27v] (62/224), IOR/R/15/1/562, http://www.qdl.qa/en/archive/81055/vdc_100024100267.0x00003f.
44 Khuri, *Tribe and State*, 88.

regarding Shaikh 'Isa's attempt to assert his jurisdiction over 'Hasawis' and 'Najdis':

> In one case, the Amir of Muharraq Island arrested and imprisoned Hasawis by order of Shaikh 'Isa who on representation argued that the Hasawis were under his jurisdiction, but he was told that this could not be recognised . . . In the other case, the Amir of Manamah took a deposit of 4 pounds from a foreign subject who was suspected of having pearls in his possession belonging to his nokhedha. On hearing the matter, the Political Agent went for the Amir and recovered the money . . . The Amir apologized.[45]

These two examples serve to show how both ethnicity and nationality came to be contested. Concerning the first case, Shi'a people in Bahrain today with links to Hasa are generally considered to part of 'Baharna' rather than a distinct group. Indeed, there have always been strong familial and marriage links between the two regions, showing the porousness within such categories. In regards to the second case, the pearl diver most probably came from Qatar or the eastern shores of the Gulf, which also have strong familial and cultural links to Bahrain, reconfirming the malleability of such categories.

These contestations over the status of 'foreign' versus 'local' subjects are confirmed by a third incident in the same year involving 'Baluchi' individuals.[46] The Political Agency reports

45 QDL, '180 Administration Report 1918 & later' [4] (7/116), IOR/R/ 15/2/951, http://www.qdl.qa/en/archive/81055/vdc_100025642677. 0x000008.
46 The term refers to individuals with historical and familial links to Baluchistan, an area located in modern-day Iran and Pakistan.

that the case related to an assault by three Baluchi servants of the ruler's son on the *Amir* in charge of Manama:

> The dispute was between the youngest brother of the Amir and the three Baluchis over some prostitutes . . . On being asked to release the Baluchis, Shaikh Isa [the ruler] stated at first that he would rather leave Bahrain himself than release the two of the three Baluchis who were chained up or to hand them over to the Political Agency, as they were born in Bahrain and were in his service and claimed that they were his subjects, but eventually his excellency gave in and the matter was amicably settled.[47]

The above examples also serve to highlight the role of another set of agents involved in events, and who would utilize, resist, and redefine the contradictions opened up by divided rule: these were ordinary non-elite individuals living in Bahrain and making a living on the islands in one way or another. At the local level, people on the ground experienced and responded to these treaties and colonial laws in different manners, testing and taking advantage of the ambiguities resulting from divided and contested sovereignty.

In hindsight, this seems expected. The ethnosectarian group one was to be classified under meant access to different legal systems and recourses of protection. Whether you were considered Persian, Hasawi, Baharna, Huwala, etc., meant being under the jurisdiction of different powers, and having access to different laws and protection forums. Thus, 'forum

47 QDL, '180 Administration Report 1918 & later' [5] (9/116), IOR/R/15/2/951, https://www.qdl.qa/en/archive/81055/vdc_100025642677. 0x00000a. Explanations in parentheses are added by me.

shopping', to borrow a legal term, was becoming a real phenomenon.[48]

There were real material advantages to be gained by some from being considered a subject under British sovereignty. For one, forced labour, which as we saw was a common phenomenon on the island, was abolished in 1904 for 'foreigners', and the British began manumitting slaves a year later. Furthermore, British jurisdiction could provide a protective force with strong coercive powers that would be able to fend off any other parties. In fact, it was the ultimate source of coercive power and protection globally, let alone locally. Forum shopping also opened up the possibility of recourse to British law and courts. In this manner, what would be considered crimes under local law might not be so under British law, and vice versa.

Different individuals would use the ambiguities opened up by divided and contested rule to their own advantage, whether material or political. The examples are numerous and well documented. In 1907, a group of 'Persians', encouraged by enforcement of British protection under divided rule, would display the imperial flag of Iran at the opening of the Manama 'Ashura' ceremonies.[49] By this act, they both challenged the ruler's sovereignty and issued a political statement on events in Iran at the time, showing their allegiance to the Qajar government, which was facing a stiff challenge from the constitutional movement there. Persian nationalism began stirring up the cocktail of divided rule in Bahrain.

There were also cases of 'Shi'a Arabs' invoking being Persian subjects in order to benefit from British protection.

---

48 Julia Clancy-Smith, *Mediterraneans: North Africa and Europe in an Age of Migration* (Berkeley: University of California Press, 2011), 216.
49 Fuccaro, *Histories of City and State in the Persian Gulf*, 169.

Furthermore, there were Persian attempts to establish an official diplomatic presence. Under the pretence that he was a
subject of Iran, the Persian merchant 'Abdul-Nabi Kal-Ewarz
issued formal documents to anyone travelling to Iran, causing
ire to both the British and the ruler.[50] Similarly, the British
Agency dealt with cases that supposedly should have fallen
under the ruler's authority. The Agency manumitted several
slaves, protected Arab women who were accused of 'dishonour-
able' behaviour (such as the famous of case of Nora[51]), and gave
refuge to merchants and individuals accused of different viola-
tions and crimes, ranging from absconding to evade debt, to
theft, to fraud.[52] The ruler, in return, decided to strike back at
that which the British most coveted: he deferred on reforming
ports and customs. Instead of installing a British officer as head
of customs as the Political Agency had requested, he kept
extending the contract given to the Indian family for farming
the port's customs.

Al-Nahda figures also tried to enter the fray, contesting
British rule and attempting to shape events towards their own
goals. Most notable was the attempt to establish a representative council in 1911, the first initiative of its kind in Bahrain and
the wider Gulf. According to al-Nabhani, the first modern
historian of the al-Khalifa family, the British tried to impose a
local firearm and slavery embargo in 1911, which led many

---

50 Khuri, *Tribe and State*, 87–88.
51 According to British officials, Nora was a Bahraini divorcee who sought
refuge at the Political Agency after she was thrown out of the house of her
lover of two years. Her father and several local notables and judges were
enraged when the Political Agent refused to hand her over to the parent,
after which she escaped and disappeared. For more see: Radhi, *The Bahrain
Judiciary*, 66–67.
52 Khuri, *Tribe and State*, 87–88.

local notables to protest.[53] They proceeded to the ruler's Majlis to demand that he put an end to British encroachments, to which he replied that he was powerless unless they formed one cohesive unit that could stand up to the British.

In response, the notables asked for the formation of a *Shura* (consultation) Council made up of their leaders and those 'of wise judgement', which would have the right to elect the legal jurists and the governors of the different regions under the ruler's control. The previously encountered 'Abdulwahhab al-Zayyani, one of the main figures of al-Nahda in Bahrain, spearheaded the drive for this Majlis. The ruler obliged and issued documents to that effect.[54] Shortly after its establishment, however, he disbanded the council. Disputably, al-Nabhani attributes this to British machinations. Seeing it as an unwelcome development, they colluded with the local judge of Muharraq, Shaikh Sharaf al-Yamani, to warn the ruler that the council was intent on removing him. The ruler became paranoid, dissolved the council, and imposed a state of near martial law, ordering the imprisonment of anyone who criticized its disbandment. The suspicious behaviour of the jurist was quickly discovered, however, and he was removed from his post, upon which he quickly hurried to the British Political Agency asking for protection.

Hence, divided rule became a terrain where different agents and forces acted, reacted, and redefined the fractured jurisdictional framework imposed by the British. The local ruler contested the parameters of divided rule: who was to be counted as a 'foreigner', and where his jurisdiction began and stopped.

53 Muhammad al-Nabhani, *al-Tuhfa al-Nabhaniyya* (Bahrain: unknown, 1923), 250–252.
54 Unfortunately very little information is available on this episode. For more see: Rashid al-Jassim, *al-Bahrain wa 'umkuha al-'araby wal Islami* (Bahrain: al-Dar al-'Arabiyya lel Mawsoo'at, 2015).

Al-Nahda figures and other notables attempted to use the situation to push for the establishment of a consultative assembly. Locals practised forum shopping, not only in terms of which law, but also which sovereign power to apply to for protection and use of their coercive powers. The British tried to keep the overall system manageable and stable, while also attempting to limit the encroachments of other regional powers, which for their part tried to use the tensions and contradictions to their advantage.

This was a convulsive mix. Much of this, as we saw, happened according to ethnosectarian identifications, which suddenly had strong social, legal, and political consequences for the individuals according to how they were identified. Divided spheres of sovereignty suddenly became a site of contestation, and the labels of either 'foreigner' or 'local', and under them 'Shi'a', 'Sunni', 'Baharna', 'Persian', etc., became apparatuses with a strategic function, as the formation of institutions, discourses, and practices emerged around these new systems of knowledge and categorization, in response to an urgency created by the new situation on the ground.[55]

The British would formally attempt to codify the system of 'divided rule' they were informally practising through the BOIC, published in London in 1913. The legislation formally established the parameters of British jurisdiction in Bahrain and their relation to the ruler. The clause relating to the Political Agent's jurisdiction over 'foreigners' was to read as follows: 'Foreigners with respect to whom the Shaikh of Bahrain has agreed with His Majesty for, or consented to the exercise of jurisdiction by His Majesty'.[56]

55 Michel Foucault, *Power/Knowledge: Selected Interviews and Other Writings, 1972–1977* (New York: Pantheon, 1980), 194–196.
56 QDL, 'File 18/77 (B Series 18/11) Annual Report on the Working of the Bahrain Order in Council', IOR/R/15/1/305, http://www.qdl.qa/en/archive/81055/vdc_100000000193.0x000116.

As the First World War erupted, British interests naturally shifted elsewhere, and the BOIC was not formally put into practice until after the end of the war in February 1919. The war years were particularly devastating for Bahrain. It was hit by outbreaks of plague in both 1915 and 1917, coupled with a general commodities shortages, as the Government of India imposed an embargo on exporting basic goods, including rice. Over five thousand people, or more than five percent of the population, died.[57] Although the repercussions of divided rule outlined above continued, British activity on the island naturally decreased, as its hands were full elsewhere. Their attention in Bahrain focused on steadying the situation during the war and keeping out imperial intrigue. As soon as the war was over, and with the Ottomans and Germans defeated, British interest in the 'Middle East' generally and Bahrain specifically was renewed, in what has been labelled as the post 'Sykes–Picot' Mandate Era. The heightened activity in Bahrain was propelled by the arrival of two new Political Agents: Major Dickson would take the helm in 1919–1921, after which Major Daly would take over until 1926. Their tenure would prove to be system shifting for Bahrain.

THE SYSTEMIZATION OF ETHNOSECTARIANISM

Harold Dickson was born in Beirut in 1881 to a British diplomatic family in the Levant. He had a blood affinity with the Anizah tribe (the same tribe al-Khalifa traced their ancestry to), as when his mother's milk failed he was attended to by a wet nurse from the tribe. Like many of the other British 'Gulfites', he

---

57 Almahmood, *The Rise and Fall of Bahrain's Merchants*, 38.

studied at St. Edward's School in Oxford and then at Wadham College, Oxford. In 1903, he then joined the First Connaught Rangers and served in Ireland for a year, after which he was transferred to India, where he joined the Indian Army, serving in Kashmir and Bikanir. Iraq was his next step during the First World War. After the war, he continued to serve in Iraq as a political officer in the Muntafiq district during the British mandate period, where he was under the leadership of Sir Percy Cox, who previously served as the Political Resident in the Gulf at Bushehr. In 1919, he was sent to be the Political Agent in Bahrain.[58]

On 5 January 1920, less than two months after his arrival, Dickson wrote a note on the political situation in Bahrain that would prove remarkably insightful to both understanding his tenure and his use of the ethnosectarian gaze.[59] He began by noting the 'curious' and 'wholly unsatisfactory' antagonistic atmosphere that existed everywhere in Bahrain towards the British Agency, with British prestige mainly relying on fear instead of respect. This was a similar conclusion to that reached by his predecessor, Colonel Bray, who wrote that there is 'considerable feeling of hostility' to the British.[60] Their conclusion was not wide of the mark, as it seemed many in Bahrain

58 'In Memoriam: Lieut. Col. H. R. P. Dickson, C.I.E, F.R.G.S.', *Journal of the Royal Central Asian Society* 46 (1959), 3–4: 195–199, http://www.tandfonline.com/doi/abs/10.1080/03068375908731667?journalCode=raaf19; 'Harold Dickson Collection', Middle East Centre of St. Antony's College, Oxford, https://www.sant.ox.ac.uk/mec/MEChandlists/GB165 -0085-HRP-Dickson-Collection.pdf.

59 QDL, 'File XXII 4 Koweit relations with Bahrain' [48r] (95/106), IOR/ R/15/5/60, https://www.qdl.qa/en/archive/81055/vdc_100033163054. 0x000060.

60 QDL, 'File XXII 4 Koweit relations with Bahrain' [46r] (91/106), IOR/ R/15/5/60, https://www.qdl.qa/en/archive/81055/vdc_100033163054. 0x00005c.

supported the Ottomans during the First World War, such inclinations being held by the ruler and his close friend the judge Sh.
Qasem bin Mehza'.[61]

After spending time gathering information from locals, he
concluded that there were two types of opposition, 'honest' and
'dishonest'. Honest opposition was malleable to be manipulated
by British power, and was mainly the result of the faulty nature of
the 'Arab character' and 'mind': unwarranted fear, pride, suspicion, and ignorance. This was no different than the case with
many other 'more or less primitive people, its degree depending
on the extent of their backwardness'. He estimated that eighty
percent of the opposition was of this type of honest opposition.
He then turned to the dishonest opposition, in which he included
relatives of the ruler, government officials, and notables of the
island. Regarding the first members of this group, he would state:

> Like all Government officials of an oriental State, we may
> expect to find abuse of authority and extortion, but
> unlike most oriental States in such close relationship to a
> European Power, we may be justly grieved to find that
> these exceed all bonds of propriety and sense of justice,
> so much so as to call forth the odium of the Arabs them-
> selves. The Amirs or Governors of the towns of Muharraq
> and Manama are officials entirely unsuited for control,
> and the power they wield is oppressive and immoral.[62]

61 The latter was such an ardent supporter of the Ottoman Khalifa that in
the midst of the First World War he threatened that anyone who was
proven not to support him would be executed, as he considered it to be
support for the British. See: al-Khater, *al-Qadhi*, 171.
62 QDL, 'File XXII 4 Koweit relations with Bahrain' [49r] (97/106),
British Library: India Office Records and Private Papers, IOR/R/15/5/
60, https://www.qdl.qa/archive/81055/vdc_100033163054.0x000062.

He then turned to describing the notables of the island, of whom he proposed a quarter were more or less friendly, while the remainder were 'definitely hostile'. This latter feeling was attributed to the war and Ottoman propaganda, 'ultra-religious feelings' amongst the Arabs, 'the natural leaning of the Persians towards intrigue', and finally the 'hopeless ignorance that exists in Bahrain'. He then followed this by attaching a 'white list' and 'black list' of individuals that he considered friendly versus hostile to British presence. In a remarkable indictment of the ethnosectarian gaze, each of the white and the black list was organized mainly across three headings: Arabs, Persians, and Indians. The British seemed to have very few friends across any ethnosectarian groupings, save for a few traders who were directly connected to British affairs.

Dickson concluded that 'an energetic and open handed policy is immediately imperative' to meet and defeat these various difficulties. These included both carrots and sticks, as well as intelligence gathering means of rule and control. Winning over hearts and minds of the public was essential through the political officer being 'the school master of public opinion and thought', and careful study and observation of the residents. Finally, an intelligence network was needed, and for this 'secret service work', he requested an annual stipend. This was similar to the conclusions of his predecessor Bray, who recommended 'the definite formation of a British party by indirect methods' in order to bolster British support on the island.[63]

The years 1919–1921 proved to be busy ones for Dickson. The BOIC was formally put into practice, as it established six

---

63 QDL, 'Historical Summary of Events in Territories of the Ottoman Empire, Persia and Arabia affecting the British Position in the Persian Gulf, 1907–1928' [33r] (72/188), IOR/R/15/1/730, http://www.qdl.qa/en/archive/81055/vdc_100022744604.0x000049.

official courts, marking the beginning of the 'rationalizing' of the legal bureaucracy in Bahrain. Following the British tradition of relying on 'local customs', the distinction between 'foreign'/'local' and ethnosectarian groupings played a major role in the shaping of these courts. First, there was the chief court, headed by the Political Resident, which had absolute jurisdiction over all foreigners in Bahrain. It was reserved for serious criminal offences and acted as a supreme court for all cases being heard in Bahrain, thus placing British sovereignty at the top of the legal structure. The district court acted as a court of first instance and for civil cases for 'foreigners', presided over by the Political Agent. The joint court was for cases involving 'foreigners' and 'locals'.

Majlis al-'Urf, also known as Majlis al-Tejara, was also acknowledged as a local institution that could hear cases of a commercial nature if called upon. However, it was inscribed that the Political Resident had the right to appoint four 'foreigners' out of its eight members in consultation with the ruler, and the ruler had similar rights for the other four to be appointed from 'locals'. There was also acknowledgement of the *Salifah* court as the reference for matters involving pearling, while the religious 'Qadhi's Court' was reserved for Muslims, and to which 'foreigner' cases could be referred if so needed. The inclusion of these 'local' institutions, albeit codified and rationalized, reflected the fact that the British had a relatively small number of staff on the island. Consequently, they had to rely on 'local institutions' to administer some of the cases.

The courts were kept extremely busy, with the number of suits increasing rapidly from 290 in 1919, to 343 in 1920, 777 in 1921, 786 in 1922, and 818 in 1923.[64] As the British admitted,

64 QDL, 'File 18/77 (B Series 18/11) Annual Report on the Working of the Bahrain Order in Council' [12r] (25/231), IOR/R/15/1/305, http://www.qdl.qa/en/archive/81055/vdc_100023067946.0x00001a.

many of these cases were pursued simply to take advantage of the new institutionalized laws and jurisdictions, since 'the fact that the advantages of taking proceedings in court which are permanently recorded, and of obtaining decrees which can be legally enforced, is becoming increasingly understood by inhabitants.'[65] Quite a significant proportion of cases were being dropped before conclusions, as the different parties would reach a settlement. Furthermore, 'the disproportionately large number of suits dropped is due to extremely floating population of the islands', as many of the suits were instigated by or against floating pearl-diving workers, who would only be around for part of the year and then abscond.[66] Hence, forum shopping reached its zenith during this period.

Similarly, appeals for British protection and use of their sovereignty by 'locals' continued, particularly by what the British identified as 'Shi'as', thus continuing the contestation of divided rule. The case of Ahmad bin 'Ali bin Khamis is emblematic in this respect. Born in 1855 in Sanabis, a village on the outskirts of Manama, he was a notable pearl merchant who owned several diving ships. He also cemented his social standing by establishing a Ma'tam in his name in the last quarter of the twentieth century.[67] In 1920, he was unhappy with the valuation the ruler's son placed on a pearl bin Khamis bought,

---

65 QDL, File 951/1912 Pt 2 'Bahrein Order in Council' [59r] (122/534), IOR /L/PS/10/249, https://www.qdl.qa/en/archive/81055/vdc_100035092757. 0x00007b.

66 QDL, 'File-No. 52 of 1922 Bahrain Order in Council' [27r] (53/62), IOR /R/15/2/948, https://www.qdl.qa/en/archive/81055/vdc_100025446172. 0x000036.

67 Hasan al-Madhoob, 'Al-Salman: Bin Khamis min Awa'el al-Mutalibeen', *Al-Wasat* newspaper, 26 March 2016, http://www.alwasatnews.com/news /1094797.html.

as this significantly affected the ten percent tax rate that the latter was required to pay. He wrote an urgent letter to the Political Agent asking for his help:

> I am a well-to-do pearl merchant of Bahrain, a Shiʿa and a subject of Shaikh ʿIsa.
>
> I, with other Shiʿas, have always been the object of secret persecution on the part of the Shaikh's family . . . My trouble is as follows . . . I bought a remarkable pearl for Rupees 42,000 . . . the transaction was entirely a gamble . . . if it has a flaw then probably it won't fetch more than Rupees 6,000 . . . Shortly afterwards I received a peremptory order from Shaikh ʿAbdulla bin ʿIsa to pay him R 4,200/- . . . I have been six days in hiding, and my friends told me fidawis are searching high and low for me.[68]

Another institution promulgated by the British in 1919, which displayed a strong ethnosectarian dimension in its formation, was the municipality council of Manama. In essence, it was an alliance between the British Agency and merchants of Manama to take away power from the ruler and the Shaikh of Manama, while also acting as a vehicle for enacting reforms that the British thought were necessary to the city. It funded its activities through taxes levied on dwellers of the city, thereby challenging the ruling family's monopoly on tax collection. Just like the ʿUrf council, its eight members were equally divided between 'foreigners' and 'locals', to be chosen by the British Political Agent and the ruler.[69]

68 Quoted in: Almahmood, *The Rise and Fall of Bahrain's Merchants*, 33–34.
69 Nominal elections that were confined to property holders were introduced afterwards in 1926.

Its make-up was formally divided along ethnosectarian lines, with the 'foreign' seats divided into specific allocations for Hindus, Shi'a Persians, and Sunni Persians, while the 'local' seats were each allocated to Sunnis and Shi'as. Consociational politics was now formally enshrined in Bahrain.

Furthermore, the British established a semi-regular police force to counteract the fidawiyya of the Shaikh of Manama. The force was headed by and staffed exclusively by 'Persians'. In this manner, 1919 was a year in which the British moved in earnest to consolidate and regulate by law its sovereign powers in Bahrain, pushing towards increased presence in the legislative (BOIC), judicial (the various courts), mercantile (Majlis al-'Urf), urban (municipality council), and coercive (police force) powers. All of these were done with heavy influences of the ethnosectarian gaze, which although already put in practice since 1904, now had a codified legal footing with real structures on the ground. Formally enshrined consociational politics became the name of the game in Manama, and this had reverberations elsewhere on the island.

The ruler was getting increasingly frustrated by British encroachment on his jurisdiction. He assigned his son Sh. 'Abdulla bin 'Isa to personally relay a letter to the Foreign Office in Britain, expressing his dissatisfaction with the situation of divided rule imposed in Bahrain. His demands were, first, equating the ruler with his neighbouring Arab rulers in having jurisdiction over all subjects except the British and subjects of other major European powers and, second, that Shaikh 'Isa alone was entitled to choose persons in Majlis al-'Urf, the trade adjudication council.[70] Sh. 'Abdulla duly travelled with the previously encountered al-Nahda figure of Qasem al-Shirawi,

70 Al-Khalifa, *Ma'a shaikh al-udaba'*, 107.

becoming the first Bahrainis to fly to the UK on an aeroplane. Unsurprisingly, these demands were rejected by the British government, claiming that British rights in this respect were clearly specified in the newly issued BOIC of 1919.[71]

By 1920, anti-Dickson actors had gathered enough support against his policies to organize a petition to the British Residency in Bushehr for his removal. This mobilization was spearheaded by the al-Nahda figure of ʿAbdulla al-Zayed, the main author of the petition, who took a very vocal stance in agitating against the British.[72] Whether because of this or for other reasons, Dickson was relieved of his duties in November 1920, to be replaced by Major Clive Daly as Political Agent in January 1921. If the opposing notables thought that Daly would follow policies that were less confrontational than Dickson's, they were soon to be in for a severe shock.

71 QDL, 'Historical Summary of Events in the Persian Gulf Shaikhdoms and the Sultanate of Muscat and Oman, 1928–1953' [29r] (62/222), IOR/R/15/1/731(1), http://www.qdl.qa/archive/81055/vdc_100023415995.0x00003f.
72 Al-Khater, al-Qadhi, 70, 87–88.

5

'FITNAH':
ETHNOSECTARIANISM
MEETS AL-NAHDA, 1921–1923

F resh from his role in the 1920 uprising in Iraq, Daly's first two years in office were also a time of turmoil in Bahrain. This was not primarily caused by economic considerations, as pearl exports, trade, and customs revenue had returned to booming after the difficulties and plagues faced during the First World War. The system was convulsing, and the previous mode of localized, personalized rule was disturbed beyond functioning. Public order was falling apart, in what the British describe as an 'abnormal wave of crime'.[1]

The events of 1921–1923 have become some the most contentious and disputed on the island, and this has reflected on the documented history of this period, with writers openly

---

1 Quoted in Almahmood, *The Rise and Fall of Bahrain's Merchants*, 52.

partisan in their analysis, often along ethnosectarian lines.[2] Indeed, the events have become part of the diverging historical narratives that different political camps in Bahrain have utilized and deployed, particularly since the 1990s. Two main causes have been put forward for the events, each emphasized by a different camp: the first holds that Daly actively engaged in agitation of the different sides, specifically using 'divide and rule' tactics along ethnosectarian lines. He would antagonize and repress opposition to his rule, while simultaneously encouraging those he labelled as the 'Shiʿa', particularly the Baharna in the villages, to protest. The other holds that heightened repression in the agricultural villages by the ruling family and some tribes, led to protests and calls for British intervention to alleviate and reform the situation. The disputes are compounded by the fact that accounts of the events were often written and recited by people who were active players in these events, raising questions of partisanship and manipulation to suit their views.[3]

Perhaps unsurprisingly, writings in English have overwhelmingly relied on and adopted the British Agents' reading of events, particularly those of Daly. This could be attributed to the extensive availability of British documents from the period, as well as the tendency of British officials to impart the image of impartial, benevolent judges standing above conflicting sides. There is considerable evidence, however, to show that Daly was a main protagonist in the events, and that at

2 The events have been the subject of several studies, which include but are not limited to: May al-Khalifa, *Sebazabad wa rejal al-dawla al-bahiyya* (Beirut: al-Muʾasasa al-ʿArabiyya lel Derasat wal Nashr, 2010); Mahdi Abdalla al-Tajir, *Bahrain 1920–1945: Britain, the Shaikh and the Administration* (London: Croom Helm, 1987).

3 This will become very evident in the developing narration.

least as much as any others, he was open to manipulating his version of events to suit his own purposes (including reports to his own bosses). Due to their neglect in most previous English accounts, Arabic sources will be relied on extensively within this particular narration.

The argument presented here will be that there is strong evidence to suggest that both of the two narrated versions above occurred simultaneously. More importantly, the main conclusion will be that these convulsive events came as the climax of the breakdown of the system of divided and contested rule, under the guise of the ethnosectarian gaze. As events will show, the British were unable to control 'foreigners', and neither was the ruler able to establish his authority over 'locals'. The conjuncture was marked by actors steadily resorting to overt contentious politics as a way of articulating their issues and grievances, with clashes and mobilization increasingly taking on an ethnosectarian dimension. The contradictions and instability that arose from the system of divided and contested rule, coupled with rising political mobilization along ethnosectarian cleavages, reached a boiling point and could no longer be sustained.

Furthermore, the events were also particularly consequential in that they crystallized the emergence of a distinct anticolonial, proto-nationalist, pro-reformist, trans-sectarian discourse, one that was spearheaded by members of the al-Nahda group. This discourse was to grow in strength and coherence over the following years, becoming the main framework that shaped the actions of both oppositional political movements and the newly emergent absolutist state for the rest of the twentieth century.

DALY, AL-NAHDA, AND ETHNOSECTARIAN MOBILIZATION

Born in 1888, Daly was a captain in the Indian Army before he moved to the Arab world. Like his predecessor Dickson, he was stationed in Iraq during the Mandate period, where he became chief political officer for the Diwaniyya District after the war ended. He developed a notorious reputation in Iraq, with opposition to his actions playing a significant role in lighting the sparks of the 1920 uprising. He oversaw tribesmen forced into British labour camps to dig rivers, insisting that tribal heads also be present. This led Gertrude Bell to comment, 'I think they were quite right to hate him – he was intolerably autocratic.'[4] He was also accused of several atrocities during attempts to quell the uprising, including burning down whole villages.[5]

He was subsequently promoted to major and sent to Bahrain directly from Iraq in 1921.[6] Learning from the problems faced by his predecessor, Daly spent his first few weeks cultivating regular contacts with the public and 'notables' of the islands. Within a few months, the 'politics of the notables' would forcefully enter the tensions arising from divided rule, under the strong aegis of the ethnosectarian gaze.[7]

4 Aula Hariri, 'The Iraqi Independence Movement: A Case of Transgressive Contention (1918–1920)', in Fawaz Gerges (ed.), *Contentious Politics in the Middle East* (New York: Palgrave Macmillan, 2015), 103–104.
5 Abbas Kadhim, *Reclaiming Iraq: The 1920 Revolution and the Founding of the Modern State* (Austin: University of Texas Press, 2012), 71–77.
6 'Maj. Clive Kirkpatrick Daly (Biographical details)', British Museum, http://www.britishmuseum.org/research/search_the_collection_database/term_details.aspx?bioId=93576.
7 'Politics of the notables' refers to a social arrangement in which urban elites play an intermediary role between centres of political power and segments of the populace. For more on the 'politics of the notables' see:

Two examples can be used to illustrate this. The first is of Khan Mohammad Sharif 'Awadhi, a Manama merchant who we encountered earlier as the British-appointed chief of the police, and who was a member and secretary of the Manama Municipal Council. His name actually appeared even earlier, when he was mentioned as the acting British Native Agent in the case involving Sayyed Khalaf and Sharida in 1897.[8] He was also an assistant and cousin to a previous Native Agent. Hence, he had a long history of involvement in the British Agency system. Given these connections and his trading activities, he came to be regarded by the British as a notable who was the head of the Persian community in Bahrain.

The 'ethnicity' of Mohammad Sharif 'Awadhi is interesting from our perspective: a Sunni, he moved to Bahrain from the region of Awadh in modern-day Iran. In present-day Bahrain, he would be classified as 'Huwala', which has come to be used as a term to include all Sunni individuals with any form of connection to the eastern coasts of the Gulf. However, back in this period Mohammad Sharif was certainly not classified as Huwala by himself, by other Huwalas, or by the British. Instead, he classified himself as Persian and under British protection, something that the Huwalas of Muharraq (where the vast majority resided) or Manama would definitely not have classified themselves as. As was the case when discussing other groups such as 'Baharna', 'Hasawis', and 'Qatifis', this serves to show how the boundaries of social categories can shift and be 'fuzzy' over time.

There were in reality significant social markers and distinctions that varied across families and regions even within each of

---

Albert Hourani, *The Emergence of the Modern Middle East* (Berkeley: University of California Press, 1981).
8 See chapter 4, 138.

these social groupings. Within the wider grouping of Huwala, for example, families could be socially identified according to region, such as Kooheji, Bucheeri, and al-Shirawi, and there could be different strands within each family. Similarly, within 'Ajams, there existed different strands within families that were demarcated by areas, such as Bushehri, Kazerooni, and Behbehani. Even the labelling of a family as part of a particular group could change depending on the time, place, and actors that made up its field of social interaction.[9] Thus, some families that could be labelled as part of 'Ajams, Baharna, and Huwala groups in Bahrain might take on a different labelling if living in other parts of the Gulf such as in Kuwait, Oman, and southern Iran, and conversely in the opposite direction. These complexities were all lost under the all-encompassing ethno-sect categories on which the British based their political institutions and readings.

The second example of the politics of the notables pertinent to our discussion is 'Abd-'Ali bin Mansour bin Rajab, a notable merchant from Manama from a well-known Baharna family. His 'notable' status was cultivated through both trade activities and connections to the corridors of power. As well as being affluent merchants, some of his family members had strong connections to British interests in Bahrain. His uncle Ebrahim bin Mohsen bin Rajab was the British Native Agent between

---

9 The examples are numerous. See, for example, the discussion on al-Madhkurs in chapter 3. Another case is the different social conceptualizations found across Bahrain, Kuwait, and modern-day UAE regarding which families belong to the Huwala as a social group, which vary considerably and are worthy of a detailed study (which unfortunately is currently lacking). For an example from Oman, some families are considered part of the Baharna ethnicity, even though many of their social roots are in Iraq. I am indebted to discussions with Rai'd al-Jamali on this last point.

1862 and 1864, the first and only 'local' of Bahrain to hold the post, as he became a naturalized British subject in Bombay and then moved back to Bahrain.[10] Furthermore, his cousin 'Abdulla bin Mohammad bin Mohsen bin Rajab was granted British protection as the agent for the British India Steam Navigation Company between 1873 and 1889 (whom we encountered previously as the individual arrested by the Shaikh on accusations of assault).[11] This cousin was also appointed by the British Indian Postal Service as sub-postmaster for Eastern Arabia. The family was also the custodian of the bin Rajab Ma'tam, one of the oldest and most famous of Bahrain.

Bin Rajab's entry into the field of contestation between the ruler and the British was through Majlis al-'Urf. The ruler appointed him in April 1919 to replace a previous local member of the Majlis, Ahmad Yateem (Sunni), supposedly within his allocation of four 'local' representatives on the Majlis.[12] Given that Yateem was seen as pro-British, the Political Agent (Colonel Bray) objected to the replacement on the grounds that he was not consulted. The ruler replied that it was his right to appoint 'local' members, causing a point of conflict between the two. By 1922, bin Rajab, who by then was identified by Daly in his letters and petitions as the 'head of the Shi'a community', had become one of the strongest supporters of British reforms in the islands.

One of these petitions that both bin Rajab and Mohammad Sharif signed provides great insight into the construction of the British ethnosectarian gaze. The petition was instigated and

10 Mohammad al-Salman, 'Al-Wakeel al-Haj Ebrahim bin Mohsin bin Rajab', *Al-Wasat* newspaper, 26 March 2013, http://www.alwasatnews.com/news/755276.html.

11 See chapter 5.

12 May al-Khalifa, *Sebazabad wa rejal al-dawla*, 451–453.

organized by Daly in June 1921, three months after his arrival, to bolster his local support. The impulse stemmed from Daly's attempts to pressure the ruler to officially appoint his son Sh. Hamad as the heir, an endeavour in which he eventually succeeded by the time of the petition.[13] Up until then, Sh. 'Abdulla was the more politically dominant of the ruler's sons in running local affairs, while Sh. Hamad was seen as being in the shadow of his more charismatic and imposing brother. However, Sh. 'Abdulla was viewed by Daly and Dickson before him as anti-British, with Hamad more open to imperial guidance. Consequently, the petition was accompanied with letters of support to shore up both Daly's and Sh. Hamad's positions. The petition explicitly singled out the latter as the head of government and worthy of praise, while his father, the ruler, did not even receive a mention.

Daly carefully picked thirty-eight 'notables' to sign the petition praising him, the ruler's son Hamad, and the Gulf Political Resident, with several individuals reportedly pressured into signing their names.[14] The structure and organization of Daly's petition provides a stunning illustration and indictment of the ethnosectarian gaze through which the British viewed and governed the island.[15] The thirty-eight signatories were carefully chosen and categorized to reflect what Daly viewed as their ethnosectarian identities and the corresponding overall sectarian demographic make-up of the island. First came a section explicitly named 'The Arab community'. It began with

13 Mahdi Abdalla al-Tajir, *Bahrain 1920–1945*, 31–33.
14 Hafedh Wahba, *Khamsoona 'Aman fi Jazeerat al-'Arab* (Cairo: Dar al-Aafaq al-'Arabiyya, 2001), 15.
15 QDL, 'File 8/2 Public petitions etc. Letters to Major Daly (P.A.) thanking him for his interest in Bahrain affairs' [6r] (11/72), IOR/R/15/2/121, http://www.qdl.qa/en/archive/81055/vdc_100023025311.0x00000c.

the two judges, Qasem bin Mehza' (Sunni) and Khalaf al-Asfoor (Shi'a). This was followed by the heads of the local tribes: al-Dawaser, al-Binalis, and al-Manna'is. Then came names of several 'Sunni' notable traders. Next was the name of 'Abd 'Ali bin Rajab, who was identified as the 'head of the Shi'a Bahrani community', followed by Haj Ahmad bin Khamis, who we encountered previously as the pearl trader from Sanabis, identified in the letter as 'a Shi'a notable'.

The petition then had a new section called 'the foreigners', and under an explicitly categorized subsection of the 'Persian community', there came a list of twelve names, headed by the aforementioned Mohammad Sharif, who was identified as 'the head of the Persian community and vice president of the municipality and member in Majlis al-'Urf'. A new subsection explicitly labelled 'the Najdi community' followed, headed by al-Qusaibi, who we came across before as the official agent of Ibn Sa'ud. Finally, there was a subsection that Daly entitled 'Indian Headmen', with two names who were identified as the leader of the 'Indian Moslem community' and the 'headman of the Hindu community'.[16]

This petition signalled that ethnosectarian politics was by now enshrined in the politics of the notables, with each ethnosect grouping represented by certain individuals, at least from the British point of view. It is significant to indicate here that the head of each 'community' that Daly identified was actually a member of Majlis al-'Urf or the Municipal Council for that community. Hence, a position within the council or Majlis gave the person the legitimacy to claim that he could head his entire

16 QDL, 'File 8/2 Public petitions etc. Letters to Major Daly (P.A.) thanking him for his interest in Bahrain affairs' [6r] (11/72), IOR/R/15/2/121, http://www.qdl.qa/en/archive/81055/vdc_100023025311.0x00000c.

'ethno-sect community'. But it is remarkable to note the near-complete absence of religious figures and Mullahs from this list of 'notables', with the vast majority being merchants of one form or another. 'Notable' thus came to be increasingly defined through relations to the sovereign powers, particularly the British and the ruler. It is also significant that nearly all of the signatories were based in the urban centres of Manama or Muharraq, with hardly any representation from the villages. Finally, this also signified the use of petitions by different sides in the to and fro of their political struggles, which would become a frequent phenomenon over the next few years.

Notably absent from the letter's signatories were the al-Nahda intelligentsia. This group was to become the main focus of Daly's subsequent antagonistic actions. He placed the members of the Literary Club in Muharraq under surveillance.[17] The first to be taken out was Qasem al-Shirawi, the poet secretary of the ruler and closest confidant of Sh. 'Abdulla, and whom Daly saw as the main schemer against the British. Daly first tried to exclude him from the Knowledge Council running the al-Hedaya school.[18] After this failed, he had Shirawi arrested on 19 November 1921 and sentenced to be deported from Bahrain for two years. This was supposedly according to the powers granted to him by the BOIC to deport 'foreigners', on charges that he 'acted in a dangerous manner to peace and good order, and has acted to excite enmity between the people of Bahrain and his Majesty (the King of England)'.[19]

17 Al-Khater, *al-ketabat al-uwla*, 95.
18 Wahba, *Khamsoona 'aman*, 35
19 QDL, 'File 5/10 Jasim Muhammad al-Chirawi and his uncle Ali bin Abdullah bin Muhammad on Black List' [23r] (47/98), IOR/R/15/2/104, http://www.qdl.qa/archive/81055/vdc_100023246775.0x000030.

To bolster these accusations, Daly arranged the signed testi-
monies of several notables he saw as supportive of his position,
including the previously encountered 'Abd 'Ali bin Rajab and
Ahmad bin Khamis, amongst others. The first testified that
Shirawi was 'a dangerous political intriguer', and the latter added
that Shirawi 'has done his best at all times to stir up trouble
against Shaikh Hamad & the (British) Agency'.[20] When
Shirawi, who was of a Huwala background, objected that he was
a Bahrain subject and thereby not a foreigner to be under British
jurisdiction of the BOIC, Daly retorted that he was Persian,
falsely claiming that he was born in Iran to bolster his ethnosectarian reading to suit his purposes. Shirawi was then deported
to India at the end of November 1921. In Bombay, he lodged an
appeal with the courts and legislatures in India, which eventually upheld his view that the BOIC did not apply to him and
quashed Daly's order, but only in June 1923 after the climax of
events.[21]

There were differences between the views of Daly (Political
Agent), Trevor (Political Resident), and the Government of India
on how to handle matters in Bahrain. While Daly was taking an
active and confrontational approach, the Government of India
did not want any interference whatsoever in the matters of 'local'

20 For the testimony of Ahmad bin Khamis and 'Abd-'Ali bin Rajab,
respectively see: QDL, 'File 5/10 Jasim Muhammad al-Chirawi and his
uncle Ali bin Abdullah bin Muhammad on Black List' [31r] (63/98), IOR
/ R / 15 / 2 / 104, http: / / www.qdl.qa / en / archive / 81055 / vdc_
100023246775.0x000040; QDL, 'File 5/10 Jasim Muhammad al-Chirawi
and his uncle Ali bin Abdullah bin Muhammad on Black List' [26r] (53/
98), IOR/R/15/2/104, http://www.qdl.qa/en/archive/81055/vdc_
100023246775.0x000036.
21 QDL, 'File 5/10 Jasim Muhammad al-Chirawi and his uncle Ali bin
Abdullah bin Muhammad on Black List' [2r] (5/98), IOR/R/15/2/104,
http://www.qdl.qa/archive/81055/vdc_100023246775.0x000006.

subjects, with Trevor being somewhere in between. Events would quickly show whose approach would prevail.[22]

In December 1921, Trevor visited Bahrain, and upon his arrival at the Agency he was met by a large deputation from some of the villages of Bahrain which, under encouragement from Daly, gathered to hand a petition to the Political Resident.[23] In it, the signatories complained about the treatment they were experiencing under the different Shaikhs in their villages, and asked for British protection and intervention. This seems to have had made a strong impression on Trevor, who increasingly came closer to Daly's viewpoint. Another similar petition followed suit on 24 January 1922.[24]

Since his brother was named as formal heir, and particularly after his confidant Shirawi was deported, Sh. 'Abdulla seemed to have increasingly resorted to violence and coercion, in the hope that this would destabilize the situation and undermine British rule. In conjunction with the petition that was handed to the Political Resident during his visit in December 1921, Daly sent a lengthy report outlining all the atrocities Sh. 'Abdulla and his fidawiyya were purported to have committed, including cases of sexual abuse.[25] The social, regional, and

---

22 See correspondence in file: QDL, 'File 19/165 I (C 18) Bahrain Reforms', IOR/R/15/1/336, https://www.qdl.qa/archive/81055/vdc_100000000193.0x000135.

23 QDL, 'File 9/4 Bahrain Reforms. Introduction of Reforms in Bahrain' [1fv] (19/224), IOR/R/15/2/131, http://www.qdl.qa/archive/81055/vdc_100023403812.0x000014.

24 QDL, 'File 9/4 Bahrain Reforms. Introduction of Reforms in Bahrain' [7v] (31/224), IOR/R/15/2/131, http://www.qdl.qa/archive/81055/vdc_100023403812.0x000020.

25 QDL, 'File 9/4 Bahrain Reforms. Introduction of Reforms in Bahrain' [4v] (25/224), IOR/R/15/2/131, http://www.qdl.qa/archive/81055/vdc_100023403812.0x00001a.

sectarian background of the victims of 'Abdulla's actions varied, but the larger part were residents of villages, particularly those under his fiefdom. Although Daly had a frequent tendency to manipulate the information he sent to his superiors, Sh. 'Abdulla had a notorious reputation in this regard, and there is little doubt that he and his fidawiyya were involved in committing many assaults.

Next on Daly's list of al-Nahda people to deport was Hafedh Wahba, the Egyptian principal of al-Hedaya school. The opportune moment arrived in January 1922. Wahba had left for the drier weather of Kuwait for a few weeks to recover from a bout of malaria. He was denied entry to Bahrain upon his return and sent back to Kuwait.[26] According to Wahba, he suspected Daly requested his deportation because he criticized Daly for beating a shopkeeper from Bastak to death.[27] The shopkeeper was accused of stealing the jewellery of Daly's wife.[28] Archival documents show that colonial officers were more concerned regarding anti-British articles on events in Bahrain that appeared in the Egyptian *Al-Akhbar* newspaper, which Daly suspected Wahba of writing.[29] Cynically, Daly feigned ignorance of the reasons for Wahba's deportation

---

26 Wahba, *Khamsoona 'aman*, 19-20. After being kicked out of Bahrain, Wahba moved to Sa'udi Arabia, where he would become a close adviser of King 'Abdulaziz ibn Sa'ud and ironically his first ambassador to the United Kingdom.

27 Bastak is a region in modern-day Iran.

28 Daly claimed he died from pneumonia after he was released from the Agency: QDL, 'File 9/4 Bahrain Reforms. Introduction of Reforms in Bahrain' [16v] (49/224), IOR/R/15/2/131, http://www.qdl.qa/en/archive/81055/vdc_100023403812.0x000032.

29 QDL, 'File 61/15 (D 40) Bin Saud: boundary settlement conference at Kuwait' [140r] (292/510), IOR/R/15/1/594, http://www.qdl.qa/archive/81055/vdc_100024111564.0x00005d.

when he relayed the news to his superior, and blamed it instead on the ruler.[30]

By this point, al-Hedaya had become a hub for anti-British sentiment. Students at the school hand-wrote posters and flyers that were posted around the cities and on houses of those seen as collaborators with the British. It seems they were encouraged in this regard by some of the more confrontational members of the al-Nahda, such as ʿAbdulla al-Zayed and Saʿad al-Shamlan, who continued to write letters and petitions denouncing the increasing British interference. This caused tension with some other members of the al-Nahda group, particularly Nasser al-Khairi, who by this point was employed by the Manama Municipality Council, and was worried that such a confrontational approach would get some of the al-Nahda group into trouble.[31]

Events continued to escalate. In February 1922, a fidawi in Manama got into an altercation with a man from a nearby village, with other Baharna overpowering the fidawi and releasing their compatriot. Many Baharna in Manama's souq initiated a strike in support. In an attempt to diffuse the situation, the ruler met a delegation of Baharna notables, who put forward thirteen requests, mainly revolving around the cessation of arbitrary taxes by different Shaikhs on the villages, and for power to be centralized and bureaucratized with the ruler. The ruler agreed to these demands except for one.[32]

---

30 QDL, 'File 9/4 Bahrain Reforms. Introduction of Reforms in Bahrain' [6v] (29/224), IOR/R/15/2/131, http://www.qdl.qa/archive/81055/vdc_100023403812.0x00001e.

31 Al-Khater, al-Adeeb al-Kateb, 107–110.

32 Al-Tajir, 'Iqd al-Liʾal, 35–36. See also: QDL, 'File 9/4 Bahrain Reforms. Introduction of Reforms in Bahrain' [9r] (34/224), IOR/R/15/2/131, http://www.qdl.qa/en/archive/81055/vdc_100023403812.0x000023.

The case of the political mobilization of the 'Baharna' provides an illustration of how mobilization based on ethno-sectarian lines could transcend other socio-economic cleavages. As previously outlined, there were significant differences in the socio-economic conditions of those who lived in urban areas vs. the villages. Nearly all of the demands in the petition were addressed towards grievances and transgressions that befell those in the agricultural villages. Many of the main drivers and signatories of this and other petitions on behalf of the 'Baharna community', however, were urban merchants from Manama. In this manner, mobilization based on a 'Baharna' identity would create a chain that would link those in an urban setting to those in the villages, bypassing other socio-economic differences between them.

THE 'FITNAH' OF 1923

Events seemed to settle for the next few months. Even Sh. 'Abdulla, who might have realized his weakened position, was seen by the British to 'have mended his ways',[33] and appeared on good terms with Daly. However, the latter became frustrated with the ruler and his sons for dragging their feet on reforms of taxes, which he thought imperative to regularize and centralize its collection. The ruler's reluctance was driven by fear of the reaction of other parties who would have opposed the proposed tax reforms. Most likely to resist were the ruler's wider family, tribes who were used to running their affairs autonomous of

33 QDL, 'File 9/4 Bahrain Reforms. Introduction of Reforms in Bahrain' [10r] (36/224), IOR/R/15/2/131, http://www.qdl.qa/archive/81055/ vdc_100023403812.0x000025.

any centralized government, as well as the nokhedha ship captains and pearl traders.

In the first group were the relatives of the ruler, particularly those who held agricultural fiefdoms that provided them with their main source of revenue extraction. The proposed tax reforms would have threatened their income flow. In the second group, the main protagonists were members of the al-Dowaser tribe, who almost uniquely within the tribes that moved to Bahrain still maintained strong cohesion by living off pearling secluded in their own town of Budaiya', with virtual independence of any influence or taxes from the Shaikh.[34] In February 1922, they approached Sh. Hamad to offer their support for the new ruler, but they received a cold shoulder from him and Daly.[35] Unhappy with developments in Bahrain, members of the tribe sent a delegation to Ibn Sa'ud to sound out his support should they decide to reallocate en masse.[36] His reply was positive, offering them a place in Dammam right across Bahrain in eastern Sa'udi Arabia should they need it, causing significant alarm to Bahrain's rulers.

Nokhedhas and pearl merchants were also expected to oppose such tax reform moves. The port economic system of al-Khalifa rule depended on giving free rein to pearl ship captains with minimal taxes, in order to encourage the main export generator and employer within the economy. Tax reform would have entailed a fundamental shift in the balance of power

34 QDL, 'File 9/4 Bahrain Reforms. Introduction of Reforms in Bahrain' [11r] (38/224), IOR/R/15/2/131, http://www.qdl.qa/archive/81055/vdc_100023403812.0x000027.

35 Al-Tajir, *Bahrain 1920–1945*, 40.

36 This delegation included Ahmad bin Lahij. For more see: al-Hadi, *A'yan al-Bahrain*, 87.

in this regard. To add to this combustible mix, a strong press campaign was launched in Iranian newspapers against the British in 1922. Several articles appeared that renewed calls for Iranian sovereignty over Bahrain and criticized British heavy-handedness, including the treatment of Persians in Bahrain and Daly's beating to death of the man from Bastak, as well as the deportations of Hafedh Wahba and Qasem Shirawi.[37] The British suspected that well-known anti-British 'Persian' traders in Bahrain were behind the articles, and they grew increasingly nervous.

These simmering contradictions of divided rule were to violently explode by the spring of 1923. In March, some members of the al-Dowaser tribe were suspected of launching an attack on the village of Barbar, which left several people injured.[38] Daly arrested the leader of al-Dowaser, who objected that he was not aware of the attacks and could not be held responsible for them. In April and May, fights broke out in Manama between members of two 'foreign groups' that were supposedly under British jurisdiction. Clashes between 'Persians', led by the previously encountered Mohammad Sharif, and 'Najdis', led by Ibn Sa'ud's representative 'Abdulla al-Qusaibi, erupted on 20 April and again from 1 to 11 May.[39] Persian newspapers in Iran were galvanized, with several

37 QDL, 'File 9/4 Bahrain Reforms. Introduction of Reforms in Bahrain' [19v] (55/224), IOR/R/15/2/131, http://www.qdl.qa/archive/81055/vdc_100023403812.0x000038.

38 QDL, 'Administration Reports 1920–1924' [158v] (321/412), IOR/R/15/1/713, http://www.qdl.qa/archive/81055/vdc_100023385511.0x00007a.

39 QDL, 'File 9/4 Bahrain Reforms. Introduction of Reforms in Bahrain' [24v] (65/224), IOR/R/15/2/131, http://www.qdl.qa/archive/81055/vdc_100023403812.0x000042.

articles and protestations published on the matter. A petition to the British Political Agency was signed by 'Persians' for protection, while different notables, all Sunnis, composed of merchants, tribal chiefs, and nokhedhas, signed a petition to the local ruler accusing 'Persians' of monopolizing and abusing Manama's police force.[40]

On 12 May, members of the al-Dowaser tribe were accused of launching another attack on the village of ʿAali, this time with deadly consequences.[41] On the same day, ʿAbdulaziz ibn Saʿud moved to Hufuf, ominously close to the shores of Bahrain. At the same time, fidawiyyas of Shaikh Khaled, the ruler's brother who had extensive fiefdoms, attacked a village in Sitra, leaving a dozen people dead, with members of the village and some other Baharna congregating on the Political Agency in uproar.[42] Ethnosectarian political mobilization had taken centre stage, and it had turned violent, with different parties contesting the volatile and unclear parameters of sovereignty and power, each trying to mobilize to its advantage. Two poles were formed, around which the different groups mobilized mainly on ethnosectarian lines, defined by the two clashing sources of sovereignty: one pole was pro-British and against the local ruler, the other was anti-British and sympathetic to the local ruler. The first framed their position in terms of considerations of social reform and fairness, while the second displayed an anti-colonial drive. To compound matters, open agitation was practised by both ibn Saʿud and the Persian government.

40 al-Khalifa, *Sebazabad wa Rejal*, 528–529.
41 QDL, 'Administration Reports 1920–1924' [158v] (321/412), IOR/R/15/1/713, http://www.qdl.qa/archive/81055/vdc_100023385511. 0x00007a.
42 Khuri, *Tribe and State*, 93–94.

In such situations, it is usually the party with the largest coercive force that is able to come out on top, and so it proved in this case. On 14 May 1923, two British military vessels arrived with the acting Gulf Political Resident Major Knox on board. On 17 May, he forcibly transferred political power to the ruler's son Hamad, and on 24 May he ordered the Indian family in charge of customs to transfer revenues to Sh. Hamad. The ruler was officially deposed on 26 May in a much-publicized ceremony. Standing on a stool higher than the ruler, Major Knox admonished him in a speech that provides one of the finest examples of the colonial ethnosectarian gaze.[43] Indeed, this speech would serve as a future map for the divide and rule ethnosectarian strategy employed by Colonial Britain in Bahrain:

> Ever since some twenty years ago, Shaikh 'Isa in his wisdom handed over to the Political Agent, the administration over and direct responsibility for foreigners, there have been practically two Governments working side by side in Bahrain. He has been open and above-board and has resulted in an enormous influx of foreigners to these Islands, and I believe that I shall not be accused of exaggeration if I say that the proportion of foreigners has during the last twenty years progressed as 20:1 and their wealth as 100:1. I really believe I am understating facts.

43 Text of the speech can be found in: QDL, 'File 9/4 Bahrain Reforms. Introduction of Reforms in Bahrain' [45r] (106/224), IOR/R/15/2/131, http://www.qdl.qa/en/archive/81055/vdc_10002 3403812.0x00006b.

Knox then turned to the representatives of what he categorized as distinct 'communities', and directed his speech to each of them. First were the rulers and the 'Sunni community', whom Knox complained had lagged behind and stood aloof from other groups. Al-Khalifa would continue to rule, Knox reassured them, with the new ruler having the full support of the British, but the 'Sunnis' had to be brought in line. He then turned to the representatives of the 'Shi'a community':

> I wish you particularly to weigh the following remarks. Much of the agitation of recent years has been fictitious. I am far from saying that you have had no cause for complaint but what I mean to say is that I cannot subscribe to the opinion that recent misrule is either more tyrannical or more flagrant than it has often been in the past. The state of these Islands, the signs of additional wealth that meet the eye everywhere around give the lie to the contention that misrule has been persistent and is increasing. We have admitted some abuses and announced our intention of fighting them.

However, Knox reminded them that this is a 'Sunni country' that was surrounded by powerful 'Sunni communities', who viewed British activities on the islands with vigilance and suspicion. Consequently, 'Sunni privileges' could not be swept away with equality established all at once.

Finally, Knox turned his speech towards 'foreigners', who were supposed to be under British jurisdiction. He assured them that this would continue to be the case:

> I believe it has been to your benefit and that you are reasonably content with it. One thing no one will deny,

that since Shaikh 'Isa, in his wisdom, entrusted foreign cases to the Political Agent, the number of foreigners, their wealth, importance and weight in the community has increased in a manner that is little short of amazing. It does not seem as if people would flock here to the extent they do, if they were dissatisfied under the conditions under which they live.

Just like the French in Tunisia, the British increasingly found themselves in a spiral trap under divided rule, as their efforts to assume greater sovereignty in Bahrain increasingly engendered contradictions that further forced the British to increase their involvement on the islands.[44] As the contradictions engendered by regional tensions, the local actors' mobilization, and the ruler's resistance increasingly began to explode and spin out of control, they had to take over the rule of local matters completely by May 1923, deposing the ex-ruler and installing his more pliant son in his place.

Shortly afterwards, al-Qusaibi was deported from Bahrain to Sa'udi Arabia. The leader of the al-Dowaser was arrested, and members of the tribe were then exiled en masse to Sa'udi Arabia. The situation remained volatile for the remainder of 1923. Sporadic violence between the different parties erupted intermittently.[45] Petitions and counter-petitions for and against the reforms vs. the *coup d'état* ensued, mainly based on ethnosect considerations.[46] There was one petition, however, that

44 Lewis, *Divided Rule*, 13–14.
45 A good overview of events can be found in: Khuri, *Tribe and State*, 93–97.
46 An example is the petition by seven Baharna merchants from Manama on 26 October 1923, representing the 'Shi'a community' and urging that the changes that 'ameliorate their conditions' should be continued: al-Khalifa, *Sebazabad wa Rejal*, 575–577.

stood out for its discourse and demands. This was a letter penned by a group calling itself the 'Bahrani National Congress', or the 'Legislative Council Group'. The discourse would mark a watershed in the history of Bahraini politics. The letter's demands were: the reinstatement of the previous ruler; the setting-up of a system of rule based on 'equality'; the setting-up of a representative council chosen by 'the people' that would take care of their interests in conducting matters relating to the institutions of government; that the British Political Agent should uphold the agreements Britain signed with Bahrain, in which it did not interfere in internal affairs; and that the congress had chosen twelve individuals to represent its demands.[47]

Furthermore, the letter adopted an anti-colonialist and nationalist discourse, explicitly highlighting 'the Arab nation' vs. 'foreigners' who were 'mischief mongers', the rule of law, as well as 'liberty' and 'reforms', in the first official written example of nationalist and democratic political demands in Bahrain. The discourse also displayed some of the exclusionary ideas that would emerge with Arab nationalism in Bahrain and the wider region, as the term 'foreigners' here explicitly referred to 'Persians', who would become one of the major 'Others' that were the target of nationalist discourse.

If one were to adopt an ethnosectarian gaze, all of those who signed this letter were Sunni merchants or members of tribes. It does seem that many of those who signed did so from a

---

47 Both an English translation of the text of the council's demand (with errors) and the text of the council's and the ex-ruler's letter can be found in the following file, which also includes Daly's replies: QDL, 'File 19/165 III (C 24) Bahrain Reforms' [43r] (92/426), IOR/R/15/1/339, http://www.qdl.qa/en/archive/81055/vdc_100024110738.0x00005b. Arabic texts can be found at: al-Khalifa, *Sebazabad wa rejal*, 553–563, 687–689.

self-interested, anti-tax, and anti-reform perspective. The two main instigators and writers of the petition, however, were 'Abdulwahhab al-Zayyani and Ahmad bin Lahij, whom we encountered previously as leaders within the al-Nahda group. The British themselves were under no illusion that Zayyani in particular was the main instigator of the petition, calling him a 'professional agitator'.[48]

Even the name of the group, Bahrani National Congress reflected a new form of emerging inchoate nationalism that was yet to crystallize clearly. Nowadays, the term 'Bahrani' would be understood to refer to someone whose background is from the Baharna social group. It would be controversial, and quite preposterous, for a group exclusively composed of Sunnis to use such a term to describe themselves. As the name of the group implies, however, this obviously was not the case back in 1923.[49] Instead, the term was employed to have the same meaning that 'Bahraini' has today, i.e. to indicate citizenship of Bahrain. Accordingly, it could be argued that the name and discourse of the Bahrani National Congress constitutes the first example of using 'Bahrainis' in such a manner to constitute a pan-Bahrain discourse of nationalism and citizenship.

48 QDL, 'File 9/4 Bahrain Reforms. Introduction of Reforms in Bahrain' [77v] (171/224), IOR/R/15/2/131, http://www.qdl.qa/archive/81055/vdc_100023403812.0x0000ac.
49 The 'Bahrani National Front', the communist party in Bahrain formed in the early 1950s, also used the term in a similar manner to the 'Bahrani National Congress', indicating a form of nationality and citizenship. This can also be contrasted with the term's usage in the letter penned in 1536 mentioned in chapter 3, where 'Bahrani' connoted coming from the islands of Bahrain, thereby showing the different and evolving meanings of the term across centuries, up to its usage today as a marker of a specific social group.

'Abdulwahhab al-Zayyani stood out in this period as one of the few figures who pushed for social and political reform towards a fairer system, while also combining it with an anti-colonial freedom drive. Most other notables active during this period split into two camps, emphasizing one of these two strands. In an effort for cross-sectarian mobilization, both he and Ahmad bin Lahij would reach out to 'Abd 'Ali bin Rajab in his position as a Baharna notable, composing a letter requesting a meeting to discuss matters and possible coordination, as the two were sympathetic to the social demands put forward in the 'Baharna Petitions' Rajab spearheaded. Their offer was refused and the letter was handed over to the British Political Agent.[50] Out of all the signatories of the Bahrani National Congress petition, Zayyani and bin Lahij would be the only ones that the British would imprison and deport to exile in India in November 1923.[51]

While in Bombay, they initiated a case with the high court to contest their exile. In a remarkable twist of history, the lawyer who took up their case was the young and up-and-coming Muhammad 'Ali Jinnah, the future founder of Pakistan. Zayyani, however, died in exile whilst still battling the courts in 1925, while bin Lahij moved to Sa'udi Arabia, finally being allowed to return to Bahrain in 1927.

Members of al-Nahda thus bore the brunt of British

50 I would like to thank Rashid al-Jassim for sharing a copy of the original from his personal collection, which can be viewed on his personal Twitter page at: https://twitter.com/rashidaljassim/status/682855895240425476.
51 QDL, 'File 5/15 Ahmad bin Lahej and Abdul Wahab Zaiyani' [9r] (17/134), IOR/R/15/2/107, http://www.qdl.qa/archive/81055/vdc_100023483757.0x000012. See also: QDL, 'File 19/165 II (C 20) Bahrain Reforms' [227r] (476/494), IOR/R/15/1/338, http://www.qdl.qa/archive/81055/vdc_100023725593.0x00004b.

coercive actions. Saʿad al-Shamlan was deported even before Zayyani and bin Lahij. He became particularly vocal during the climax of events, verbally confronting Daly on more than one occasion, as well as playing an active role in trying to prevent tribes from relocating away from Bahrain. He was placed under house arrest with his livelihood cut off, and subsequently he was deported by the Political Agent to Bombay, accused of playing a role in instigating the conflict between the 'Persians and Najdis'.[52]

The events of 1923 caused significant hardship for the al-Nahda group. Daly kept the Literary Club in Muharraq under close surveillance by spies.[53] Many of those in exile went bankrupt, and quarrels began to emerge. Saʿad al-Shamlan and ʿAbdulla al-Zayed publicly attacked Judge Qasem bin Mehzaʿ in newspapers for refusing to sign the Bahrani National Congress petition.[54] In an ironic twist of fate, Nasser al-Khairi, who at this point was working in the Manama municipality, was tasked by Cox with reading the Arabic translation of his speech at the deposing of Shaikh ʿIsa. This led to a palpable break between him and the rest of the group, which saw him as having sold out to the British.[55] Only Sh. Ebrahim, the patron of the Majlis, and his son Sh. Mohammad continued their friendship with him, something that Khairi complained bitterly about until his death shortly afterwards in 1925.

For his part, Sh. Ebrahim opted to stay out of overt political agitation, given his background as a member of the ruling

---

52 Al-Hadi, *Aʿyan al-Bahrain*, 340–343.
53 Al-Khater, *al-ketabat al-uwla*, 164–166.
54 Al-Khater, *al-Qadhi*, 82–87.
55 Al-Khater, *al-Adeeb al-kateb*, 97.

family. Privately, however, he made his views very clear through his letters to ʿAbdulla al-Zayed, who was trading in Bombay while the climax of events ensued:

> Truth to be said, your homeland and people are in consecutive struggles, as the foreigner's hand plays with them like a child messes with his toy. He pleads with some of them to wear down some of the others, and most are in ignorance of the scheming against them. A few less are in a conundrum, where they do not think of helping the public but are more concerned for their personal safety. This I am sure is not new knowledge to you, for it is how you previously knew your people and homeland to act, and my words serve nothing but to deepen your already known woes.[56]

ʿAbdulla al-Zayed was very vocal in his disapproval of events, writing several poems denouncing the situation. After hearing about the death of Zayyani in 1925 in exile, he authored one of his most famous poems, 'Who is for the Cause?':

> Who is for the cause after your death?
> It has been buried, for there are no words or deeds left.
> The people are slumbering in ignorance
> Enticed by the enemy to his side.[57]

---

56 Al-Khater, *al-ketabat al-uwla*, 103.
57 Al-Khater, *Nabeghat al-Bahrain*, 198. Arabic text:

من للقضية بعد موتك إنها
دفنت فلا قول ولا أفعال
والقوم في نوم وفي جهل وفي
صف العدو أمالهم فأمالوا

His ire would be directed particularly against Daly, to whom he would compose a poem in his (dis)honour:

O Britain, is there any justice in what has happened
Is a victim to be burned and his killer honoured?
Would London acquiesce
If hordes of German police took it over?
So please excuse us if we complain
And a strong love runs in our veins
Since when has Bahrain been a piece of your lands
For you to depose its ruler whose virtues are countless?
You have returned us to the age of the Tatars
As lightning crash and earthquakes thunder.[58]

The (by now) ex-ruler would also try to contest his deposition, sending several letters, including to the Gulf Political Resident and the Government of India, protesting his case. He would endorse the demands of the aforementioned Bahrani National Congress group in their entirety, including the representative parliament and equality of treatment, explicitly demanding that 'the people' be consulted on who should be leader.[59] The

---

58 Ibid., 230–233. Arabic text:

(بريطانيا) هل في العدالة ما جرى
أيحرق مقتول ويكرم قاتله
أترضى إن وفيت لندن أن ترى
بوليساً من الألمان تغدو جحافله
لذا فاعذرونا إن شكونا وإن سرى
لأوطاننا حب تضوع خمائله
متى كانت البحرين بعض بلادكم
فيعزل ملك لا تعد فضائله
أعدتم لنا عهد (التتار) منتظما
صواعقه تهوى وتدوي زلازله

59 al-Khalifa, *Sebazabad wa rejal*, 589.

Political Resident replied that they were under no obligation to consult anyone in their decision, given they were the ones who had previously installed him in 1869.[60] 'Abdulwahhab al-Zayyani would then initiate cases in the courts of the Government of India in Bombay, making the congress's and ex-ruler's demands the subject of an international to and fro that would end in vain with his death. Ironically, the birth of a modern nationalist discourse for a representative form of rule in Bahrain came from a faction aligned with the ex-ruler, the head of the old order. Of course, by this point he was not the ruler any more, but one of the opposition, a symbol to them of a usurped power and an anti-colonialist drive.

The events of 1922–1923 have been well documented in English, with most of the narration based on the British archives and the accounts of Daly and Knox.[61] As a counter-narrative to these colonial documents, it is instructive to present the events through the writings of a local historian, Mohammad 'Ali al-Tajir, whom we encountered previously as one of the founders of the initiative for the first library and literary club in Bahrain. If one were to go by the colonial ethnosectarian gaze, the expectation is that he would be pro the British reforms and against the ruler, given that he was a Shi'a Bahrani. Instead, he would write:

60 Trevor commentary on letter: QDL, 'File 9/4 Bahrain Reforms. Introduction of Reforms in Bahrain' [79r] (174/224), IOR/R/15/2/131, http://www.qdl.qa/en/archive/81055/vdc_100023403812.0x0000af.
61 The most famous of these probably relates to the Najdi Persian incident, which has usually been given from a British colonialist archive perspective, with the discourse on this particular incident being a masterpiece of ethnosectarian and frankly, racist discourse: QDL, 'File 19/165 I (C 18) Bahrain Reforms' [58r] (128/528), IOR/R/15/1/336, http://www.qdl.qa/en/archive/81055/vdc_100023840573.0x000081.

The sole reason for the recent coup is the Western glut-
tony for overtaking the Eastern Kingdoms under a
curtain of deception, flimsy excuses, and commercial
and political means. The appearance is that of love,
compassion, sincerity, and enchanting promises, while
its substance is treachery, deception, betrayal, disunity,
and the creation of problems so that the situation reaches
a point where they can appropriate the country without
the significant costs that are necessary in warfare; and to
have outward excuses to counter any accusations that
great countries are attacking small emirates and overtaking them by force. And this is a microcosm of colonialists' policy generally regarding colonies.[62]

Al-Tajir then proceeds to describe the imperial rivalries that
entangled Britain during the First World War. After the war's
end Britain returned its focus towards Bahrain, as it rolled up its
sleeves for the moment of action and 'took off the lamb's fleece
and appeared in its true form'. The 'cunning' Dickson becomes
a central character in his narrative:

(He) was as fluent in Arabic as a native, and he took to
meeting individuals from the people (*al-ahali*) to mould
from them an instrument through which to gain his
political motives . . . For he would show compassion and
sympathy for the situation of the oppressed and present
them with promises of ending servitude; and that the
time of gaining freedom, independence and regaining
trampled rights and stolen lands is imminent . . . And
these seeds that he laid started growing . . .

62 Al-Tajir, '*Iqd al-Liʾal*, 151.

This became too much to bear for the government, and so it sent a complaint to the British Gulf Resident. Dickson was then replaced by Daly, which for al-Tajir was like jumping out of the frying pan and into the fire. Al-Tajir has no reserve in displaying his disdain for Daly, whose machinations on the island now become the focus of his narration:

> He pretended for a year to be stupid and simple. He created the bait for the local government, which was fooled by his appearance of stupidity, and took it as an opportunity to increase its power and to discipline some members of the people that were tempted by his predecessor 'Dickson', without having a just reason or them having committed a crime. And henceforth the going became heavy, and that – the silence of the British Political Agency – was the biggest factor for indulging in oppression.

At that moment, when Daly had achieved what he wanted by gaining the government's trust, he cast aside the appearance of stupidity and appeared in his true form, hatching his plan of enticing groups from the people (*al-ahali*) to mobilize against the ruler:

> It was then that Major Daly schemed the plan of division according to the policy of the adage 'Divide and Rule', where he created middlemen and brokers (*Samasira*) to entice the two sides against each other. And whenever someone was oppressed and solicited Daly for help, he would reply by saying 'Aren't you men and they are men? Face them with the same and fight fire with fire! If you lack weapons, we will provide you with those so that you

achieve your vengeance from them.' . . . And so you can
see the extent to which this policy aims at horrible
dangers.[63]

The above passages are important not because they present a
counter-narrative to the British account of events, accusing
Dickson and Daly of creating middlemen and intentionally
fomenting divide and rule; for it is not the main intention of
this study to vouch for the validity of the different versions of
what happened. What is more important for our purposes is its
complete rejection of the ethnosectarian framework that we see
in British documents. Instead of reducing social agents to
simply their sects and ethnicity, thereby becoming 'Shiʿa',
'Sunnis', 'Najdis', 'Persians', etc., al-Tajir is careful to label this as
'divide and rule', and to point out that the categories used, such
as 'foreign', etc., are socially produced constructions, which
were turned into the paramount variables in politics by British
rule. This is important to emphasize, for if al-Tajir was simply
reduced to his ethno-sect background of Bahrani Shiʿa, as the
British tended to do, then the above narration would be hard to
swallow. However, if we remember that al-Tajir was a member
of the al-Nahda group in Bahrain, and one of the founders of
the first public library and literary club, such a narration of
events makes sense.

To press the point further, it is useful to compare al-Tajir's
narration of events, which are emphatically against the British
actions, with those of a compatriot historian who was also part
of the al-Nahda. Nasser al-Khairi was a Sunni, if one were to
classify him by sect. Paradoxically from the viewpoint of a colonial ethnosectarian gaze, however, Khairi was actually

---

63 Al-Tajir, 'Iqd al-Liʾal, 152–153.

sympathetic to some of the reforms instituted by the British, and he blamed the ruler for the events leading to his deposition.[64] What he shares with al-Tajir, however, is his rejection of the ethnosectarian gaze of the British, and a realization that these were social constructs. Both authors would use the word 'fitnah' to describe the events narrated between 1904 and 1923, a choice of phrase that depicts an unnatural, sinister situation of strife, with an extreme impact on society and the people who experienced it.

None of these social intricacies and variation within the thoughts and actions of the al-Nahda group, or indeed any other social actors, mattered from the colonial ethnosectarian viewpoint. Differences in each individual's stance regarding the primacy of anti-colonial vs. social fairness issues, between being more pro-ruler or anti-British, between taking a more nationalist vs. Islamist ecumenical reform stance, or simply differences in their personal circumstances and interests, were all relegated and hidden in the background. They were robbed of their agency, and what was revealed instead as primary in categorizing each individual was his designated sect and ethnicity, which ultimately defined and articulated his position and worth as a social agent from the British colonial point of view.

64 Al-Khairi, *Qala'id al-Nahrain*, 422–431.

POSTSCRIPT: THE RISE
OF ABSOLUTISM AND
NATIONALISM, 1923–1979

T he actions of the al-Nahda group amounted to little in the immediate aftermath of the *coup d'état*. They were a relatively small circle, their discourse and thought was yet to coalesce into something coherent, and most importantly, they were no match for the might of British gunboats. Modernized absolutist rule under the guidance of British imperialism was rapidly being consolidated, and the change in the political system would be reflected geographically. No longer was Muharraq the seat of rule, which shifted instead to Manama, where both the new ruler and the British Political Agency would be based. The British were not interested in replacing the rule of al-Khalifa, nor in a democratic setting, but in 'reforming' the current system so that it was stable and compatible with their own interests. The ex-ruler's son Sh. Hamad would be installed as the new head. Weak, with few local allies and many more enemies, including within his own family, the new ruler depended almost entirely on British support to bolster his position.

THE RISE OF MODERNIZED ABSOLUTISM

Although al-Khalifa rule was nominally transferred from the ex-ruler to his son, the British radically reshaped the system of government over the rest of the decade. The old order that was based on a constellation of diffuse, decentralized forces was rapidly dissolved. In its place sovereign power was monopolized in the shape of the new ruler, the figurehead of state, with the Political Agent and other British officers dictating things behind him. The strategy rested on two pillars: centralizing political power in the state under the ruler, combined with administrative and economic 'reforms', a blueprint that would become a pillar of state-building in all the Gulf Arab States in the twentieth century. Political power would now flow from top to bottom. A professionalized, centralized bureaucracy would run the affairs of the state, most importantly in revenue collection and the coercive apparatuses. Paramount was the ability to deal with any opposition that might arise to this mode of rule. British officials identified the authoritarian strand within local al-Khalifa rule, and rationalized and modernized it, thereby infusing it with all moments of political power.[1] Modernized absolutism would be born for the first time in Bahrain and the wider Gulf.

The British wager was that the new modernized mode of government, under the guidance of 'benevolent imperialism', would drive economic and social gains and thus defeat any

1 Mahmood Mamdani, 'Historicizing power and responses to power: indirect rule and its reform', *Social Research* (1999).

opposition. Daly introduced a set of drastic reforms aimed at rationalizing the state bureaucracy, monopolizing power in its hand, as well as alleviating some of the more blatant social hardships in the land. A professionalized police force inspired by the Muscat Levy Corps was set up, first staffed by Baluchis and then by Indian Punjabi recruits. Courts were regularized and a civil code introduced, based on those in India and Sudan. Customs were centralized and placed under a British officer. A surveyor from India was brought in to carry out cadastral mapping, centralizing property documentation under a newly established Tapu Land department. There were now standardized state budgets, with the ruling family's share of state revenues limited to half, with the rest used to fund the fledgeling state bureaucracy.[2]

Extra-state militias and coercive forces were ended, and the individual powers of judges such as Qasem bin Mehza' were significantly reduced and transferred to the state's courts. Debt inheritance by the families of pearl divers was banned, interest rates on their loans lowered, and regular pearl diving contracts introduced. Similarly, there were now regularized contracts and property holding documents that determined the relationship between agriculturalists and the estate holders, including the different al-Khalifa Shaikhs.

Daly's rule in Bahrain would end in 1926 after an assassination attempt, which only succeeded in injuring its target. In the same year and upon Daly's suggestion, the British would recruit a private British 'Adviser' for the Shaikh, the infamous Charles

---

2 Summaries of the reforms can be found in: QDL, 'File 9/1 Institution of Reforms & Sunni opposition intrigues' [149r] (314/504), IOR/R/15/2/127, https://www.qdl.qa/archive/81055/vdc_100023321443.0x000073; QDL, 'File 19/165 III (C 24) Bahrain Reforms' [159r] (324/426), IOR/R/15/1/339, https://www.qdl.qa/archive/81055/vdc_100024110739.0x00007b. The same files also include extensive details on the reforms.

Belgrave, who would be the executive in chief and effectively the country's first prime minister for the next thirty years. The Political Agency officially no longer had a hand in running affairs for local subjects, although strong communication and joint work between the 'Adviser' and the Agency continued unabated.

Throughout this period, British colonial officers were under no illusion that they were the supreme authority that was intimately involved in running local affairs in Bahrain. Although the particular mode of rule included many unique traits that catered to the local scene, the overall blueprint was based on colonial rule in the Indian (Native) Princely States, combined with elements from British rule in Arab areas such as Iraq and Sudan.³ Bahrain frequently became a subject of explicit comparison with Indian Native States such as Kalat and Tonk, with some officers stationed in Bahrain also previously serving there.⁴ The personal judgements and dictates of the British officers on the scene (particularly the Adviser, the Political Agent, and the Gulf Resident) played a crucial role in shaping

3 For more on Princely States in India see: Barbara N. Ramusack, *The Indian Princes and Their States* (Cambridge: Cambridge University Press, 2004).
4 Thus, in 1929 the Government of India wrote to the Political Residency in Bushehr complaining that Bahrain had 'actually more British administration than in an ordinary Indian State even than (for instance) in Kalat, though Kalat is a frontier State, in which imperial considerations dictate a comparatively marked degree of direct interference'. The Political Agent in Bahrain replied that he had served previously in Tonk, and that Bahrain was in need of more British presence than either of the two previously mentioned States due to regional intrigues and the heavy workload from internal affairs. QDL, 'File 9/1 Institution of Reforms & Sunni opposition intrigues' [143r] (302/504), IOR/R/15/2/127, https://www.qdl.qa/archive/81055/vdc_100023321443.0x000067.

Bahrain's version of modernized absolutism. They had considerable leeway in constructing the new system's legal and administrative infrastructure, under the watchful eye of the Government of India and Whitehall. In fact, colonial rule was so dominant that the stationed officers themselves came to see it as more extensive than direct British rule elsewhere in the empire. Hence, Whitehall could be forgiven for including Bahrain in its consular instructions for British Protected States, even though the island never officially became one.[5]

British officials across the empire's institutions were very much aware of the extent of their interference, which for a short while alarmed the Government of India and the Foreign Office. The justification given for such extensive interference rested on four rationalizations: firstly and most importantly, Bahrain was the 'Keystone of British position in the Gulf' due to its economic weight, but more importantly because of regional intrigues surrounding the islands.[6] This required Britain's imperial interests in the Gulf to be vigorously defended by direct physical presence in Bahrain. Particularly worrying were the perceived threats from Ibn Sa'ud and the Shah in Iran, as well as other Western imperial forces.

Secondly, British rule was justified by the belief that it was materially beneficial to an island previously beset by 'despotic' and mismanaged government. They were alleviating hardships through social and economic reform that they believed to be

5 QDL, 'File 19/165 III (C 24) Bahrain Reforms' [152r] (310/426), IOR /R/15/1/339, https://www.qdl.qa/archive/81055/vdc_100024110739. 0x00006d.
6 QDL, 'File 9/1 Institution of Reforms & Sunni opposition intrigues' [144r] (304/504), IOR/R/15/2/127, https://www.qdl.qa/archive/81055/vdc_100023321443.0x000069. The same file contains detailed correspondence between various branches of British imperial administration regarding justification for British rule in Bahrain.

popular with many social segments on the island. In this manner, Bahrain was held by British officers as a model of enlightened absolutist rule that could be exhibited to the rest of the region. Thirdly, interference and reforms were by now far too advanced to be reversed, and there were no locals that were trusted or competent enough to take over (particularly since many of those who could potentially qualify were part of the antagonistic al-Nahda group). Other Arabs, whether from Yemen, Egypt, Syria, Palestine, or Iraq, were deemed too politically dangerous to be given such roles.[7] Thus, British interference necessitated further British interference. British white and Indian officers were needed to continue running the state, while amenable locals, particularly from the ruling family, had to be trained to eventually take over sometime in the future.

Finally, the possibility of oil, particularly after its discovery in Iran and Iraq, gave British boots on the ground an added strategic priority. After extensive discussions between the Foreign Office in Whitehall, the Government of India, the British Residency in Bushehr, and the Political Agency in Bahrain, all parties came to the conclusion that British rule in Bahrain was here to stay. It did not make political sense, however, to formally declare Bahrain a Protectorate, as that would have caused significant alarm throughout the Gulf and beyond. Instead, the optimum course was for Bahrain to nominally remain under an independent Shaikh, with the British running affairs on the ground. The British Viceroy in India summed up the matter well in a 1929 letter to the Secretary of State for India in London, concluding that although the 'British

7 QDL, 'File 9/1 Institution of Reforms & Sunni opposition intrigues' [171r] (358/504), IOR/R/15/2/127, https://www.qdl.qa/archive/81055/vdc_100023321443.0x00009f.

element is stronger than in an ordinary Indian district let alone an Indian state', there was no 'question of relaxing our essential hold on Bahrain'.[8]

However, the remainder of the 1920s were challenging years economically for Bahrain, particularly after the collapse of the pearling market with the advent of Japanese cultured pearls and the global Great Depression. After a few difficult years, the discovery and export of oil in 1932 changed the situation completely, giving the newly established government independence in terms of revenue from merchants and other local parties. These revenues would be coupled by a continued drive to rationalize the governmental bureaucracy, whose high posts would increasingly be staffed by British officers and other member of the ruling family, in a system that has been described as 'dynastic monarchism'.[9] From the British point of view, Bahrain would rapidly become the role model of modernized absolutism for its neighbours in the Gulf.

THE RISE OF NATIONALISM

Bahrain was the first of the Gulf Arab States to discover oil, largely saving it from the harsh economic situation that its neighbours faced in the 1930s. The new oil industry in many ways took over from the pearl industry, both as the major employer on the island as well as becoming its main export generator. Pearl divers as an economic class would rapidly

8 QDL, 'File 9/1 Institution of Reforms & Sunni opposition intrigues' [187r] (390/504), IOR/R/15/2/127, https://www.qdl.qa/archive/81055/vdc_100023321443.0x0000bf.
9 Michael Herb, *All in the Family: Absolutism, Revolution, and Democracy in Middle Eastern Monarchies* (New York: SUNY Press, 1999).

disappear, and instead a new class of workers in the oil indus-tries began emerging.[10]

Such rapid social and economic transformations reflected onto the political scene, as several episodes of political mobili-zation ensued. First came the 1932 pearl divers' uprising for better social and monetary working conditions. This was not the first time pearl divers engaged in militancy, as the labour-intensive nature of their industry meant that they constituted by far the most organized workforce in Bahrain. Then came the 1934 'Baharna petition', as some Baharna notables demanded the reformation of Shi'a courts and having a separate school for Shi'as. The demands also included greater Shi'a-based repre-sentation in the Manama Municipality Council and Majlis al-'Urf, based on the claim that Shi'as constituted the majority of the population. This marked the emergence of ethno-demo-graphic 'minority' vs. 'majority' arguments onto the local politi-cal scene.[11]

Ethno-sect-defined political mobilization in Bahrain among non-state actors would largely manifest in Shi'a-centric

10 For a summary of social and political movements in Bahrain during the remainder of the twentieth century, which the analysis presented here largely derives from, see: Omar AlShehabi, 'Political Movements in Bahrain Across the Long Twentieth Century', in J. Hanssen and A. Ghazal (eds.), *The Oxford Handbook of Contemporary Middle-Eastern and North African History* (Oxford: Oxford University Press, 2017).

11 Such arguments have returned to prominence in the local political scene since the 1990s, particularly after the emergence of the 'political naturalization' issue, where the ruling regime has been accused of granting thousands of Bahraini citizenships in order to reshape the ethno-sect demographic make-up of the country. For more see: Omar AlShehabi, 'Demography and Bahrain's unrest', *Report for the Carnegie Endowment for International Peace* 16 (2011), http://carnegieendowment.org/sada/43079.

movements in the twentieth century.[12] The agricultural villages' unique historical experience of direct extractive repression under members of the ruling family would increasingly inter-act with the rising social (and eventually political) importance of the religious institutions of 'Ashura' processions, Ma'tams, and the clergy, as well as emerging Shiʻa-Islamist movements in the wider region. This provided the socio-economic back-drop that shaped the emergence of political discourses, organi-zations, movements, and traditions to articulate and address Shiʻa-centric political grievances and goals in the twentieth and twenty-first centuries.[13] In contrast, there was a marked lack of political and social movements self-identifying and shaping their political discourse and mobilization primarily as 'Sunni' in the same period, even though tribal affiliation for some could still constitute a form of political identification.[14]

A new nationalist movement emerged in 1938. Strikes erupted at the local oil company Bapco, protesting against a crackdown by Belgrave on alleged underground youth and labour movements. The company fired the striking workers, and subsequently eight notable members of both sects, four Sunni and four Shiʻa, got together to put forward a list of demands to the government. These included the formation of

12 For a similar analysis in Iraq of Shiʻa-centric mobilization see: Fanar Haddad, 'Shiʻa-centric state building and Sunni rejection in Post-2003 Iraq' (Paper, Carnegie Endowment for International Peace, 2016), http://carn-egieendowment.org/2016/01/07/Shiʻa-centric-state-building-and-sunni-rejection-in-post-2003-iraq-pub-62408.
13 For a study that looks at the political traditions of Shiʻa Islamism in the Gulf in the twentieth century see: Laurence Louër, *Transnational Shiʻa Politics: Religious and Political Networks in the Gulf* (New York: Columbia University Press, 2008).
14 This would markedly change with the February 2011 protests, where a new 'Sunni' consciousness, although still inchoate, would emerge.

an elected legislative body, reforming the courts so that judicial matters were in Bahraini hands, replacing foreign police with locals, and forming a committee to represent workers in the oil company.[15] This marked the first time that both 'Sunnis' and 'Shi'as' would explicitly present themselves as putting forward common nationalist demands in a jointly signed statement.

Two leading members of the group were Sa'ad al-Shamlan, back from exile, and Ahmad al-Shirawi, the cousin of Qasem al-Shirawi. Thus, after a few years in the doldrums between exile and a worsening economic situation, in which many lost their status as affluent members of society, some figures from al-Nahda would return to the political scene. The seeds they sowed would grow to form the basis of the biggest political movements on the islands until the 1970s.

The changing socio-economic conditions in many ways worked to favour al-Nahda ideals. The spread of their discourses and demands multiplied rapidly with the increasing availability of standardized schooling, roads, radios, newspapers, and other forms of mass communication that became staples of society. In addition, there was increased militancy and labour consciousness among workers in the oil industry, honed by contact with organized labour from abroad, in addition to importing the militancy of the pearl workers, many of whom switched now to working in the oil industry. This provided fertile ground for al-Nahda ideals, and consequently its ideas and discourses ceased to be confined within a small circle of the intelligentsia, spreading between the newly emergent professional and working classes and beyond.

The field where the al-Nahda reformers probably had the longest lasting impact in Bahrain and the wider Gulf was the

---

15 Almahmood, *The Rise and Fall of Bahrain's Merchants*, 80–81.

introduction of institutionalized education in local society. Al-Hedaya school quickly opened another branch in Manama in 1921, and by 1927 there were four al-Hedaya schools around the island. The first local school for girls followed in 1928 amidst much objection. The initial site was in Muharraq in the house of 'Abdul Rahman, a relative of 'Abdulwahhab al-Zayyani, before moving to its own purpose-built place. The same year also saw the first group of four Bahrainis sent for higher education to the American University of Beirut, amidst British terpidation.[16] The following year, a group of Shi'a merchants opened the al-Ja'fariyya school in Manama, the first school catering specifically to Shi'as only.

Throughout the 1920s, the education committee continued to exercise independence from the government in running the schools. This never sat well with the British Adviser, Belgrave, who was worried about the Arabist and anti-colonial ideas propagated in the schools and continued to view institutionalized education in Bahrain with mixed feelings until his departure in the mid-1950s.[17] In 1930, the Adviser and the government forcibly took over education oversight from the committee. 'Uthman al-Hourani, the popular Syrian headmaster of al-Hedaya school (who came to Bahrain on the recommendation of the legendary Syrian modernist Sate' al-Husri), was dismissed and deported from Bahrain.[18] Large demonstrations ensued and were forcibly

16 QDL, 'File 9/1 Institution of Reforms & Sunni opposition intrigues' [189r] (394/504), IOR/R/15/2/127, https://www.qdl.qa/archive/81055/vdc_100023321443.0x0000c3.

17 See: Charles Dalrymple Belgrave, *Personal Column* (Beirut: Librairie du Liban, 1972).

18 Sati' al-Husri was an influential Arab nationalist thinker who played a central role in setting up the educational systems of many countries of the Arab world. For more on 'Uthman al-Hourani see chapter 4.

put down. A more amenable head of schools, the Syrian Fa'ik Adham, was installed. Over the next few years, modern schools catering specifically to Shi'as only were abolished and unified with the rest of the educational system, and Belgrave eventually put his wife in charge of women's education. The ruler's brother Sh. 'Abdulla bin Isa, who by now was fully on board with the government, continued in his post as head of education for the rest of the decade. Standardized institutional education rapidly expanded throughout Bahrain, with enrolled students reaching more than a thousand by 1935, and the first school located in the villages opening in the same year.[19] Schooling eventually became mandatory for all the population, and by the end of the twentieth century Bahrain would boast the highest literacy rates in the Arab world.

The other field in which the Bahraini al-Nahda left an indelible mark is in mass media. Looming large in this domain is the figure of 'Abdulla al-Zayed, who brought the first modern printing press to Bahrain in 1932. He was responsible for launching the first periodical on the islands, the weekly *Al-Bahrain* magazine, in 1939. With al-Zayed its only editor, the magazine was beset by financial problems, a lack of paper supplies during the Second World War, and very close scrutiny by British officials.[20]

---

19 The best resource on the history of education in Bahrain is: Abdul Hamid al-Muhadeen, *al-Khurouj min al-'Utma* (Beirut: Arab Institute for Research and Publishing, 2003). For Belgrave's take on the events leading to the government takeover of education see: QDL, 'Government of Bahrain Administrative Report for the Years 1926–1937' [26r] (51/86), IOR/R/15/1/750/1, https://www.qdl.qa/en/archive/81055/vdc_100024140826.0x000034.

20 It seems that British officials actively provided material to be included in the magazine. It is unclear whether al-Zayed was a willing partaker or instead was pressured to distribute British-sanctioned material. I am particularly indebted to discussion with Talal al-Rashoud, Wafa al-Sayyed, and Rashid al-Jassim on this matter.

The periodical only lasted until 1945, and al-Zayed died shortly afterwards in 1946.[21] The publication, however, set the stage for the flourishing of printed media in Bahrain in the following decade, as a host of newspapers and magazines mushroomed in the 1950s onwards. These publications involved individuals who worked with al-Zayed and were directly mentored or inspired by the early al-Nahda group, and who in turn also went on to lead political mobilization in the country.[22]

The strategies and tactics of the state and its colonial backers were also modified in the face of these social and political changes. The use of the ethnosectarian gaze now had to be reconciled with the new form of modernized absolutism that was being sculpted on the islands, which faced the task of ruling over all 'local subjects' regardless of their ethnicities and sects. The way these tensions were consolidated (but never resolved entirely) in Bahrain was through entrenching absolutism via the monopolization of sovereign power and the conception of the nation in the head of the state, while the population was to be governed through vertical segmentation based on the ethno-sectarian gaze. From here onwards, the population was to be seen as a collection of ethnicities and sects,[23] watched from the top by a sovereign with a bird's eye view, who held these groups together under his conception of the nation. Any movements

21 For more on al-Zayed's publishing activities see: Mubarak al-Khater, *Nabeghat al-Bahrain 'Abdulla al-Zayed* (Bahrain: Government Press, 1988).

22 *Al-Qafela* and *Al-Watan*, for example, were two prominent newspapers in the 1950s, in which many of the leading figures in the National Unity Committee of 1953–1956 actively participated, including 'Abdul Rahman al-Baker and Mohammad Qasem al-Shirawi.

23 Abdulhadi Khalaf, 'Contentious Politics in Bahrain: From Ethnic to National and Vice Versa', paper presented at the Fourth Nordic Conference on Middle East Studies, Oslo, 1998.

that would arise against this absolutist rule and its image of the nation would be reduced to their elements of ethnicities and sects and dealt with accordingly.

Thus, in keeping with their deeply ingrained views, the British would pass down the reading and labelling of all political movements in ethnosectarian terms, with the biggest source of opposition now seen as the 'Sunnis' of Muharraq. Belgrave labelled the 1938 movement as one mainly driven by 'Huwala', whom he would classify now as 'Persian'. For his role, Sa'ad al-Shamlan would derogatorily be called a 'negro'.[24] Belgrave moved to divide the movement by courting its 'Shi'a' and 'Baharna' leaders through granting reform in Shi'a courts, in return for a promise that they would suspend their support for the movement.[25] On the other side, the 'Sunni' members were imprisoned, tortured, and exiled. Belgrave arrested Sa'ad al-Shamlan and Ahmad al-Shirawi, accusing them of instigating the protests in Bapco, and after a period of imprisonment and hard labour they were evicted to India where the former would spend his remaining days.[26]

'Divided rule' also continued under the new system, but by this point the 'contested sovereignty' part and the associated instability was largely resolved, at least in regards to the relations between the local ruler and the British. Both were now on the same page, largely drafted by the latter. Britain continued to

24 QDL, 'Government of Bahrain Annual Report for Year 1357 (March 1938 – February 1939)' [104r] (45/80), IOR/R/15/1/750/3, http://www.qdl.qa/en/archive/81055/vdc_100024140827.0x000008.

25 QDL, 'Government of Bahrain Annual Report for Year 1357 (March 1938 – February 1939)' [104r] (45/80), IOR/R/15/1/750/3, http://www.qdl.qa/en/archive/81055/vdc_100024140827.0x000008.

26 Interview, Noora al-Shirawi. Also: Al-Hadi, A'yan al-Bahrain, 359–361, and Fouziyya Matar, Ahmad al-Shamlan, 49–54.

exercise jurisdiction over foreigners, while the ruler theoretically exercised sovereignty over locals, with Belgrave the Adviser running affairs in the background. However, proclamations, laws, and courts tended to be harmonized over time between the two jurisdictions, with both the emblem of the local government and the British Political Agency appearing on official government proclamations during the rest of the 1920s. Over time, Britain even tended to hand back more and more jurisdiction over subjects to the ruler, given that the two systems were largely reconciled.

This was further strengthened by the fact that nationalities and passports had become a common feature across the region and the world through the 1930s. As state borders in the region hardened, the centuries-old movement of people across the shores and ports of the Gulf became subject to the dictates of state passports, nationalities, and citizenship laws. In tandem with the advent of the oil industry, most of the 'foreigners' arriving in Bahrain now increasingly came from the Indian subcontinent carrying British passports, as the flow of people into the island morphed and expanded beyond the areas surrounding the Gulf. No longer was there the same level of heightened contestation and fuzziness regarding who was a 'foreigner' vs. 'local' that occurred in the early period of divided rule, a time in which, as we saw, no such modern political categorizations existed, and when the vast majority of people came from areas surrounding the Gulf.

However, this did not mean that regional tensions and contradictions around the newly emergent system of states, nationalities, and passports ceased to appear. Examples include Iran continuing to refuse recognition of Bahraini sovereignty and passports. On the other side of the Gulf, Dubai began issuing passports without consulting with the British, creating a market for passports and a rich arena for forum shopping. This was often used by pearl divers, gold smugglers, and other agents looking for legal loopholes across the region.[27]

A notable new development within the newly forming state in Bahrain was the emergence of a nation-building discourse. True, it was slanted to a particular reading of the nation and its traditions, as well as being in many ways inchoate and halting, but the appearance of such a discourse is unmistakeable. As the nationalist current gained strength regionally and globally, and the ideas of self-determination gained wider currency in the world, such resonance had its effects on the state in Bahrain. Commonalities rather than ethno-sect differences were increasingly emphasized, at least in the official discourse. Terms such as 'Bahraini' and 'national' began appearing at an increasing rate from the 1930s onwards in its official publications, strengthened by the issuance of corresponding nationality laws and passports.

In fact, it would not be too far off to postulate that in the new emergent climate of nationalism, a remarkable trait of official state discourse is the near-complete absence of overt ethno-sect terminologies such as 'Sunni' and 'Shi'a' when talking about 'citizens'. This is in complete contrast to the manic obsession of British officials with ethnosectarian categories in the first quarter of the twentieth century, where nearly every single document and correspondence is filled with discussions of

---

27 Another prominent contestation surrounding nationalities was the emergence of the issue of the 'Bedoons' (Stateless) in the region: individuals from the region, largely from socio-economic backgrounds that prevented them from obtaining passports and nationalities when they were first issued, who ended up being stateless subjects. For a study on the Bedoon in Kuwait see: Claire Beaugrand, *Stateless in the Gulf: Migration, Nationality and Society in Kuwait* (London: I.B.Tauris, 2017).

'Sunnis' vs. 'Shiʿas' vs. 'Baharna' vs. 'Huwala'.[28] This intentional hiding of an overtly sectarian narrative would be a prevalent feature of state discourse from the 1930s, and would continue until today in modified forms.[29] 'Bahraini' would in many ways become the ambivalent opposite to the ethnosectarian gaze, both from the viewpoint of political movements as well as the regime, and it would become a concept open to contestation between the different parties in Bahrain's political scene. From the state's perspective, the first nationality law of Bahrain, enacted in 1937, had no mention of ethnicities or sects whatsoever, and instead based nationality on a combination of both the principles of *jus soli* and *jus sanguinis*.[30] Anyone who was born in Bahrain, or whose father or paternal grandfather was born in Bahrain, or who had resided in Bahrain for ten or more years, was entitled to Bahraini citizenship.[31]

This ascendancy of 'nation-building' reflected several factors. First and most obvious was the strength of the emergent nationalist discourse, both locally, regionally, and internationally. This was a time of anti-colonial and nationalist fervour, and the main

28 This ethnosectarian obsession of British officials in Bahrain would continue well into the 1970s. For example, see the report sent by the British embassy after the legislative elections of 1973, in which all elected members were classified primarily by ethnicity and sect: *The British National Archives*, FCO 8/2180.

29 This can be easily verified by picking up any official newspaper and browsing state proclamations across its issues, whether from the 1970s or the twenty-first century. While talk of 'citizens' and 'nationals' abound, there is rarely any overt discussion of nationals in ethnosectarian terms.

30 *Jus sanguinis* refers to citizenship by 'right of blood' or ancestry, usually determined by paternal lineage. *Jus soli* refers to citizenship based on 'right of soil', or the land where a person is born. Over time, the citizenship law in Bahrain would be modified so that the first would become more dominant.

31 Husain AlBaharna, *The Legal Status of the Arabian Gulf States* (Manchester: Manchester University Press, 1968), 125.

opposition movements were increasingly taking on a nationalist flavour. Secondly, states with defined boundaries became increasingly the norm in the world, and this was no different in Bahrain. Finally, and probably most importantly, the state had to try to impose hegemonic rule over its population. Governing them purely as different and warring ethnicities and sects, instead of also as a unified set of national citizens, would not be too conducive in this matter. State official discourse would become filled with terms such as 'citizens', 'nationals', and 'Bahrainis', while 'Sunni' and 'Shi'a' subjects would gradually take a back seat from the 1930s onwards. When sects had to be mentioned, they were usually indirectly referred to as 'al-ta'ifatain al-kareematain' (the honourable two sects), instead of overtly mentioning Sunnis and Shi'as, a practice that continues until today.[32]

The new mode of rule even actively sought to co-opt and involve individuals influenced by the al-Nahda group. This is not too surprising, given that many of the involved families historically had close relationships with the al-Khalifa, and they were some of the earliest to receive standardized education. Probably the most prominent example is that of Yousuf al-Shirawi, the son of Ahmad al-Shirawi. Even though he imprisoned and exiled his father, Belgrave took him under his wing as a mentee, and Yousuf eventually became one of the leading figures in the Bahraini government apparatus for nearly half a century, holding the position of Minister of Development amongst many others.[33]

32 See for example the following news article from the Northern Area Municipality from 6 June 2015: 'Tantalek min zera'at dur al-'ibada fi madinat Hamad', Northern Area Municipality, http://websrv.municipality.gov. bh/north/pages/newsDetails_en.jsp?param=644.
33 For a brief overview on Yousuf al-Shirawi see: 'Yousuf Ahmad al-Shirawi', Al-Wasat newspaper, 4 February 2004, http://www.alwasatnews.

However, ethnosectarian readings continued to play a dominant role in defining the regime's strategy and discourse in
times of strong internal opposition and crises. Learning from
what the British implemented in the first quarter of the twentieth century, sectarian cleavages in such cases would continue to
be a vital, and indeed the predominant tool resorted to by the
regime to fragment opposition movements along sectarian
lines. Such sectarian discourse and practice by the state was
used to fragment the opposition in the 1938 movement, and it
would be used again to fragment movements in the 1950s, the
1970s, the 1990s, and most recently during the 2011 political
explosion. Thus, the state increasingly tried to impose a particular hegemonic version of obedient citizens and nationals, which
it never succeeded entirely in achieving due to contestation by
oppositional forces, while at the same time resorting to the
ethnosectarian gaze whenever any emergent movement threatened its monopoly on political rule.

Ethnosectarianism would also interact and reverberate
regionally across the Gulf. During the rise of the Shah's expan-
sionary nationalist and state policies in the 1920s and early
1930s, the Arabs of the Muhammarah region in Iran would
experience increasing harassment after the deposition of their
leader Shaikh Khaz'al. A petition was organized by leaders of
the 'Baharna community' in Muhammarah to Bahrain's ruler
and British officials, pleading for assistance to step up to their
aid. Many moved to the islands during this period. Writing

---

com/news/362061.html. Another notable example is 'Abdulaziz al-
Shamlan of the NUC, who after returning from imprisonment and exile in
1972 was publicly welcomed by the government and took up several offi-
cial positions, including ambassador to Egypt. For more see: Abdalla al-
Madani, 'Min al-Manfa ela al-Safara: Hekayat Mu'ared Watani Sharif', *Al-
Ayam* newspaper, 11 April 2014, https://goo.gl/Swc8D9.

about the situation, the British Adviser Belgrave declared that 'the Baharna would rather die than become Persian subjects'.[34] Such statements, like those of his predecessors who stated that 'all Shi'as are Persians', 'the Huwala are without solidarity amongst themselves', or claimed that all of the Baharna wanted to be under British jurisdiction, are more useful as an indication of the ethnosectarian essentializing mentality of their utterers, rather than being accurate reflections of the subaltern they professed to help.

The hardening nationalist discourse and policies in Iran after the Shah seized power in 1921 increasingly reverberated in Bahrain. The Shah refused to acknowledge the existence of most of the Gulf Arab States throughout the 1920s and 1930s, declined to accept their passports and visas, and began putting forward claims that Bahrain was part of Iran. Iranian nationalism took root within a small but significant group of individuals in Bahrain, who came to identify themselves as Iranian, particularly concentrating in the city of Manama.[35] Considered foreigners with British jurisdiction under the ongoing system of divided rule, self-identified 'Persians' in Manama continued to run their own school, and a large proportion continued to hold Iranian passports. Some organized scout groups and held parades in which pictures of the Shah and the Iranian flag were raised, causing ire to the British officials and the local ruler.[36]

34 Louis Allday, 'Britain's Interest in Bahrain', *Qatar Digital Library*, http://www.qdl.qa/en/britain%E2%80%99s-%E2%80%98interest%E2%80%99-bahrain.
35 Iranian nationalism as a political phenomenon emerged mainly in the city of Manama. In contrast, it was nearly non-existent in other areas where individuals who self-identify as 'Ajam also resided (e.g. Muharraq).
36 QDL, 'File 9/11 Grant of Passports and Permits by the Bahrain Government and Treaty with Persia relative to withdrawal of claim to'

The state eventually restricted the right to own property to local citizens in the late 1930s, largely in order to force self-identified 'Persians' to obtain Bahraini citizenship. In turn, this increase in the number of 'Persians' with Bahraini citizenship did not sit well with proponents of Arab nationalism, and many came to see them as a fifth column. It was nationalism, rather than sectarianism, that would emerge as the dominant framework and the point of contestation in local politics for the next half-century.

From their side, the al-Nahda-inspired political movements would grow over time and prove to be the biggest thorn in the side of the new colonialist-absolutist regime for the next forty years. Just as the state was to invent and hone its traditions[37] of nation-building and governance, so would these political movements create and build their own traditions of resistance that would continue to be carried, modified, and passed down the decades until this day.[38] In many cases, there were direct familial lineages, where such discourses and demands were inherited generation after generation, and moulded and adapted according to the new situations they faced.

The unfolding decades saw the drifting apart of two strands that were previously merged in the writings of Mohammad 'Abduh and the founding group of al-Nahda in Bahrain, with each establishing its own set of traditions across people, space, and time. On the one hand were those who held on to Islamic principles and saw Islam as the basis

---

[20r] (41/150), IOR/R/15/2/138, https://www.qdl.qa/en/archive/81055/vdc_100023045639.0x00002a.

37 Eric Hobsbawm, Terence Ranger (eds.), *The Invention of Tradition* (Cambridge: Cambridge University Press, 2012).

38 Karma Nabulsi, *Traditions of War*. I am particularly indebted to Abdel Razzaq Takriti for his thoughts on this topic.

for political and societal reformation. This would be crystallized in Egypt with the founding of the Muslim Brotherhood in 1928. On the other hand, there were those who believed that political life needed to be run according to secular norms. For most, the secular principle that should govern society was that of nationalism, becoming the precursor to many of the nationalist and leftist groups that would emerge throughout the twentieth century in both Bahrain and the wider Arab world.[39]

The first strand to take concrete political party form in Bahrain was that of the Islamist reformists, encapsulated in the establishment of a chapter of the Muslim Brotherhood in Bahrain under the name of the al-Islah Society in 1941. This was the first institutionalized political movement in Bahrain, which began as a society set up by students of al-Hedaya school. The contacts between the Brotherhood in Egypt and Bahrain seem to stretch to an even earlier time. The June 1937 monthly periodical of the Brotherhood stated that the nineteenth district for Brotherhood activity in the Islamic World included the islands of Bahrain. Their representative was mentioned as Sh. Mohammed bin Ebrahim, the son of the poet with the celebrated Majlis in Muharraq.[40]

The first president of al-Islah was Sh. Khaled bin Mohammed bin ʿAbdulla al-Khalifa, the son of Sh. Mohammad bin ʿAbdulla, the first president of the Literary Club, and the grandson of Sh. ʿAbdulla bin Isa, the deposed ruler's son. His brother Sh. Isa bin Mohammad would become the leading figure in the society, holding its presidency for more than five decades from 1963

---

39 Hourani, *Arabic Thought*, preface, vi.
40 'Al-Ikhwan al-muslimoon fi Qatar wal Bahrain', *Al-Majalla*, 11 June 2013, https://goo.gl/X878Tg.

until his passing away in 2015.[41] The society was never to play a dominant role in Bahraini politics, and was distinguished from Muslim Brotherhood organizations elsewhere by the close involvement of individuals from the ruling family in its founding and leadership. It did, however, herald the establishment of the first Islamist political movement in Bahrain, directly tracing its first roots to al-Nahda.

The second, 'secularizing' wing would manifest itself most clearly in movements based on linguistic nationalism, and more specifically Arab nationalism, where all who spoke Arabic constituted a nation.[42] In this manner, 'Arab' was not defined primarily based on a racialized or blood-lineage interpretation, but on the primacy of the spoken tongue.[43] This strand was to become the dominant political strand by the 1950s, with al-Nahda sowing the first seeds of Arab nationalism and a pan-Bahraini identity; one that transcended sect and made colonial Britain its enemy, and reform of local rule the centre of its demands.

This was a revolutionary period in the Arab world, with Jamal ʿAbdul Nasser in Egypt propelling the rising tide of Arab nationalism. In Bahrain, the movement would crystallize itself in the establishment of the National Union Committee (NUC) during 1953–1956, the largest political movement in Bahrain's history, which would display comparative demands and a similar, nationalist, anti-colonial, anti-authoritarian discourse to the

41 Iman Ahmad, ʿAl-Ikhwan al-muslimoon fil Bahrain wa idarat al-tahawwulat al-rahina', *Egyptian Institute for Political and Strategic Studies*, 13 January 2016, https://goo.gl/MN6Zc6.

42 Hourani, *Arabic Thought*, 341.

43 Hence, it could theoretically also include individuals who self-identified as ʿAjam and spoke Arabic, despite its lack of appeal to many of them in Bahrain.

movements of 1923 and 1938. The demands put forward included the establishment of an elected legislative body, a general legal code, labour unions, the reformation of the court system, as well as the favouring of Bahraini as opposed to foreign workers in the oil company. As was the case with other Arab nationalist movements in the Gulf, its discourse was chequered with an anti-'Persians' streak, whose notables were accused of colluding with foreign powers and the British-backed local regime.[44] In Bahrain, this was strengthened by the fact that the leaders of Iran kept on claiming their sovereignty over the islands.

Nationalism in Bahrain has tended to present itself in two traditions that often overlapped, with each ebbing and flowing in strength across the unfolding twentieth century. In addition to linguistic nationalism based on Arab identity, civic nationalism would also become a central feature of these political movements, focusing their goals on activating citizenship based on public participation in decision making.[45] Just like the movements in 1923, 1938, and the latter ones in the 1970s and the 1990s, the NUC would put forward demands for reforms and representation in government and worker unions, issues that would continue to be central platforms of political movements throughout the twentieth century.

Reflecting its sensitivity to underlying sectarian tensions, the NUC emulated the 1938 movement and elected eight leaders, four Sunni and four Shi'a, to represent its demands. One of

44 It is worth mentioning that this streak was trans-sectarian, as it was displayed by many Arab nationalists from both sects.

45 Rogers Brubaker, 'The Manichean myth: Rethinking the distinction between "civic" and "ethnic" nationalism', in Hanspeter Kries, *Nation and National Identity: The European Experience in Perspective* (West Lafayette, Indiana: Purdue University Press, 1999), 55–71.

the most charismatic leaders and dynamos of the movement was ʿAbdul ʿAziz al-Shamlan, the son of Saʿad al-Shamlan, who would inherit his father's anti-colonial and reformist fervour. Another notable member of the NUC was Mohammed al-Shirawi, the son of Qasem al-Shirawi. He headed its labour chapter and was its chief negotiator in establishing Bahrain's 1957 Labour Law, the first labour law of its kind in the Gulf.

Once again, and as they have done across time and generations, the British and the regime would continue in periods of political crises to reduce people's identities and actions to an elemental ethnosectarian unit of analysis, upon which they would measure the person's value, position, and tendencies to act. The strongest base of the NUC was in the urban areas, particularly in Muharraq, and given that most of the originators of the NUC and its supporters were 'Sunni', if one were to employ an ethnosectarian lens, Belgrave attempted to divide the movement on that front.[46] He accused the NUC of mainly being driven by Huwala and Sunnis. He labelled ʿAbdulaziz al-Shamlan, the son of Saʿad, as the son of a disreputable 'negro'. In a case of deja vu, he would try to create a Shiʿa-notables counter-bloc to the NUC, which this time would not fully succeed in splitting the movement by sect.[47] Finally, when violent protests broke out in November 1956 to denounce the tripartite aggression against Egypt after the nationalization of the Suez Canal, he used them as an excuse to arrest and deport

46 Interview, Jasem Murad and ʿAli Rabia, 4 September 2017. The two main drivers of the NUC, ʿAbdulrahman al-Baker and ʿAbdulaziz al-Shamlan, had initially encountered great difficulties in convincing notable Shiʿas to publicly join the NUC, until Ebrahim al-ʿUrayyedh suggested that they approach Sayyed ʿAli Kamaluddin, a religious cleric, who agreed to join.
47 Khalaf, 'Contentious Politics'.

the leaders of the NUC, with some sent into exile on the island of St Helena.[48]

The dissolution of the NUC marked a shift in Bahraini political movements from civic nationalist, reformist, and public demands towards a more radical agenda of clandestine organizations for the overthrow of the regime. Two movements dominated the scene during the 1960s and the 1970s. The first was the National Liberation Front (NLF), a chapter of the Communist Party that had strong ties to the Iranian Tudeh party and the Iraqi Communist Party. The second was the Movement of Arab Nationalists (MAN), which aimed to liberate Palestine and the wider Arab World by revolutionary means. Both movements attracted hundreds of cadres from across Bahrain's regions and social backgrounds. Many of these members were directly inspired by the NUC, and in many cases had familial and neighbourly connections with them. Such is the case, for example, with Ahmad al-Shamlan, the nephew of Sa'ad al-Shamlan and a noted member of the Movement of Arab Nationalists in the 1960s, before switching to the communist National Liberation Front in the 1970s.[49] As a poet, he became noted for penning the words of 'Tareekuna' (Our Way), a celebrated anthem of nationalist and leftist movements in Bahrain, thus helping cement the radical traditions inspired by al-Nahda across time and generations.[50]

48 For more on the NUC see: Omar AlShehabi, 'Divide and Rule in Bahrain and the Elusive Pursuit for a United Front: The Experience of the Constitutive Committee and the 1972 Uprising', *Historical Materialism* 21.1 (2013): 94–127, 100–102.

49 He then also became a prominent member and lawyer in the 1990s constitutional movement, which once again would display similar nationalist and reformist demands.

50 Ahmad al-Shamlan and Majeed Marhoon, 'Tareekuna', https://www.youtube.com/watch?v=VViLGQTO6rQ, uploaded by YouTube user Silveroo85.

THE RISE OF THE PETRO-MODERNIST
STATE AND ISLAMISM

In 1968, Britain announced its intention to withdraw from areas east of the Suez Canal, and Bahrain was granted independence in 1971. As *Pax Britannica* formally came to an end in the Gulf, the ruling family became more assertive locally, although British influence continued to play a significant role, particularly in supervising internal policing matters. A new ally appeared for the regime in the shape of the United States of America, which chose the islands to station its navy's Fifth Fleet. The influence of Sa'udi Arabia also began to loom large on its smaller neighbour. Consequently, the newly independent regime was firmly anchored within the US–Sa'udi alliance in the emerging global order of the Cold War.

The year of independence also marked the establishment of the Constitutive Committee (CC) for the General Federation of Workers in Bahrain, the first organized public mass movement in Bahrain's independent era, as well as being the first public movement in Bahrain's history where sect considerations did not play any role in its creation whatsoever.[51] This period was the zenith of the secular nationalist and leftist movements, as ethnosectarian considerations were relegated to the back seat. As the industries and sectors in Bahrain's economy expanded, so did the labour movements situated within them. The CC capitalized by initiating a public drive towards the establishment of a General Union to represent workers. This also served as an impetus for the clandestine formation of labour syndicates within the different industries. One of CC's core leaders was 'Ali al-Shirawi, the son of Mohammed and the

51 Omar AlShehabi, 'Divide and Rule'.

grandson of Qasem al-Shirawi, who was actively involved in setting up the teachers' syndicate, thereby continuing to carry his ancestors' al-Nahda political traditions, albeit in modified forms.

The rising labour militancy was led in large part by the NLF and the Popular Front for the Liberation of Oman and the Arabian Gulf (PFLOAG), the heir to the MAN as it moved left-wards and adopted a Marxist-Leninist ideology. By this point, the support base that these movements drew from had extended rapidly across the cities and villages of Bahrain, drawing individuals from a diverse set of social backgrounds. Thus, the secretary general of the PFLOAG in exile was Abdulrahman al-Noaimi, whose family hailed from one of the notable tribes of the Arabian Peninsula, and his comrade in charge of foreign relations was 'Abdul-Nabi al-'Ekri, who grew up in the village of al-Daih. The direct familial connections to the early al-Nahda roots continued to play a significant role. For example, a leading member in the Arab-Marxist PFLOAG, a union leader, as well as a participant in the Dofar revolution in nearby Oman was 'Abdulmen'em al-Shirawi, the brother of the aforementioned 'Ali.[52]

The CC's request for a union licence was not granted, and the simmering situation culminated with the workers' uprising and strikes of 1972. The authorities arrested the leaders of the CC and put down the protests. However, the activities of the CC, along with British and Kuwaiti pressures for some cosmetic reform, opened the way for a promise to establish the Constituent Assembly of 1972, a partly elected assembly that was tasked with drafting a constitution for the country.

---

52 Ibid., 100–107. Interviews with 'Abdulmen'em al-Shirawi, 'Ali al-Shirawi, and 'Abdul-Nabi al-'Ekri.

This was followed by elections for the legislative National Assembly, in which leftists and nationalists would constitute the largest bloc, coupled with a strong presence of Shi'a clerical figures representing the villages. The democratic experiment did not last long, and the government dissolved the assembly and declared a state of emergency that lasted for the next twenty-five years. As it cracked down on the nationalists and leftists, arresting and torturing many of their members, it successfully obtained acquiescence from the main Shi'a clerical political figures in not opposing its escalating repression.[53]

The 1973 oil boom coupled with American and Sa'udi backing gave the regime increasing confidence in its authoritarianism, which manifested itself in a new form of modernized absolutism, heralding the rise of the petro-modernist emirate.[54] By this point, the previous coercion-heavy social relations of production, centred around pearl diving in the urban areas and agriculture in the villages, had disappeared nearly completely from the islands. Work for citizens was instead replaced by expanding employment in the bureacracy of the welfare state, financed by the burgeoning oil revenues, with rapid social transformations ensuing. Fordist modes of consumption became the norm, as people emptied from the historic cities of Manama and Muharraq and moved to newly built villas in the suburbs.

Geographically, Bahrain began turning into one overarching metropolitan area that encompassed the historic city centres, new suburban areas, and the villages. This was greatly facilitated

---

53 'Ali Rabee'a, *al-Tajruba al-Maw'uda* (Bahrain: unknown, 2010).
54 Omar AlShehabi, 'Histories of Migration to the Gulf', in Abdulhadi Khalaf et al. (ed.), *Transit States: Labour, Migration & Citizenship in the Gulf* (London: Pluto Press, 2015), 3–38.

by the rapid rise in ownership of cars, and the associated road network system across the island. Although education and health provision also quickly expanded in the agricultural villages from their previous deficit compared to the urban areas, material riches and gains grew at a much lower pace and continued to lag behind other areas of Bahrain, creating visible income and wealth inequalities across the land. Jobs for nationals were mainly concentrated in the public sector and state-owned enterprises, which over time began displaying an ethnosectarian streak in their composition.[55] Most jobs in the private sector of family-owned companies, on the other hand, were populated by newly arrived migrants who were regulated under the Kafala labour sponsorship system.[56]

The recalibration of the local socio-economic scene coincided with significant changes on the regional front, and this would be reflected in a structural reorganization of the local political scene. As the Cold War between the United States and Soviet Union heated up, the former came to regard Islam as a potential bulwark against communism in the region and beyond, taking a friendly approach towards Islamist movements. While the crackdown against nationalist and leftist movements intensified during the 1960s and 1970s in Bahrain

55 There are no official statistics based on sects and social groupings, reflecting the new state's aversion towards overt ethnosectarian discourse. However, popular perception perceives the formation of different ethnosectarian pockets in the local economy, with tribal members seen as concentrating in the military, Huwala in banking, Baharna in health, water, and electricity, and 'Ajams concentrated in the local airline Gulf Air and the aluminium smelter Alba.

56 'Kafala' refers to the set of practices and laws that govern the importation of migrant labour to the Gulf in the oil era, under which each migrant worker has to have a local 'Kafeel' (sponsor) who acts as his legal guardian.

and the wider region, Islamist movements on the other hand were tolerated and sometimes even supported.[57] The year that is usually given in regional historiography as the watershed moment for the rise of Islamism is 1979, as revolution erupted in Iran with the subsequent takeover of rule by Shi'a clerics.[58] This was followed a few months later by the seizure of the Grand Mosque in Mecca by Juhayman al-'Utaybi, which catalysed the Sa'udi 'Sahwa' movement and the increasing turn towards exporting Salafism. The Soviet invasion of Afghanistan also commenced in December 1979, becoming a rallying cry for Islamist forces across the region. These three seismic changes are usually seen to have spectacularly marked the rise of the Islamist current and the receding of the 'secular' strand. One year later, the Iran–Iraq war would ignite and continue for another eight years. There were now global and regional factors that would cross-feed with local politics and influence its sectarianization.

Correspondingly, the state's ethnosectarian readings of the opposition movements would also change. While 'Sunnis' were

57 A notable example would be the cleric Hadi al-Modarresi, who settled in Bahrain in 1969 after fleeing the Ba'ath in Iraq. He cultivated close connections with members of the ruling family in the early 1970s, even appearing on national TV. Modarresi would eventually become a lightning rod for many oppositional Shi'a Islamist movements and one of the most vocal opponents of the ruling family, calling for its overthrow.

58 There is a need for in-depth political histories of Bahrain and the Gulf from the 1980s onwards, including the rise of sectarianism, with much of the prevailing historiography for this period in need of re-examination. For example, there is not necessarily a direct and linear relationship between sectarianism and the rise of Islamism, as this study has demonstrated in the case of the colonial era. Furthermore, a detailed look at the linkages between the colonial and the post-independence eras becomes crucial, including at the regional, state, and political movements level.

viewed by the British and the local rulers as the main source of opposition from the 1920s to the 1950s, culminating with the rise of nationalist and leftist movements in the 1960s and 1970s, Shiʿa Islamists were now identified as the new largest threat to the regime as the 1980s wore on. Particularly, religious clerics and their supporters based in the villages, previously seen by British officials as a conservative force that could be amenable to cooperation, would now constitute the backbone of the opposition until recent times, particularly since the 1990s uprising. In turn, the regime's repression would increasingly target the opposition based on their ethno-sect identities.

As the American–British invasion of Iraq in 2003 propelled sectarianization across the region, the ruling family in Bahrain placed itself firmly within the Saʿudi camp, while many of the opposition established links with the Islamic Republic of Iran and the Shiʿa-centric political forces that now dominated politics in Iraq. The regime cracked down on widespread protests during 2011, and as the misnamed 'Arab Spring' gave way to regional conflicts, Bahrain became a key fault line in the Saʿudi–Iranian rivalry. A modified form of sectarianism would once again dominate the political field of the islands, as the new international, regional, and local dynamics fed into the roots planted in the colonial era. The ethnosectarian gaze would re-emerge as the primary lens through which to read and practise politics in Bahrain.

CONCLUSION: STATE AND SOCIETY BETWEEN SECTARIANISM AND NATIONALISM

T he lineages of modern sectarianism in Bahrain can be traced to the period of the first quarter of the twentieth century, when colonial involvement reached its height through divided and contested rule. When the British forcibly entered local political affairs at the turn of the century, the islands were experiencing an unprecedented pearling and trading boom during the global age of capital. The corresponding rapid rise of the cities of Manama and Muharraq manifested itself in a distinctive urban–rural divide, both socially and politically. Agricultural villages were ruled as fiefdoms by senior members of the ruling family, imposing direct taxation and corvée on their inhabitants. The situation differed markedly in the towns, as taxes on traders and craftsmen were kept comparatively low. However, pearl divers who composed the majority of the working population were subject to debt-bondage by ship captains and financiers, with little interference from the ruling family.

This urban–rural social scene was woven within an intricate web of locality, kinship, class, madhhab, and profession, producing a fragmented system of popular politics and patronage. Overall, domestic political rule was largely decentralized and personalized with minimal bureaucratic structures, showing significant customized variation based on the context and individuals involved. Region-wise, politics were dictated by temporary alliances and tribute payments in the midst of other tribal confederations and larger imperial forces, above all the rising *Pax Brittanica* in the Gulf's waters. The ultimate aim of the rulers was to navigate such regional intrigues and maintain domestic rule over a diverse social scene, so that they could maximize taxes extracted from subjects under their jurisdiction.

British officials came to read this complex social landscape primarily in ethnosectarian terms. They perceived society to be made up of two distinct 'communities' that formed the basic building blocks to understanding the local population: Sunnis and Shi'as. Each sect was subdivided into large ethnic groupings, ruled overall by the al-Khalifa family. When Britain forcibly claimed sovereignty over all 'foreigners' in Bahrain, it came to define 'foreignness' primarily through these ethnosectarian groupings. Thus, sects and ethnicities defined the main groups in societies, which in turn were accordingly categorized as 'foreign' and 'local' subjects under British or domestic sovereignty. Laws, institutions, discourses, and actions rapidly formed around this colonial ethnosectarian gaze under the new system of divided rule. Other actors contested the fuzzy parameters of this field both locally and regionally, including the ruler, Ibn Sa'ud, the Qajar empire, local notables, and ordinary people. Ethnosectarian mobilization increasingly dominated the unstable political conjuncture, which would spectacularly explode by 1923 as events spiralled out of control and British officials took over complete rule.

Thus, by 1923, Bahrain in the eyes of the British had become an unruly collection of warring ethnicities and sects, surrounded by regional intrigues, and headed by an ineffective, weak, and despotic ruler. This had to be put an end to and the system reorganized. The British acted decisively to 'reform' political power in a modernized manner they perceived to be both more manageable with regard to their interests and fairer to the different ethno-sect 'communities' on the islands. They turned to the mode of rule in the Indian Princely States as a blueprint to sculpt the new form of authoritarianism in Bahrain. The previous political regime was rapidly dismembered and rebuilt through a centralized bureaucracy run by British officers, with the new ruler nominally at the top. Modernized absolutism was thus born for the first time in the Gulf.

Ethnosectarianism was not the only form of political mobilization to emerge in this period. As the al-Nahda renaissance took root in Bahrain during the early twentieth century, a group of intelligentsia emerged that articulated a dynamic mix of anticoloniaism, Arabism, ecumenical Islam, and civic reform. The British colonial apparatus and the local regime it oversaw came to see them as the biggest source of political opposition, with their ideals, actions, and traditions laying the foundations for the nationalist and leftist trend that would dominate the oppositional political scene in Bahrain over the next half-century. The contradictions, overlaps, and contestations that emerged between ethnosectarianism, colonialism, absolutism, and al-Nahda ideals came to define the modern political terrain of Bahrain, their ramifications still powerfully felt today.

POLITICAL POWER, THE STATE,
AND ETHNOSECTARIANISM

The colonial period that marked the rise of modern sectarianism in Bahrain long predated the rise of Islamism or the oil rentier state, concepts that have dominated explanations of sectarianism for the past few decades. However, it is important to acknowledge that this should not be seen as supporting a linear teleological argument for sectarianism that can be read from 1900 until events today. While understanding these historic roots is important, the causality chain should not be overplayed, as several new factors have entered into the calculus over the years, including the discovery of oil, independence, the contestations of the Cold War, the rise of Islamism, the 'War on Terror', the war in Iraq, the Saʿudi–Iranian rivalry, and the repercussions of the Arab uprisings of 2011.

Indeed, one of the main themes of this book is the importance of periodizing events and placing them within their historical context. Political developments in society are not predetermined, but take on a much more open-ended and contingent dimension across space and time. It matters greatly that the events discussed here occurred in the first quarter of the twentieth century, a juncture that predates the advent of the modern state or fully formed nationalism in the Gulf region, and which was instead marked by expanding British imperialism, with a heavy influence of the ethnosectarian gaze. It is unlikely that the state and sectarianism would have followed the same path if direct British involvement had come, for example, fifty years later, or if it was applied to a population with a different social composition than Bahrain.

This often forgotten truism applies equally to the period that is the focus of this book. Most previous writings on the events of 1920–1923 have taken the British narration at face value, viewing them as neutral observers that were witnessing and describing life on the islands as it had been from time immemorial. However, our narration makes clear that the second half of the nineteenth century was in many ways a dynamic period in Bahrain, both in terms of the economic growth and social relations that developed throughout its decades. It is also essential to emphasize that rather than being non-intrusive observers of the situation, the British played a major role in determining how events developed on the ground. This was both through direct intervention, as well as indirectly through the unintended consequences and reactions of other social actors to their imposing presence.

Drawing on Edward Said's insights and applying them to Bahrain's context, the colonial outlook on the islands was not neutral, but a particular orientalist lens that was marked by prevalence of the ethnosectarian gaze.[1] In its essence, the gaze viewed and ordered social relations of power based on reified categories of sects and ethnicities. This in turn would affect developments on the ground, influencing how other social agents perceived and reacted to these categories.[2] These social relations of power were not abstract, but as this work strived to show, they were embodied in concrete networks of people, institutions, laws, wars, and trade. Thus, ethnosectarianism became a form of mobilization to contest the distribution of social power along parameters of ethnicities and sects, whether for British colonial officers, senior members of the ruling

1 Said, *Orientalism.*
2 Such a process has sometimes been referred to as 'dynamic nominalism', whereby many social actors came to interact, react, and reshape the political categories that colonial authorities had initially fashioned. For more see: Chakrabarty, *Habitations of Modernity,* 86.

family, regional actors, or social groups that were previously on the margin. This distribution of power was not even, nor did ethnosectarianism emerge haphazardly, as behind the crystallization of ethno-sect parameters lay specific patterns of domination and conflict in political, economic, military, and ideological affairs.[3] It is in these material networks of social power that ethnosectarianism found the sustenance to emerge and grow.

Given its centrality to political power in the modern era, the nature and role of the state emerge as crucial to understanding ethnosectarianism. In Bahrain's case, the state was exemplified both by the social relations around the ruling family and the British colonial regime, which after the contestations of divided rule were fused together in the new system of modernized absolutism. The tendency to classify, label, and order different subjects into clearly demarcated categories such as 'citizens' vs. 'foreigners', or 'migrants' vs. 'refugees', is a hallmark of the tools of government and rule in any modern state. Such categorizations take on a new dimension when they are enshrined into laws and formal institutions, which serve to sharpen the categories' cleavages and create legal and political consequences to being labelled in one group rather than another.

In many cases such legal categorizations can play a role in the production of political subjects that alter their perceptions of themselves and others around them in society. Such social identities, never completely fixed and always prone to changes and slippage in meaning, were redefined and came to signify

---

3 Michael Mann's conceptualization of social power is helpful in this regard. For more see: John A. Hall and Ralph Schroeder (eds.), *An Anatomy of Power: The Social Theory of Michael Mann* (Cambridge: Cambridge University Press, 2006).

new social and political relations.[4] While intersections and overlaps existed between class, sects, professions, geography, and kinship across space and time in Bahrain, the elevation of ethnosectarian categories by the British above all others and enshrining them into legal and political state institutions catalysed sectarianism to become the dominant game in the early twentieth century. If the ingredients that could allow sectarianism to emerge existed beforehand locally, then colonial divided rule shaped the 'field' on which the game was to be played out, and the parameters of this field were to be ethnosectarian.

Furthermore, events in Bahrain during this period highlight that if the nature and the construction of the state play an important role in laying the ground for the rise of ethnosectarianism, then just as crucial are periods marked by the dissolution of the prevalent mode of government. Such situations allow for a reconfiguration of the relations of power, and the reinvention of networks of locality, kin, and patronage.[5] A crisis of the state above can be connected with the state of the streets below through an acute manifestation of ethnosectarianism.[6] As the previously decentralized, personalized form of governance began disintegrating under British-imposed divided rule, ethnosectarianism emerged as the main form of

4 Stuart Hall, 'Race: the Floating Signifier', Lecture at Goldsmiths College, University of London, 1996, https://youtube.com/watch?v= OtkTkdiF5ZY.

5 Aziz al-Azmeh, 'Sectarianism and Antisectarianism', Keynote address at the Rice University/University of Houston Conference on Arab Traditions of Anti-Sectarianism, 2017, https://www.strikingmargins.com/news-1/ 2017/12/20/prof-aziz-al-azmeh-sectarianism-and-antisectarianism?format=amp.

6 The phrasing is borrowed from: Stuart Hall, *Selected Political writings: The Great Moving Right Show and Other Essays* (Durham, North Carolina: Duke University Press, 2016), 153.

political mobilization in Bahrain. British colonial officers acted decisively to recalibrate the distribution of power and heavily concentrate it in 'the sovereign' under the newly constructed absolutist state. Hence, given a suitable environment of the destabilization of the old order, social actors can re-engineer power relations for sectarianism to emerge as the new politics, whereby ethnicities and sects become the new boundaries for the contestation of power, even if they played a marginal and confined role previously. If we were to instinctively jump to a comparison with the Arab world in our current age after the Iraq 2003 invasion and the 2011 Arab uprisings, such rise of ethnosectarianism amidst the atrophy of previous modes of government finds strong echoes.

An obvious set of questions might come up in this respect: was the emergence of ethnosectaraniasm inevitable in Bahrain? At a more generalized level, could one argue that ethnosectarianism is an inevitable product of any modern state with multiple sects or ethnicities, given the tendency of any state to resort to the classification and ordering of its subjects? If we look at racism as a subset of ethnosectarianism, can we not follow Foucault in saying that any state is racist by its very nature? Does not every state, by definition, categorize particular people as part of its polity, to whom its sovereignty applies, versus 'foreigners'? Is it not the fundamental nature of any state to elevate and focus its care on certain groups that it 'makes live', while having no qualms in relegating or even 'letting die' individuals that do not fall into those groups?[7]

Answering questions about the generalized prevalence and inevitability of sectarianism can only be done through a deep

---

7 Michel Foucault and François Ewald, *'Society Must Be Defended': Lectures at the Collège de France, 1975–1976*. Vol. 1. (New York: Macmillan, 2003).

excavation of several case studies across time and regions. A priori, however, there is little reason to believe this to be the case. The fact that states may categorize people into those who are part of their polity versus 'foreigners' who are excluded, does not entail that all states formally enshrine difference – let alone ethno-sect difference – as a basis of governance *within* their own polity. In fact, many visions, principles, and traditions explicitly argued for the opposite outlook, including civic nationalism and republicanism, advocating instead for ideals of equal and inclusive political citizenship regardless of sect or ethnic background.[8]

Neither is it more convincing to restrict the inevitability of ethnosectarianism to Bahrain, the Gulf, or the Arab world. Such a reading betrays a fatalistic orientalist view of the region as inherently sectarian, while implicitly arguing the pointlessness of any alternative visions and those who fought for them. As our story showed, these competing visions of governance were very much evident in the case of Bahrain, and at several junctures had a marked influence on the state and its politics. Primary amongst them were the demands of civic nationalism advocated by some members of al-Nahda, which continued to inspire many subsequent political groups in Bahrain until today.

Under such ideals, individuals enter the political arena a priori as equal citizens who share membership of one polity. Contrast this with state-sponsored ethnosectarianism as practised in early-twentieth-century Bahrain, which at its heart aimed to produce and reproduce differences between social actors based on

8 This is also not to speak of states that employed ideals of ethnic homogenization. For more on the different scales and ideals of rule employed by empires and states see: Jane Burbank and Frederick Cooper, *Empires in World History*, introduction and chapter 5.

hardened concepts of sects and ethnicities. Each social actor entered the political arena primarily as a member and representative of his sect and ethnicity vis-à-vis other ethnicities and sects. What defined his political value was his ethnosectarian background, and particularly *its inherent difference* to other ethnicities and sects in the political field. The state enshrined and encouraged such a reading whether in terms of the consociational setup of courts, laws, city councils, or its definition of what constituted a 'local' vs. 'foreign' 'subject'. Hence, if equal citizenship for individuals who are a priori part of the same polity is at the heart of the concept of civic nationalism, then enshrined differences between a priori separate groups of ethnicities and sects represents the essence of state-formalized ethnosectarianism.

It becomes evident that empirically reducing the experience of multi-sect states to ethnosectaranism tends to overlook their differences and unique traits across time and space, whether in Bahrain or elsewhere. Surely just as relevant for any analysis should be highlighting the experience and thoughts of the diverse range of political actors and their degree of success in putting forward their ideals, including those that contested and fought such sectarian political categorizations and pushed for alternative visions of rule.

One possibly useful historical comparison would be contrasting the situation in Bahrain in the first half of the twentieth century with areas of similar socio-demographic make-up in the rest of the Gulf at the same period. Particularly of relevance are Kuwait and the Eastern Province of Saʿudi Arabia. A quick first glance suggests that in both cases, and especially in Kuwait and al-Hasa, it is noteworthy there was a relative lack of politics predominantly driven by ethnosectarianism during the twentieth century until the 1970s and the rise of the Islamist wave.

There were two notable differences in each case when compared to Bahrain in the first half of the twentieth century. With regard to the Eastern Province, the ruling al-Saʿud family did not personally appropriate many of the privately owned farms in the agricultural areas when they took over the province from the Ottomans without physical resistance in 1913.⁹ Instead, most of the previous owners continued in their social relationships with those who worked on the farms.¹⁰ Many of the local notables continued to interact with the new rulers in social and political relations that were not too dissimilar from those that existed in the Ottoman period. Consequently, there was not the same direct line of repression as existed between the ruling family and the residents of the agricultural villages in Bahrain in the early twentieth century. Furthermore, neither the Eastern Province nor Saʿudi Arabia were subjected to British colonialism, and so divided or indirect colonial rule was never an issue to contend with.¹¹

9 Studies in English are few, and they are hampered by the current dominance of highly polemic depictions that tend to reductively essentialize the politics of the Eastern Province as one overwhelmingly and almost singularly driven by state-sectarianization and unmitigated repression ever since the beginning of the Saʿudi third state in the early twentieth century. For a contemporary depiction of life under Saʿudi rule during this period by an American see: Paul Wilberforce Harrison, *The Arab at Home* (New York: Thomas Y. Crowell Company, 1924).

10 Although the new state did take over lands previously owned by the Ottoman state, as well as imposing general *Jihad* taxes of its own on the population to replace those of the Ottoman Empire.

11 Of course, one of the most (in)famous features of the al-Saʿud-ʿAbdul Wahhab alliance is a strong Islamic puritan streak that many past Western orientalists found reminiscent of the Reformation, and which is commonly referred to today as 'Wahhabism'. Certain manifestations of Wahhabism did exhibit strong polemics and attacks against different schools and sects of Islam, and these polemics seem to have ebbed and flowed in their

One exception was during the crisis in relations between some residents of Qatif and Ibn Sa'ud in the late 1920s, during his conflict with the Ikhwan forces and the imposition of high taxes across the kingdom in the midst of the government's fiscal crisis. These events are also notable for the involvement of British officials. During the tensions, some individuals from Qatif would seek refuge in Bahrain, and British officials there would debate whether the Shi'a of Qatif were 'Baharna', and thereby entitled to claim 'refugee' status in Bahrain. This case would also show how issues of socially produced identities, forum shopping, and divided rule could criss-cross boundaries and feed into events elsewhere in the Gulf.[12]

Kuwait officially signed a 'protection' agreement with Great Britain in 1896, but unlike in Bahrain British officials never had much involvement in local affairs until the discovery of oil in the late 1930s, and even then it never reached the extent it did in Bahrain. Most obviously, the British did not depose any rulers, nor did they install British 'advisers' that had a monopoly on running local affairs. More significantly, they did not

---

importance and influence on the mode of political rule across the three Sa'udi states. They seem to have taken on a more prominent role, for example in certain periods of the first Sa'udi state and at the end of the twentieth century. The different manifestations and evolution of political rule across the three Sa'udi States is an under-researched topic that requires much further study.

12 It is also noteworthy that the mobilization was confined to Qatif and did not involve other areas in the Eastern Province such al-Hasa, which indicates that specific localized factors might have been more influential in driving the events. I am indebted to Sultan al-Aamer and Ahmed al-Owfi for illuminating this point. For the point of view of British officials based in Bahrain see: QDL, 'File 19/163 I (C 33) Bin Saud's relations with Shaikh of Bahrain. Nejdi Agent's activities in Bahrain' [133r] (272/412), IOR/R/15/1/334, http://www.qdl.qa/en/archive/81055/vdc_100023515109.0x000049.

claim jurisdiction over a large proportion of the local population. When Britain passed the Kuwait Order in Council in
1925, using Bahrain's 1919 BOIC as the blueprint, it also
claimed jurisdiction over 'foreigners' in Kuwait. There was one
fundamental difference, however. Unlike in Bahrain, where the
ruler's jurisdiction was limited to whatever social groups the
British defined as 'local subjects', the ruler in Kuwait insisted
that his jurisdiction was defined to cover all Muslims, with the
exception of subjects from India. In return, British jurisdiction
was limited to non-Muslim subjects and those from India.

This meant that the pool of people to which the Order in
Council applied in the pre-oil era was minuscule compared to
Bahrain, where the British claimed jurisdiction over roughly
half of the population. At the time of issuance of Kuwait's 1925
Order in Council, it only applied to three Indian 'petty traders',
compared to the British claiming jurisdiction over seventy
thousand people in Bahrain in 1923.[13] A similar situation
applied to the other Orders in Council in the rest of the Gulf
Arab States. Indeed, no other Gulf Arab State would experience
the same extent of British colonial rule and interference as
Bahrain until the 1960s.[14]

Furthermore, agricultural areas and relations were not
extensive in Kuwait, with the ruling family being an integral
part of setting up the urban town of Kuwait from its beginning

13 QDL, 'File 18/110 (B Series 18/12) Annual Report on the Working of
the Kuwait Order in Council', IOR/R/15/1/308, http://www.qdl.qa/
archive/81055/vdc_100022744559.0x000008.
14 Between 1965 and 1970, Britain would depose and replace three rulers
in Abu Dhabi, Sharjah, and Oman. By that point, however, the outlook of
British imperialism would differ significantly from the ethnosectarian
framework which prevailed in the early 1900s in Bahrain under divided
rule.

in the early eighteenth century. Hence, there were not the same relations of repression intersliced with sect, kinship, and geography as was the case in the relationship between the ruling family and residents of the agricultural villages of Bahrain. Given these factors, it might not be so surprising that ethnosectarian mobilization was not predominant in Kuwait until the rise of Islamism in the 1970s.[15]

Once again, one exception was characterized by heavy British involvement. In 1938, and during the Majlis movement spearheaded by notable merchants for an elected body to control legislative and executive powers, demands were put forward to reduce the rising 'Persian' immigration at the time. British officials would float the idea of offering protection and passports to 'Shi'as' in Kuwait, and some notables of the Shi'a faith would petition to be granted such passports and protection.[16]

What about possible regional comparisons that did experience ethnosectarian mobilization in a manner similar to Bahrain? The two cases that come immediately to mind would be Lebanon since the mid-nineteenth century, and more recently Iraq post the 2003 US invasion. Lebanon has long been

---

15 Instead, the notable socio-political mobilization in Kuwait would be along Bedouin/Hadar (Urban) cleavages, and even in this case it was never as pronounced as the Sunni/Shi'a political dichotomy in Bahrain.

16 Reflecting the rising Arab nationalist mood at the time, the activities of *al-Majlis* members were anti-Persian rather than anti-Shi'a, as borne out by the fact that there were Arab Shi'a members in the movement (I am indebted to Talal al-Rashoud for drawing attention to this point). Thus, 'Persians' became one of the main 'others' for movements influenced by Arab nationalism in Kuwait, as was the case in Bahrain. For the British point of view on these events, including offering passports to 'Shi'as', see: QDL, 'File 4/20 I Koweit Situation' [274r] (551/707), IOR/R/15/5/205, https://www.qdl.qa/archive/81055/vdc_100044487755.0x000098.

held as the ultimate, and in many ways unique, manifestation of institutionalized sectarianism in the Arab world. There are some similarities between Lebanon and Bahrain. Both experienced formally enshrined sectarian consociational politics at some point during the twentieth century under the strong dominance of Western imperial powers. The similarities, however, should not be overplayed. Lebanon's enshrinement of sectarianism in formal consociational politics stretches for more than a century and a half, existing in one form or another from at least 1840 until today. In contrast, Bahrain's experiment with formal consociational politics had its peak between the 1900s and 1920s, and was completely abandoned within a decade in favour of outright modernized absolutist rule. As was previously pointed out, politics dominated by ethnosectarianism generally declined throughout the period of the 1930s to the 1970s, before making a gradual return during the remainder of the twentieth century, and particularly after the 2003 invasion of Iraq and the 2011 protests.[17]

During this period, heightened ethnosectarian tensions were generally confined to times of political crises for the regime and the colonial order, in which they would often resort to ethnosectarian mobilization to counter any oppositional movements, as was the case in 1938 or 1953–1956, with varying degrees of success. As I have argued, it is important not to project the current predominance of sectarianism in Bahrain, nor that in the early 1920s, onto other periods of the nineteenth and twentieth century. This is a common practice within the current literature on Bahrain, the two periods being taken as representative of the entire modern political history of Bahrain,

17 For more on the 2011 protests see: Omar AlShehabi, 'Political Movements'.

and often juxtaposed on each other. In reality, they are two distinct periods of uniquely heightened ethnosectaranism, sharing some commonalities but also significant differences. As highlighted, it is important to emphasize that ethno-sects were not the dominant mobilizing parameters in local politics in other periods, whether at the state or popular level, for a diverse range of political forces, many of them non-sect based and sometimes even explicitly anti-sectarian, took centre stage.

It would seem at first glance that post-2003 Iraq would provide a better case for comparison than Lebanon. Just like Bahrain in the early 1900s, it is a society whose main religious sects were Shi'as and Sunnis. Its preceding political system was similarly not dominated by such confessional considerations, while it also exhibited high levels of repression. It was subjected to a Western occupation dressed in the guise of 'liberal interventionism', deposing the old order and catalyzing the emergence of a political system largely based on ethnosectarian readings of the local society. The similarities should not be overplayed, however, as both the levels of repression carried out during Saddam's rule, and the subsequent destruction that was imposed by Western forces on Iraq, were on a completely different scale to those in early-twentieth-century Bahrain. The significant role of sect-based Islamist forces, as well as Kurdish nationalist movements in post-invasion Iraq, further complicates such a simple analogy, as well as factoring in the surrounding regional developments during this period. The need for a detailed and attentive historiography that fights the urge to make essentializing generalizations remains paramount. The fact remains, however, that in both post-2003 Iraq and early-twentieth-century Bahrain, sectarianism became the dominant force in politics after the destabilization of the old political regime and the imposition of a political system by Western imperial forces, that read politics mainly based on such ethno-sectarian categories and enforced such readings on the ground. This process enabled and gave primacy to political actors that also employed such ethnosectarian readings in their political mobilization.

It is worth re-emphasizing that developments in any of these countries cannot and should not be read as self-enclosed units of analysis that stand aloof from the surrounding context. Throughout this book, I have taken pains to illustrate how dynamics in the region and the globe interacted with those in Bahrain, emphasizing that developments on the islands should not be read in isolation from these factors. Whether through stressing *Pax Brittanica* and the 'age of capital' that reigned supreme during the nineteenth century, or highlighting the decline of the Ottoman and Qajar empires in the same period, or narrating the rise of the Sa'udi state and Iranian nationalism, or focusing on the interactions between the figures of al-Nahda across the Arab world, it becomes essential that these regional and global dynamics are placed at the centre of the story.

Ever since the 2003 invasion of Iraq, the ethnosectarian gaze has re-emerged as the pre-eminent lens through which to view events in Bahrain and the Gulf, particularly after the 2011 mass protests, which have been coloured and depicted largely in sectarian terms. It is important to keep in mind the roots of this gaze in the case of Bahrain. Twentieth-century forms of sectarianism on the island were not a continuation of an age-old form of political mobilization, but a modernist one whose roots were sculpted during the period of divided and contested colonial rule in the early twentieth century. Concurrently, this period witnessed the birth of nationalist, anti-colonial, and trans-sectarian discourses that traced their roots to al-Nahda in the wider Arab world, and which would sow the first seeds of modern nationalist, leftist, and Islamist movements on the islands.

It is essential to understand that colonialism, absolutism, nationalism, and sectarianism did not arrive as fully formed projects into Bahrain. Thus, sectarianism was not exclusively only a form of colonialist gaze and knowledge, nor only a reality that existed in a precolonial past.[18] It was, instead, a conjunctural product of both precolonial and colonial factors, but in which the newly unfolding colonial order provided the main impetus and institutional setting that drove it forward. As was stressed in this book, there was significant overlap in sect, geography, class, and life experiences for many that would have provided strong breeding grounds for ethnosectarian mobilization to thrive locally. Sectarianism is both a colonialist knowledge and a local knowledge that were produced conjointly.

Instead of putting forward a pre-established dichotomy between different sects and ethnicities, foreigners and locals, colonizer and colonized, collaborators and resisters, this book tried to uncover the system of divided and contested rule that played out in Bahrain as an arena of exchange, manoeuvring, and contentious politics, where actions by different actors take on a much more open-ended dimension; where pre-existing conditions, regional forces, the politics of the notables, forum shopping by ordinary locals, as well as actions of local and regional rulers all played out and cross-fed with each other. Social categories, labels, and grouping were shown to be emergent, provisional, contested, and morphable over time. The crucial point, however, is this: the distribution of power in this arena was not even, and the arena itself was largely contested

18 For a similar argument regarding sectarianism in Lebanon see: Makdisi, *The Culture of Sectarianism*, 7–8.

and reconstructed by the colonial power and its system of divided rule and the ethnosectarian gaze. The dice were loaded.

On the flip side, it was important to show that although the game was rigged towards the predominance of sectarianism during this period of British colonial rule, such an outcome was not preordained. One of my main goals was to shed light on the origins of movements that were able to face and transcend such sectarianism, in large part succeeding in driving forward an alternative reading of society for the half-century that followed the events in this book. Such movements articulated instead discourses of nationalism, anti-colonialism, anti-absolutism, and civic-based change. In this age that has become obsessed with framing the politics of Bahrain, the Gulf, and the wider Arab world mainly in categories of ethnicities and sects, excavating and recentring such radical movements that transcend sectarianism, in all of their complexities, contradictions, and shortcomings, becomes ever more crucial.

BIBLIOGRAPHY

ARCHIVES

Qatar Digital Library, http://www.qdl.qa
The British National Archives
Sakhr Software Archive of Arabic Literary and Cultural Magazines, http://
archive.sakhrit.co/AllMagazines.aspx
Personal collection of Mr Rashid al-Jassim

INTERVIEWS

Abdul-Nabi al-Ekri, ex-PFLOAG member, 11 and 22 June 2010.
Abdul Hamid Al-Muhadeen, former teacher at al-Hidaya school and writer,
28 October 2017.
Jasem Murad and Ali Rabia, former Bahraini MPs who were active in several
political movements, 4 September 2017.
Hasan Radhi, leading Bahraini legal expert, 30 September 2017.
Abdulmenem al-Shirawi, ex-PFLOAG and grandson of Qasem al-Shirawi,
19 November 2010.
Ali al-Shirawi, ex-PFLOAG and grandson of Qasem al-Shirawi, 26 November
2010.
Noora al-Shirawi, writer and daughter of Ahmad al-Shirawi, 19 September 2017.

251

LITERATURE IN ARABIC

The Noble Quran

Abdulla, Hassan, 'al-Wujood al-Britany wal Hukm al-ekta'iy wal Islahat fil Bahrain', (unknown: unknown, 1999), https://goo.gl/es6XYf.

Ahmad, Iman, 'Al-Ikhwan al-muslimoon fil Bahrain wa idarat al-tahawwulat al-rahina', *Egyptian Institute for Political and Strategic Studies*, 13 January 2016, https://goo.gl/SbfPXp.

Al-Alawi, Mohammad, 'Bushehri: al-Manama 'asimat al-'aza' al-Bahraini', *Al-Wasat* newspaper, 5 November 2014, http://alwasatnews.com/news/933706.html.

Al-Ansari, Jalal Khaled Haroon, *Tareekh 'Arab al-Huwala wal 'Utoob* (Beirut: Al-Dar al- 'Arabiyya lel Mawsoo'at, 2011).

——, 'Ajdaduna al-Ansar', *Shabakat al-Tawwash*, http://alharoon.blogspot. qa/2014/05/blog-post_27.html.

Mohammad Jaber al-Ansari, *Al-Fikr al-'Arabi wa Sera' al-Addad* (Beirut: al-Mu'asasa al-'Arabiyya lel Derasat wal Nashr, 1999).

Al-Bahrani, Yousuf, *Lu'lu'at al-Bahrain fil Ijazat wa Tarajem Rijal al-Hadeeth* (Bahrain: Maktabat Fakhrawi, 2008).

Al-Baqshi, Ahmad, 'Al-Ehsa'yoon fil Bahrain awaset al-qarn al-'eshreen', *Maraya Alturath*, https://malturath.wordpress.com/2013/04/12/الإحسائيون-في-البحرين-أواسط-القرن-الع/#more-369.

Al-Basri, Othman, *Saba'ek al-'Asjad* (Doha: Hasan al-Thani Centre for Historical Studies, 2007).

Al-Bassam, Khaled, *Rejal fi jaza'er al-lu'lu'* (Beirut: Arab Institute for Research and Publishing, 2007).

Al-bin 'Ali, Rashid bin Fadhel, *Majmoo' al-fadha'el fi fan nasab wa tarikh al-qaba'el* (Qatar: Bader Publishing, 2007).

Al-Ghatam, Khalifa, 'Amir al-souk', *Bahrain Historical and Archaeological Society*, 10 June 2016, https://www.youtube.com/watch?v=70t1Z8m XMqA.

Al-Hadi, Bashshar, *Al-fadhel Al-'Utoob* (Bahrain: unknown, 2009).

——, *A'yan al-Bahrain fil qarn al-rabi' 'ashar al-hijri*, vol. 4 (Bahrain: Jam'iyyat al-Imam Malek bin Anas, 2008).

——, 'Al-Madares al-Ahliyya fil Bahrain', *Shar'ia Teaching in the GCC Countries Conference*, http://www.rogulf.com/play.php?catsmktba=14.

——, 'Al-Shaikh Mubarak bin Khalifa al-Fadhel mo'asses qaryat al-Malkiyya', *Medwanat Bashshar al-Hadi,* 11 September 2010, http://bashaaralhadi. blogspot.com/2010/09/blog-post_11.html.

Al-Jassim, Rashid, *al-Bahrain wa 'umkuha al-'araby wal Islami* (Bahrain: al-Dar al-'Arabiyya lel Mawsoo'at, 2015).

Al-Jazeeri, Mahmood, 'Al-Nashaba: Mudaifa' awwal Ma'tam fil Bahrain', *Al-Wasat* newspaper, 14 October 2015, http://www.alwasatnews.com/ news/1035536.html.

Al-Khalifa, May, *Ma'a shaikh al-udaba' fil Bahrain Ebrahim bin Mohammad al-Khalifa* (London: Riad al-Rayes Books, 1993).

——, *Ma'at 'am min al-ta'leem al-nethami fil Bahrain* (Beirut: Arabic Institute for Research and Publishing, 1999).

——, *Sebazabad wa rejal al-dawla al-bahiyya* (Beirut: al-Mu'sasa al-'Arabiyya lel Derasat wal Nashr, 2010).

Al-Khater, Mubarak, *al-Qadhi al-ra'is al-Shaikh Qasem bin Mehza'* (Bahrain: Government Press, 1975).

——, *al-ketabat al-uwla al-hadeetha li muthaqqafi al-Bahrain 1875–1925* (Bahrain: unknown, 1978).

——, *al-adeeb al-Kateb Nasser al-Khairi* (Bahrain: Government Press, 1982).

——, *Nabeghat al-Bahrain 'Abdulla al-Zayed* (Bahrain: Government Press, 1988).

Al-Khairi, Naser, *Qala'id al-Nahrain fi Tarikh al-Bahrain* (Bahrain: al-Ayyam Publishing, 2003).

Al-Madani, Abdulla, 'Min al-Manfa ela al-Safara: Hekayat Mu'ared Watani Sharif', *al-Ayam,* 11 April 2014, https://goo.gl/RzGjwm.

——, 'Kab ee r Al - ' a jam fil Bahrain', *Al-Ayam* newspaper, 2 May 2014, https://malturath.wordpress.com/2014/05/02/ كبــير-العجــم-في-البحــري/#more-1075.

Al-Madhoob, Hasan, 'Al-Salman: Bin Khamis min Awa'el al-Mutalibeen', *Al-Wasat* newspaper, 26 March 2016, http://www.alwasatnews.com/ news/1094797.html.

Al-Muhadeen, Abdul Hamid, *al-Khurouj min al-'Utma* (Beirut: Arab Institute for Research and Publishing, 2003).

Al-Nabhani, Muhammad, *al-Tuhfa al-Nabhaniyya* (Bahrain: unknown, 1923).

Al-Raihani, Amin, *Muluk al-'Arab* (Beirut: Dar al-Jeel, 1987).

Al-Salman, Mohammad, 'Al-Wakeel al-Haj Ebrahim bin Mohsin bin Rajab', *Al-Wasat* newspaper, 26 March 2013, http://www.alwasatnews.com/news/755276.html.

Al-Sayyed Salman, Al-Sayyed Hashem, *Ghayat al-Maram fi Tarikh al-A'lam* (Bahrain: Manshoorat Maktabat al-Madani, 2004).

Al-Sebe, Wesam, 'Mohammad 'Ali al-Tajer ... hekaya min al-madhi', *Al-Wasat* newspaper, 17 December 2013, http://www.alwasatnews.com/news/838698.html.

Al-Shubaili, Abdul Rahman, 'Muqbelan min al-Thukair', *Asharq al-Awsat* newspaper, 20 November 2011, http://archive.aawsat.com/details.asp?section=19&article=650680&issueno=12045#.WNEX3PmGM2w.

Al-Tajir, Mohammad, *'Iqd al-Li'al fi Tarikh Awal* (Bahrain: al-Ayyam, 1994).

Al-Waqt newspaper, 'Tarikh al-'irq al-Farsi fil Bahrain', 28 October 2009.

Antoon, Sinan, 'Al-Sukkan al-asliyoon wal baqiyya: eshkaliyyat al-mustalah', *As-Safir*, 22 March 2016, http://assafir.com/article/482731.

Kadhim, Nader, *Taba'e' al-Istimlak* (Beirut: al-Maktaba al-'Arabiyya lel Derasat wal Nashr, 2007).

——, *Isti'malat al-Dhakira fi Mujtama' Ta'addudi Mubtala bi-l-Tarikh* (Bahrain: Maktabat Fakhrawi, 2008).

Khuri, Ebrahim and Ahmad Jalal al-Tadmuri, *Saltanat Hurmuz al-'arabiyya al-mustakilla Vols. 1 & 2* (Ras al-Khaimah: Markaz al-Derasat wal Wath'eq, 1999).

Matar, Fouziyya, *Ahmad al-Shamlan seerat munadel wa tareekh watan* (Beirut: Arab Institute for Research and Publishing, 2009).

Rabee'a, Ali, *al-Tajruba al-Maw'uda* (Bahrain: unknown, 2010).

Rida, Rashid, *al-Manar*, Volumes 16 and 17 (1331–1332).

Seddiq, 'Abdulrazzaq Mohammad, *Sahwat al-Fares fi Tarikh 'Arab Fares* (Beirut: Matba'at al-Ma'aref, 1993).

Unknown, 'Al-Ikhwan Al-Muslimoon fi Qatar wal Bahrain', *Al-Majalla*, 11 June 2013, https://goo.gl/t3EAE9.

Unknown, 'Portrait Ebrahim al-'Urayyedh', *Al-Wasat* newspaper, 20 October 2012, http://www.alwasatnews.com/news/166180.html.

Unknown, 'Portrait Yousuf Ahmad al-Shirawi', *Al-Wasat* newspaper, 4 February 2004, http://www.alwasatnews.com/news/362061.html.

Unknown, 'Tantaleq min zera'at door al 'ebada fi madinat Almuharraq', Northern Area Municipality, 6 June 2015, http://websrv.municipality.gov.bh/north/pages/newsDetails_en.jsp?param=644.

Wahba, Hafedh, *Khamsoona 'Aman fi Jazeerat al-Arab* (Cairo: Dar al-Aafaq al-Arabiyya, 2001).

Yateem, Abdalla Abdulrahman, *al-Manama al-madina al-'arabiyya* (Bahrain: University of Bahrain, 2015).

LITERATURE IN ENGLISH

Abisaab, Rula Jurdi, *Converting Persia: Religion and Power in the Safavid Empire* (London: I.B.Tauris, 2004).

Al-Azmeh, Aziz, 'Sectarianism and Antisectarianism', keynote address at the Rice University/University of Houston Conference on Arab Traditions of Anti-Sectarianism, 2017, https://www.strikingmargins.com/news-1/2017/12/20/prof-aziz-al-azmeh-sectarianism-and-antisectarianism?format=amp.

Al-Baharna, Husain M., *The Legal Status of the Arabian Gulf States* (Manchester: Manchester University Press, 1968).

Al-Khan, Waheed Ahmed bin Hasan, *Aghani al-ghaws fil bahrain* (Doha: Markaz al-turath al-sha'bi, 2002).

Allday, Louis, 'Britain's Interest in Bahrain', Qatar Digital Library, http://www.qdl.qa/en/britain%E2%80%99s-%E2%80%98interest%E2%80%99-bahrain.

Almahmood, Mahmood, *The Rise and Fall of Bahrain's Merchants in the Pre-Oil Era* (Washington, D.C.: MA thesis, American University, 2013).

Al-Naqeeb, Khaldoun, *Society and State in the Gulf and Arab Peninsula: A Different Perspective* (London: Routledge, 2012).

Al-Otabi, Mubarak, *The Qawasim and British Control of the Arabian Gulf* (PhD thesis, University of Salford, 1989).

Al-Qasimi, Sultan Muhammed, *The Myth of Arab Piracy in the Gulf* (Abingdon: Routledge, 1988).

Al-Rashoud, Talal, *Modern Education and Arab Nationalism in Kuwait, 1911–1961* (London: PhD thesis, SOAS, 2017).

Al-Rumaihi, Mohammed Ghanim, *Bahrain: Social and Political Change Since the First World War*, Vol. 5 (London: Bowker, 1976).

AlShehabi, Omar Hesham, 'Demography and Bahrain's unrest', *Report for the Carnegie Endowment for International Peace 16* (2011), http://carnegieendowment.org/sada/43079.

——, 'Divide and Rule in Bahrain and the Elusive Pursuit for a United Front:

The Experience of the Constitutive Committee and the 1972 Uprising', *Historical Materialism* 21.1 (2013): 94–127.

——, 'Histories of Migration to the Gulf', in Abdulhadi Khalaf et al. (ed.), *Transit States: Labour, Migration & Citizenship in the Gulf* (London: Pluto Press, 2015): 3–38.

——, 'Political Movements in Bahrain Across the Long Twentieth Century', in Hanssen, J., and Ghazal. A. (eds.), *The Oxford Handbook of Contemporary Middle-Eastern and North African History* (Oxford: Oxford University Press, (2017).

——, and Saleh Suroor, 'Unpacking "Accumulation by Dispossession", "Fictitious Commodification", and "Fictitious Capital Formation": Tracing the Dynamics of Bahrain's Land Reclamation', *Antipode* 48.4 (2016): 835–856.

AlShehabi, Saad Hesham, *The Evolution of the Role of Merchants in Kuwaiti Politics* (PhD thesis, King's College London, 2015).

Al-Tajir, Mahdi Abdalla, *Bahrain 1920–1945: Britain, the Shaikh and the Administration* (London: Croom Helm, 1987).

Anderson, Benedict, *Imagined Communities: Reflections on the Origin and Spread of Nationalism* (London: Verso Books, 2006).

Ashcroft, Bill, Gareth Griffiths, and Helen Tiffin, *Post-Colonial Studies: The Key Concepts* (London: Routledge, 2013).

Banton, Michael, *Racial Theories* (Cambridge: Cambridge University Press, 1998).

Beaugrand, Claire, *Stateless in the Gulf: Migration, Nationality and Society in Kuwait* (London: I.B.Tauris, 2017).

Belgrave, Charles Dalrymple, *Personal Column* (Beirut: Librairie du Liban, 1972).

Bishara, Fahad Ahmad, *A Sea of Debt: Histories of Commerce and Obligation in the Indian Ocean, c. 1850–1940* (Durham, North Carolina: PhD thesis, Duke University, 2012).

Boehmer, Elleke, *Colonial and Postcolonial Literature: Migrant Metaphors* (Oxford: Oxford University Press, 2005).

Brubaker, Rogers, 'The Manichean myth: Rethinking the distinction between "civic" and "ethnic" nationalism', in Kries, Hanspeter, *Nation and National Identity: The European Experience in Perspective* (West Lafayette, Indiana: Purdue University Press, 1999): 55–71.

Burbank, Jane, and Frederick Cooper, *Empires in World History: Power and the Politics of Difference* (Princeton: Princeton University Press, 2010).

Chakrabarty, Dipesh, *Habitations of Modernity: Essays in the Wake of Subaltern Studies* (Chicago: University of Chicago Press, 2002).

Chomsky, Noam, speech at FAIR 25th anniversary meeting, https://www.youtube.com/watch?v=yY3yVQ0sxXo.

Clancy-Smith, Julia, *Mediterraneans: North Africa and Europe in an Age of Migration* (Berkeley: University of California Press, 2011).

Dirks, Nicholas B., *Castes of Mind: Colonialism and the Making of Modern India* (Princeton: Princeton University Press, 2011).

Eriksen, Thomas Hylland, Ethnicity and Nationalism: Anthropological Perspectives (London: Pluto Press, 2002).

Fisher, Michael H., *Indirect Rule in India: Residents and the Residency System 1764–1857* (Oxford: Oxford University Press, 1998).

Foucault, Michel, *Power/Knowledge: Selected Interviews and Other writings, 1972–1977* (New York: Pantheon, 1980), 194–196.

——, *Security, Territory, Population: Lectures at the Collège de France 1977–1978*, Vol. 4 (Basingstoke: Macmillan, 2009).

Fuccaro, Nelida, *Histories of City and State in the Persian Gulf: Manama Since 1800* (Cambridge: Cambridge University Press, 2009).

Gellner, Ernest, *Nations and Nationalism* (Ithaca: Cornell University Press, 2008).

Grummon, Stephen R., *The Rise and Fall of the Arab Shaikhdom of Bushire 1750–1850* (Baltimore: PhD thesis, John Hopkins University, 1986).

Haddad, Fanar, 'Shi'a-centric state building and Sunni rejection in Post-2003 Iraq' (Paper, Carnegie Endowment for International Peace, 2016), http://carnegieendowment.org/2016/01/07/Shi'a-centric-state-building-and-sunni-rejection-in-post-2003-iraq-pub-62408.

——, ' "Sectarianism" and Its Discontents in the Study of the Middle East', *Middle East Journal* 71.3 (2017): 363–382.

Hall, John A., and Ralph Schroeder (eds.), *An Anatomy of Power: The Social Theory of Michael Mann* (Cambridge: Cambridge University Press, 2006).

Hall, Stuart, *Selected political writings: The great moving right show and other essays.* (Durham, North Carolina: Duke University Press, 2016).

——, 'Race: the Floating Signifier', Lecture at Goldsmiths College,

University of London, 1996, https://youtube.com/watch?v=OtkTkdiF5ZY.

——, 'The Neoliberal Revolution', *Cultural Studies* 25.6 (2011): 705–728.

Hannah, Matthew G., *Governmentality and the Mastery of Territory in Nineteenth-Century America* (Cambridge: Cambridge University Press, 2000).

Hanssen, Jens, *Arabic Thought beyond the Liberal Age: Towards an Intellectual History of the Nahda* (Cambridge: Cambridge University Press, 2016).

Hariri, Aula, 'The Iraqi Independence Movement: A Case of Transgressive Contention (1918–1920)', in Fawaz Gerges (ed.), *Contentious Politics in the Middle East* (New York: Palgrave Macmillan, 2015), 103–104.

Harris, William, *Lebanon: A History, 600–2011* (Oxford: Oxford University Press, 2014).

Harrison, Paul Wilberforce, *The Arab at Home*, Vol. 4, No. 5 (New York: Thomas Y. Crowell Company, 1924).

Harvey, David, 'Between Space and Time: Reflections on the Geographical Imagination', *Annals of the Association of American Geographers* 80.3 (1990): 418–434.

Herb, Michael, *All in the Family: Absolutism, Revolution, and Democracy in Middle Eastern Monarchies* (New York: SUNY Press, 1999).

Hobsbawm, Eric, *The Age of Capital: 1848–1875* (London: Weidenfeld & Nicolson, 1975).

——, *The Age of Empire: 1875–1914* (London: Weidenfeld & Nicolson, 1987).

——, and Terence Ranger (eds.), *The Invention of Tradition* (Cambridge: Cambridge University Press, 2012).

Hourani, Albert, *Arabic Thought in the Liberal Age 1798–1939* (Cambridge: Cambridge University Press, 1962).

——, *The Emergence of the Modern Middle East* (Berkeley: University of California Press, 1981).

Kadhim, Abbas, *Reclaiming Iraq: The 1920 Revolution and the Founding of the Modern State* (Austin: University of Texas Press, 2012).

Kaiksow, Sarah, *Threats to British 'Protectionism' in Colonial Bahrain: Beyond the Sunni/Shiʿa Divide* (Washington, D.C.: MA thesis, Georgetown University, 2009).

Khalaf, Abdulhadi, 'Contentious Politics in Bahrain: From Ethnic to National and Vice Versa', paper presented at the Fourth Nordic Conference on Middle East Studies, Oslo, 1998.

Khaldun, Ibn, *The Muqaddimah: An Introduction to History* (Princeton: Princeton University Press, 1969).

Khuri, Fuad I., *Tribe and State in Bahrain: The Transformation of Social and Political Authority in an Arab State* (Chicago: University of Chicago, 1980).

Krimly, Rayed Khalid, *The Political Economy of Rentier States: A Case Study of Sa'udi Arabia in the Oil Era, 1950–1990* (Washington, D.C.: George Washington University, 1993).

Lewis, Mary D., *Divided Rule: Sovereignty and Empire in French Tunisia, 1881–1938* (Berkeley and Los Angeles: University of California Press, 2013).

Lorcin, Patricia, *Imperial Identities: Stereotyping, Prejudice and Race in Colonial Algeria* (London: I.B.Tauris, 1995).

Lorimer, John Gordon, *Gazetteer of the Persian Gulf*, Vol. 1 and Vol. 2, 1908.

Louër, Laurence, *Transnational Shi'a Politics: Religious and Political Networks in the Gulf* (New York: Columbia University Press, 2008).

Low, Charles Rathbone, *The Land of the Sun* (London: Hodder and Stoughton, 1870).

Makdisi, Ussama, *The Culture of Sectarianism: Community, History, and Violence in Nineteenth-Century Ottoman Lebanon* (Berkeley and Los Angeles: University of California Press, 2000).

——, 'The Mythology of the Sectarian Middle East', Center for the Middle East at Rice University, 2017, http://www.bakerinstitute.org/media/files/files/5a20626a/CME-pub-Sectarianism-021317.pdf.

Mamdani, Mahmood, *Citizen and Subject: Contemporary Africa and the Legacy of Late Colonialism* (Princeton: Princeton University Press, 1996).

——, 'Historicizing Power and Responses to Power: Indirect Rule and its Reform', *Social Research* 66 (1999), 859, 870.

Martin, Vanessa, *The Qajar Pact: Bargaining, Protest and the State in Nineteenth-Century Persia* (London: I.B.Tauris, 2005).

Momen, Moojan, *An Introduction to Shi'i Islam: The History and Doctrines of Twelver Shi'ism* (New Haven: Yale University Press, 1985).

Nabulsi, Karma, *Traditions of War: Occupation, Resistance, and the Law* (Oxford: Oxford University Press, 2005).

Nakash, Yitzhak, *The Shi'is of Iraq* (Princeton: Princeton University Press, 2003).

Obama, Barack, 'State of the Union Address 2016', Mic, https://mic.com/

articles/132466/state-of-the-union-transcript-2016-obama#. DDupWynlZ.

Onley, James, 'The Politics of Protection in the Gulf: The Arab Rulers and the British Resident in the Nineteenth Century', *New Arabian Studies* 6 (2004): 30–92.

——, *The Arabian Frontier of the British Raj: Merchants, Rulers, and the British in the Nineteenth-Century Gulf* (Oxford: Oxford University Press, 2007).

Owen, Roger, *The Middle East in the World Economy, 1800–1914* (London: I.B.Tauris, 1993).

Palgrave, William, *Personal Narrative of a Year's Journey Through Central and Eastern Arabia (1862–1863)* (London: Macmillan, 1871).

Quijano, Aníbal. 'Coloniality of Power and Eurocentrism in Latin America', *International Sociology* 15.2 (2000): 215–232.

Radhi, Hassan Ali, *The Bahrain Judiciary* (London: Kluwer Law International, 2003).

Ramusack, Barbara N., *The Indian Princes and Their States* (Cambridge: Cambridge University Press, 2004).

Rich, Paul J., *Creating the Arabian Gulf: The British Raj and the Invasions of the Gulf* (Plymouth: Lexington Books, 2009).

Said, Edward, *Orientalism* (New York: Vintage, 1979).

Salloukh, Bassel, *The Politics of Sectarianism in Postwar Lebanon* (London: Pluto Press, 2015).

Scudder, Lewis R., *The Arabian Mission's Story: In Search of Abraham's Other Son* (Grand Rapids: Wm. B. Eerdmans Publishing, 1998).

Simpson, Adam, Nicholas Farrelly, and Ian Holliday (eds.), *Routledge Handbook of Contemporary Myanmar* (Abingdon: Routledge, 2017).

Spivak, Gayatri Chakravorty, 'Can the Subaltern Speak?', in Morris, Rosalind (ed.), *Can the Subaltern Speak? Reflections on the History of an Idea* (New York: Columbia University Press, 1988): 21–78.

Takriti, Abdel Razzaq, *Monsoon Revolution: Republicans, Sultans, and Empires in Oman, 1965–1976* (Oxford: Oxford University Press, 2013).

Traboulsi, Fawwaz, *A History of Modern Lebanon* (London: Pluto Press, 2007).

Unknown, 'Harold Dickson Collection', Middle East Centre of St. Antony's College, Oxford, https://www.sant.ox.ac.uk/mec/MEChandlists/ GB165-0085-HRP-Dickson-Collection.pdf.

Unknown, 'In Memoriam: Lieut. Col. H. R. P. Dickson, C.I.E, F.R.G.S.', *Journal of the Royal Central Asian Society* 46 (1959), 3–4, http://www.

tandfonline.com/doi/abs/10.1080/03068375908731667?journalCode
=raaf19.

Unknown, 'Maj. Clive Kirkpatrick Daly (Biographical details)', British
Museum, http://www.britishmuseum.org/research/search_the_collec-
tion_database/term_details.aspx?bioId=93576.

Vahman, Fereydun, and Garnik Asatrian, 'Lorimer, David I. In Persia',
Encyclopedia   Iranica,   http://www.iranicaonline.org/articles/
lorimer-david-i-in-persia.

Weiss, Max, *In the Shadow of Sectarianism* (Cambridge, Massachusetts:
Harvard University Press, 2010).

Winter, Stefan. *The Shiites of Lebanon under Ottoman Rule, 1516–1788*
(Cambridge: Cambridge University Press, 2010).

INDEX

263